READY...
SET...
RETIRE!

Also by Raymond J. Lucia

BUCKETS OF MONEY®: How to Retire in Comfort and Safety

New Beginnings/Hay House Titles
of Related Interest

HOW TO RUIN YOUR FINANCIAL LIFE, by Ben Stein

SUZE ORMAN'S INSURANCE KIT

SUZE ORMAN'S WILL & TRUST KIT

YES, YOU CAN BE A SUCCESSFUL INCOME INVESTOR!:
Reaching for Yield in Today's Market, by Ben Stein and Phil DeMuth

YES, YOU CAN GET A FINANCIAL LIFE!:
Your Lifetime Guide to Financial Planning,
by Ben Stein and Phil DeMuth

YES, YOU CAN STILL RETIRE COMFORTABLY!:
The Baby-Boom Retirement Crisis and How to Beat It,
by Ben Stein and Phil DeMuth

$ $ $

All of the above are available at your local bookstore, or
may be ordered by visiting the distributors for New Beginnings Press:

Hay House USA: www.hayhouse.com®
Hay House Australia: www.hayhouse.com.au
Hay House UK: www.hayhouse.co.uk
Hay House South Africa: orders@psdprom.co.za
Hay House India: www.hayhouseindia.co.in

$ $ $

READY...
SET...
RETIRE!

Financial Strategies
for the Rest of Your Life

RAYMOND J. LUCIA, CFP®
with Dale Fetherling

NBP
NEW BEGINNINGS PRESS
Carlsbad, California

Published by: New Beginnings Press, Carlsbad, California

Distributed in the United States by: Hay House, Inc.: www.hayhouse.com • **Published and distributed in Australia by:** Hay House Australia Pty. Ltd.: www.hayhouse.com.au • **Published and distributed in the United Kingdom by:** Hay House UK, Ltd.: www.hayhouse.co.uk • **Published and distributed in the Republic of South Africa by:** Hay House SA (Pty), Ltd.: orders@psdprom.co.za • **Distributed in Canada by:** Raincoast: www.raincoast.com • **Published in India by:** Hay House Publications (India) Pvt. Ltd.: www.hayhouseindia.co.in

Editorial supervision: Jill Kramer • *Design:* Tricia Breidenthal

Library of Congress Cataloging-in-Publication Data

Lucia, Raymond J.
    Ready-- set-- retire! : financial strategies for the rest of your life / Raymond J. Lucia with Dale Fetherling.
        p. cm.
    ISBN-13: 978-1-4019-1206-2 (hardcover)
    ISBN-13: 978-1-4019-1207-9 (tradepaper) 1. Retirement income--Planning. 2. Finance, Personal. 3. Investments. I. Fetherling, Dale, 1941- II. Title.
HG179.L828 2007
332.024'014--dc22   2006023096

Hardcover ISBN: 978-1-4019-1206-2
Tradepaper ISBN: 978-1-4019-1207-9

10 09 08 07   4 3 2 1
1st edition, March 2007

Printed in the United States of America

To Jeanne . . .
my loving wife of 34 years,
who gave me family time
during evenings, weekends,
and even on vacations
so I could write this book.

— Ray

Contents

Foreword

Ray Lucia doesn't look like a financial type. He's not a thin, anemic-looking guy with suspenders, horn-rimmed glasses, and flinty blue eyes. Nor does he *sound* like a financial type. His voice is rich, sonorous, and alive, like that of the rock singer and guitarist he is. (He has the "battle of the bands" awards to prove it, handed to him by a member of The Who.)

Ray's sound and message are never boring, never number crunching, never dry statistics. When he talks, it's more like Pete Townshend singing. Maybe a bit frank, but not boring in the slightest.

What comes out of Ray when you meet him and listen to him is the exact opposite of what comes out of most gurus of financial planning: Ray is as warm and magnetic as they are cold, cold, cold. Ray is a people person, and he exudes concern about the people in this country like an old-fashioned country priest. He may know more than you do about (financial) salvation, but he's never going to hold it over your head. He's going to help you with what he knows because he cares about his people, those who come to him for advice and counsel.

And, wow, does he know a lot! He knows about investments, about their track records, about their future prospects, about how they're taxed, and about how they should be held. He knows about retirement vehicles—his *spécialité de la maison*—of every description. He knows them so well that when I talk to him, I—who have studied this area for decades and have written books about it—am staggered by my own limitations. (He never makes me feel bad about them, though.)

Ray knows about rules, about taxes, about ways to stick it to the tax man and save your family first. He knows how to guard your future by accumulating savings in different forms, how to make sure you don't outlive your money, and how to provide a cushion for your retirement future against inflation by maximizing your returns from stocks while keeping liquid in the short and medium run. His strategy is called "Buckets of Money." It's the future, and it works.

The easy way to say it is that there's almost nothing Ray doesn't know about retirement planning. And he knows this above all: that people do not care how much you know until they know how much you care. Ray cares. He's already rich and already has a beautiful wife, so he's not in it to pay his bills. He's in it to help, and help he does . . . at his seminars, in his money-management work, and in this book about retirement.

Presented in the same readily accessible, warm, and caring way Ray conducts his life, in expository paragraphs, conversations, and give-and-take, Ray tells us what we need to know in every possible dimension. This book is Ray on the printed page: a rock star of personal finance, available to you, understandable by you—optimistic, upbeat, and right on target.

I wish I'd written it. I didn't, but Ray did, and now it's your job— and your pleasure—to read it. You really can't consider yourself ready to prepare to retire until you've read this book. Go ahead. Be good to yourself.

— **Ben Stein**

$ $ $ $ $

Introduction

Retirement, despite what you might have heard, is more than a number. And it's not so much a destination as it is a journey, a process, a plan in the making, and a work in progress. Whether you're already retired, about to retire, or a part of that massive wave of baby boomers whose retirement is coming up faster than you probably ever imagined, you need a strategy.

It wasn't always so. Remember how retirement used to be called "the golden years"? Pretty much the only strategy then was to kick back. It was to be the fun time, when you could relax and do what you never had the leisure to do when you were younger. You know, like sign up for yoga lessons; read great books; play with the grandkids; and maybe take long, meandering trips in a RV.

You hardly ever hear it described that way now. Instead, retirement is usually painted as complicated and emotion laden, almost more of a burden than a liberation. It doesn't need to be *that* complicated, but of course, to forge a good retirement you need to figure out a few things that our parents didn't need to wrestle with. They experienced cataclysms, including the Depression and World War II, which shaped their financial reality. Despite these hardships, that generation endured and felt optimistic enough about the world to populate it with individuals such as you, me, and our peers. If your parents were like mine, they frequently reminded you of how difficult things used to be, perhaps recalling how they walked barefoot to school through the snow and wrote their school lessons with a piece of charcoal before the flickering light of the fireplace. Okay, so they exaggerated a little.

But the point is, times *were* different then. Our folks scraped together a living, many staying at one job all their working lives so they could reap a pension and that Social Security check they were counting on. They probably lived within their means, too. After all, that's what they'd been taught.

Their environment reinforced those lessons in thrift. Credit cards weren't as widely available then. No one had ever heard of an interest-only mortgage. And, in fact, debt was largely viewed as something to be avoided. As a result, our parents didn't refinance their house every few years; instead, they tried to pay off the loan. Saving was in their DNA, even if they didn't yet know what DNA was.

A Different System

Today, most of us work under a much different system. Neither our employers nor our government gives us much of a guarantee about retirement. Debt is as plentiful and, to many, almost as necessary as oxygen. "Charge it," we say, whether it's a 42-inch plasma TV, a college education, or a no-down-payment home loan. We plan to play catch-up.

As frequent victims of layoffs, or just susceptible to the siren song of better opportunities, we change jobs, or even careers, almost as often as our grandparents changed socks. Most of us receive no education in personal finance unless we pursue it as an occupation. If we look to the popular media for advice, we're usually met with headlines like THE 10 BEST FUNDS TO BUY *Now!* or we watch TV talking heads rant about stocks we've never heard of and may never hear of again.

Despite this precarious fiscal foundation, we're bombarded by marketing messages suggesting that success is measured by the car we drive, the house we live in, the clothes and jewelry we wear, and the air freshener that masks the smell of something rotten coming from beneath our financial house of cards. But now, having spent decades accumulating assets—homes, cars, boats, and businesses—we need to begin to disburse those assets in a way that can be sustained over 25, 30, or even 40 years of retirement. And that's where the problem lies: We've spent too much and saved too little. We didn't get this way overnight. In the early '80s, the savings rate was more than 8 percent. Now, to put it charitably, the rate is about 0 percent.

It's not just that we aren't saving enough. We're *not*. Or that we're buying too much on credit and squandering our wealth. We *are*. And both of those are bad. But more important, we've got no financial strategy to protect on the downside.

$ $ $

This book aims to get you out of paralysis and into doing something regardless of your situation. It differs from many others in that it doesn't just give you a scolding, and it doesn't give you a hot stock tip or predict which mutual funds are set to soar. In fact, this book may not mention *any* specific stocks or mutual funds. Instead, it will offer you financial strategies. Because that's what you need.

Most of us spend too much time trying to outguess the market and not enough thinking about our long-term financial future. *Money* magazine columnist Jason Zweig (January 2005) calls this tendency by investors the "inverse law of attention." He explains, "The less important something is to their long-term financial results, the more attention they pay to it. And the more important it is, the less care they give it." For example, Zweig adds, "For every hour you've spent trying to guess which investments will earn a big return, you've probably spent less than a minute thinking about your investment taxes. And yet managing taxes wisely is the simplest way to raise your returns."

What Zweig says about our focus is true. What's more, we concentrate too much on today, tomorrow, and next year and not enough on two years or even two decades from now. Making a killing on that penny stock shouldn't be your main concern. Making sure you never run out of money should be. That's what this book is about.

Start with a Strategy

I've studied the financial markets for more than 30 years. I've gotten to know thousands of listeners who've called my radio show to ask about stock-market investing. I've heard numerous horror stories. I've also watched the late-night, get-rich-quick infomercials that I find akin to those flaky diets that promise Eat More and Lose Weight! I've looked at hedge funds, timing systems, proprietary software programs, rolling stocks, options, channel investing—you name it. I've read dozens of books and hundreds of research papers on the subject of asset allocation, market timing, technical analysis, and portfolio management. In fact, I'm quite confident that I've explored much of the available scientific data to try to produce for my clients a better rate of return at an equal or lower risk.

And what have I concluded? That you need to start with a strategy that gives you the means as well as the discipline and/or courage to hold your long-term investments for years. First, find ongoing short- and intermediate-term investments that will provide years of inflation-indexed income for your daily needs. Once those income needs are handled, you can afford to allow your long-term investments, such as stocks and real estate, to grow unhampered by the market's ups and downs.

If you buy quality, well-diversified investments, keep your trading fees and taxes low, and hold for the long term, statistics suggest that you have a reasonable degree of assurance (although not a guarantee) that an amount invested in the broad stock market today should buy at least the same goods and services 20 years from now as long as that investment is left untouched, and dividends and capital gains are reinvested.

But remember, not just *any* stock investment does that. You can't simply pick any couple of stocks and succeed, even if you're really lucky. Becoming a successful stock investor depends on:

- How long you invest for (your time horizon)

- How varied your stock portfolio is (your diversification)

- How you spread your wealth among stocks, bonds, real estate, and cash (your asset allocation)

By augmenting that basic strategy with others that I'm going to present to you in this book, you can get the tools you need to win at the retirement game. I'm going to show you entirely new ways to allocate your money, ones that involve lowering risk and/or lowering taxes. I want to show you how to get the right kinds of assets in the right accounts and how to come up with a workable withdrawal strategy in retirement. I also want to introduce you to some little-known concepts, such as:

- Nontraded, low-leveraged real estate investment trusts (REITs) that can provide a stable income stream and create a hedge against inflation.

- 72(t) elections that permit a fixed amount to be withdrawn at regular intervals from retirement accounts before the age of 59½ without penalty.

- Equity-indexed and guaranteed-principal annuities that ensure a return but may pay more if the stock market does well.

- A way to lower taxes on the sale of appreciated company stock in your 401(k).

- An investment in low-income housing credits that can help you taxwise even as you help others.

- An insurance strategy for high-income individuals that provides tax-free retirement income and/or a lump-sum benefit for their heirs or favorite charity when they die.

And I'll let you in on many more techniques I've personally used and/or have used successfully as a financial advisor to help more than 5,000 retirees (or near retirees) over the course of three decades.

What This Book Contains

Part I sets the stage. First, it shows why some of the most popular investing methods, such as trying to time the market or using technical analysis, don't consistently work. Then in Chapter 2, I outline the factors that will most influence your retirement: how much you save and for how long, how you allocate your assets, what kind of return you get, and what you lose in taxes and expenses. Then "a self-interview" follows in Chapter 3 so that you can see what you're up against as you set your own retirement goals.

The middle of the book begins with an extended dialogue with "John and Chris," a hypothetical couple in whom you may see something of yourself. John and Chris know a bit about investing but not as much as they'd like. While fairly conservative, they're savvy enough to understand that they must take some risk to maximize returns. Although they'd like to leave something to their kids and to charity, they don't want to scrimp so much that they don't enjoy a comfortable retirement. And they're eager to learn about this overall strategy that would provide for both income and growth. Part II finishes with an exploration of other strategies to make your money last—everything from how to best tap into your home equity, to ways to draw down your retirement accounts, to ideas on how to maximize the benefits of rental property.

Subsequent chapters in Part III delve into things such as planning your estate, giving and/or receiving an inheritance, and how to find financial advisors who will do the best job for you.

And, finally—a topic dear to my heart—how to not just invest well, but live well . . . and enjoy every moment of what I hope is your long and fruitful retirement.

$$$$$

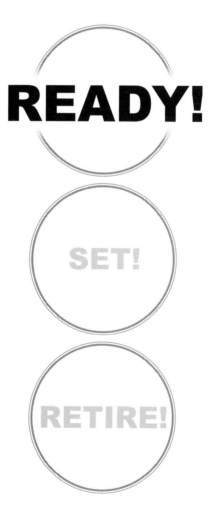

PART I

READY!

SET!

RETIRE!

CHAPTER ONE

Why You Need Strategies, Not Stock Tips

I magine that it's late 2004. You're in your 60s and saving for retirement in a 401(k) plan. Maybe you're planning to quit your job soon. You take a peek at your account balance at the end of 2004, and what do you find? That despite regular contributions and an expected growth in stocks, your savings has actually shrunk over the previous five years.

That's right. The average account balance for those in their 60s was $136,400 at year-end 2004, down from $143,161 at year-end 1999, according to a study by the Employee Benefit Research Institute and the Investment Company Institute. In effect, these soon-to-be-retired workers had run in place for five years. Instead of having something like a quarter of a million dollars set aside for retirement, they hadn't even been able to hold on to what they'd amassed five years earlier.

For those workers, crunch time had indeed arrived. They needed a new strategy—quick. Their old strategy probably was just to shovel money into their retirement account and let the stock market do the rest. Clearly, that didn't work. Now their new plan would most likely need to include some previously unimaginable options . . . like working longer, moving to a less expensive (and perhaps less desirable) part of the country, taking out a reverse mortgage, or something else that they hadn't planned on. Instead of retiring in comfort and safety, they find that they may need to just keep on . . . keepin' on.

Ought to Be Doable

Retirement looms ahead for all of us. We don't want to become hostages to the vagaries of the stock market, so we each need to come up with a plan that gives us steady income in the short term and smooths out the market's peaks and valleys over the long run. To come up with a workable strategy is doubly important now that our government and our employers can no longer be counted on to bail us out.

Many people—and you're probably among them—worry about outliving their savings. A survey by the Guardian Life Insurance Company reported that 80 percent of baby boomers, for example, are concerned about having adequate retirement income. But half said that they aren't sure how much money they'll need—and fewer than one in four (24 percent) said they were on track to amass sufficient retirement savings.

Yet this goal of creating a reasonable retirement, while it will take some work, ought to be doable for most of us. You don't need to be an investing genius, but you do need to pick a good mix of investments, and over the long term they need to perform well, though not spectacularly well. Creating such a mix and fashioning a decent retirement ought to be within the reach of motivated, intelligent individuals.

However, that will mean becoming financial adults now and seeking to become more investment savvy, something we haven't always been too keen on. For instance, many really don't know how to save or understand how money compounds or how inflation eats away at savings. According to the Guardian study, 76 percent of all boomers believe that saving $100 a month from age 30 to 65 will yield greater returns than saving $100 a month from age 21 to 30. In truth, because of compounding, the younger investor who saves from age 21 to 30 will have a larger nest egg when he or she turns 65. Also in the Guardian study, 76 percent said they would be satisfied with an investment that grew from $10,000 to $15,000 over 20 years. While that's a 50 percent gain, it's only 2.5 percent annually, less than the historical rate of inflation. Result: You'd end up with less purchasing power, not more.

So we must become better students of money. We also need to acquire a better sense of the big picture. So before I get into the specifics of what you need to do, let's look at how you're going to be affected by ongoing changes in financial affairs and how the usual ways of investing aren't stacked in your favor.

Social Security

Social Security reform, including the system's very future, is going to be debated over the next several years. Trustees who oversee Social Security predict that by 2040 the trust fund will be depleted, and payroll taxes will cover only about 73 percent of the promised benefits. One of the biggest reforms being offered up is privatization, meaning that workers would be able to divert some of their Social Security taxes into their own investment accounts. By investing on their own, taxpayers should be able to build up more money for retirement over the long haul than the scant returns earned under Social Security, or so the idea goes.

I'm all for giving Americans the freedom to work hard and build up assets. That's a big part of what has made America great. But letting workers divert some portion of their Social Security payroll taxes into individual accounts so they can invest in stocks? For some, that may be a good idea. But most people would need some serious financial education.

Privatization would be a plus for the financial industry, but would it be good for the *workers?* It might if investors properly diversify and buy and sell wisely . . . and if they have the discipline to be successful investors. But the evidence shows that they often don't. While many investors swear that they're buy-and-hold to the core, most are what are called "accidental" market timers. And those accidents are costly.

Dalbar Inc., a financial-services information firm, found that the average equity investor earned 3.51 percent annually between 1984 and 2003. That's slightly better than inflation (about 3 percent) during those two decades, but far short of the 12.98 percent annual gain for the Standard & Poor's 500 (S&P 500). (Investors did better in 2004, earning 12.6 percent, according to Dalbar.)

But isn't that long-term figure scary? Despite the fact that stock-market returns far exceeded inflation, the returns of most fund investors didn't. That's because they buy when a sector is hot, then they sell in a panic when it starts dropping. Thinking he or she is being smart and defensive, the average investor dumps stocks on the downturn and buys what the media buzz says is the next Big, New Thing. But of course, by that time the hot stock or hot fund is starting to cool. And so it goes, in a downward spiral.

The average holding period, Dalbar found, was just over two years. That, in itself, is a recipe for disaster. Is that how we want folks to invest their Social Security money? Is that better than the current system of having the government invest this money in Treasury bonds? Those bonds now pay about 5 percent. But higher returns—even for savvy investors—come with higher risks.

So, I'm sad to say, here's the honest truth: Privatization of Social Security, even if it works, won't come soon enough for most of us. Even if the problem of too many beneficiaries being supported by too few workers is fixed, Social Security just isn't going to be enough. After all, the system was always intended to play a supporting role, not be the main attraction. Increasingly, it's up to you to make sure you have some other actors in your drama.

Defined-Benefit Pensions

In days gone by, company-paid pensions—known as *defined-benefit* plans as opposed to the self-directed *defined-contribution* plans like 401(k)s—didn't warrant much thought. A pensioner just cashed his or her monthly check and hoped for an occasional hike in benefits. But poor stock-market results and low interest rates on fixed income have hampered the return on pension investments. Plus, many companies with aging workforces have failed to set aside sufficient assets to pay the promised benefits. Meanwhile, the number of active workers covered by company pensions is fast declining. That's because employees are now less likely to stay at one firm for a long time. This is both because pension plans are costly to run, and at some firms they've taken a backseat to stock options and other benefits.

As a result, less than half of households receive pensions, down from two-thirds 20 years ago. And if you're lucky enough to have one, you'd be wise to keep an eye on your former employer's financial well-being.

The fiscal health of America's private pension plans worsened again in 2005, according to the federal agency that's assigned to pick up the pieces. U.S. firms have underfunded their defined-benefit plans by a total of $450 billion, the Pension Benefit Guaranty Corporation

(PBGC) reported. The PBGC took over 120 defined-benefit pensions in the past year and now covers 1.3 million active and retired workers. When it takes over a pension system, benefits are usually cut, sometimes severely.

What's more, PBGC is not a bottomless well. While it collects roughly $600 million a year in premiums from the private sector, that's far short of what's needed to pay the pensions of companies that default. As a result, PBGC itself now runs a $23 billion deficit. While the PBGC is charged with making sure that pensioners get at least the minimum benefits, that may be a good deal less than you planned on. And with the rescuer now in need of a life preserver, that's an added reason for being watchful.

What does all of this mean for you? Probably nothing if your employer is in good financial shape. But if it's a shaky company or in an unstable industry, you should take steps to protect yourself. You can do so by studying your pension plan's benefits compared to the maximum benefit offered under the PBGC. Compare retirement ages for each plan. Scrutinize all notices and statements, ask questions, get regular updates as you near retirement, and—*yes!*—build independent savings.

Defined-Contribution Plans

Defined-contribution plans, such as your 401(k), are another matter. With these plans, employees or employers (or both) make contributions. The investments are usually employee directed, and there's no guaranteed payout.

But when fully vested, the account legally belongs to the employee, which means that you're generally protected even if your employer goes bankrupt. So your investing habits will most likely pose more risk to that nest egg than any employer mishandling. (Much more on those investing habits later.)

While 401(k)s are becoming more like pensions, with more firms automatically enrolling workers and some plans now offering annuity options, they're really quite different. You—not your employer—invest the money. What you get in retirement depends on how much you contribute and how well you manage that sum.

Thus, the burden is on you to educate yourself and perhaps consult a financial advisor to see if you're investing the right amounts in the right vehicles. Generally, you want to contribute as much as you're allowed in 401(k) and 403(b) plans, as well as maxing out on post-tax Roth IRAs. Diversify your investments and become a bit more conservative as you near retirement. Avoid holding more than, say, 20 percent of your 401(k) in your company's stock. You don't want an Enron-like situation to bring down your entire retirement.

Not What the Pundits Say

Research has proven that a diversified portfolio of stocks (and real estate) has consistently provided, over the long term (20 years or so), what's called a real rate of return—that is, a gain above and beyond the rate of inflation. According to Ibbotson Associates, there has never been a 15-year period when an investment in the broad stock market, as measured by the S&P 500 index, produced a negative return. Further, there has never been a 20-year period when the stock market hasn't produced a rate of return that didn't exceed the rate of inflation. So if investors want to minimize the risk of losing money in their equity portfolio, they should diversify, and plan on investing for a minimum of 15 to 25 years.

This buy-and-hold advice may be contrary to your instincts. It's also contrary to much of the advice, solicited or not, that we receive. Most of us want to move money around when things aren't going our way. And many pundits think they can predict with reasonable accuracy when to be in or out of the market. "Buy great stocks and do your homework," they urge, "then sell when they're no longer great stocks."

But that assumes you can analyze the ups and downs of companies as well or better than full-time professionals and determine what to buy, when to buy, and, more important, what and when to sell. Even the professionals have a tough time doing that consistently. Some investors, professional or otherwise, follow strict buy-and-sell disciplines, read stock charts religiously, have proprietary timing models, and employ sophisticated technical and fundamental analyses. Others subscribe to magazines and newsletters to help them decide how to invest, and listen regularly to the financial TV and radio shows. Armed with this often-pseudo intelligence, they manipulate their portfolios in the hopes of becoming the next Peter Lynch or Warren Buffett. Some of the exceptionally lucky ones are successful; most are not. In truth, most individual investors have neither the experience, the discipline, nor the same tools available to them to compete with the pros.

Timing Doesn't Work

Trying to time the stock market is a fool's game. Numerous studies by university professors, economists, and market gurus have come to this same conclusion. However, a large industry—comprised of timing newsletters and services, software, magazines, and seminars—makes big profits based on the notion that there's an easy way to get rich. Just buy low and sell high! Unfortunately, there's no simple way to do that.

Again, to quote *Money* magazine columnist Jason Zweig (December, 2003):

> The key to market timing is finding a valuation tool that can reliably tell you . . . when the stock market is overvalued. And many of the world's best investing minds . . . have put market history under a microscope, looking for just such a measure.
>
> Price/earnings ratios, price-to-book value, dividend yields and even the ratio of stock prices to the replacement value of corporate assets . . . can all be used, with perfect reliability, to show when the stock market was overvalued. Unfortunately, it does not appear that any of them can be used to indicate, with reasonable reliability, when the stock market is or will be overvalued.

Further, listen to your common sense. If a certain trading method really worked, wouldn't everybody begin using it? Then, of course, it would no longer work. Attempting to help you get wealthy is a multi-billion-dollar industry. That makes the promoters rich but leaves most investors holding the empty bag. Beating the broad stock market in the short term, after subtracting fees, bid/offer spreads, commissions, and taxes is extremely difficult.

Fundamental Analysis

Wall Street has mostly shunned the timers as well as the technical analysts, who analyze historical statistics to identify promising stocks. Instead, many pros prefer something called "fundamental analysis." Fundamentalists look at a company's earnings growth, price-earnings (PE) ratio, sales growth, cash position, book value, insider buying, and a host of other indicators in search of potential profitability and a higher stock price.

But even fundamental analysis may not always be a good predictor. For example, you would assume that if corporate profits are rising, then the stock market would also be rising. However, as *The Wall Street Journal* reported, a study by Ned Davis Research concluded that just the opposite has happened. Looking at historical data, researchers found that as company earnings were declining, stock prices were actually increasing—the exact opposite of what logic and most fundamentalists would predict.

Why? Because stocks generally move up or down in anticipation of future events, whether good or bad. For example, let's say that Google or Intel is believed to be headed for strong quarterly earnings. There's a good chance that those stocks, as well as the entire tech sector, will rise in anticipation of better days ahead. But by the time the earnings actually materialize, it's likely already discounted into the stock's share price. Information travels so fast in the marketplace today that as soon as the news hits the wire, it's instantly digested worldwide and discounted into the share price. This is called an "efficient market."

In fact, on Wall Street almost everything seems to work exactly the opposite of how you might think. Good economic news, for example, usually means higher interest rates are coming, and stocks often go down with the higher interest rates. If a money manager hits it out of the park one year, tons of money pours into his or her fund, and that usually causes underperformance and disappointment the next year. Thus, individual investors may be sorely disappointed if they rely exclusively on earnings growth and fundamental analysis, prior track records, or a guru's recommendations to help select the right stocks or mutual funds. Even the selections of the most highly touted stock pickers often lose their value when the hullabaloo dies down.

What's an Investor to Do?

So if neither market timing, technical or fundamental analysis, or hot tips from market gurus work consistently, what's an investor to do? The short answer is: Buy quality, well-diversified investments as part of a strategy that gives you the means as well as the discipline and/or courage to hold them for years. Exhibit discipline and patience, and work at keeping your investment fees and your taxes low.

That's the gist of my Buckets of Money plan that I outlined in my book *BUCKETS OF MONEY: How to Retire in Comfort and Safety* (John Wiley & Sons, 2004). In brief, the strategy entails investing for long-term growth so you can build a secure, lifetime retirement income.

You do that by placing short- and intermediate-term, relatively safe investments in accounts—known as Bucket Nos. 1 and 2—that will provide you with an inflation-indexed income for a period of years. Into Bucket No. 3, meanwhile, you put long-term, growth-type investments, such as stocks and real estate. The key is to spend your safe money first (Buckets Nos. 1 and 2). That buys you the time—at least 10 to 20 years—to allow Bucket No. 3 to grow. The longer you leave Bucket No. 3 alone, the lower the risk of a persistent and substantial decline in your portfolio. Sounds simple, and it is. As the Dalbar study showed, most investors tend to overmanage their holdings, hurting performance far more than they help it. But Buckets of Money helps them buy time by encouraging them to be more patient and to follow a more successful prescription for investing.

To further minimize the risk of a significant or prolonged decline, you should diversify your Bucket No. 3 among asset classes, styles, and even money managers. Also keep in mind that making a 10 to 20 percent allocation to REITs (real estate investment trusts) can help mitigate some of the overall market volatility. (According to Ibbotson, equity REITs correlate positively with large and small company stocks about 25 percent of the time. This means that 75 percent of the time when stocks are declining, REITs are on the rise, or at least not declining as much. This was especially significant during the big decline from 2000 to 2002. REITs posted some of their best performances, while stocks were recording some of their worst. The combination of the two—owning both stocks and REITs—produced significantly better results than a 100 percent allocation to stocks.)

You can also reduce stock-market risk by investing in types of stocks that don't necessarily move in lockstep. International and small-cap stocks, for example, when added to a portfolio of large stocks, tend to reduce volatility, lower risk, and increase the potential return.

Lowering volatility is important, because in a bear market a diverse portfolio tends to lose less than a concentrated one. Ironically, losing less in down markets is more important than making more in an up market. For instance, a portfolio that gains 50 percent one year, then loses 50 percent the next is still down 25 percent over the two-year period. It's often said that the best way to win in investing is to keep from losing. And the best way to do that is to diversify. That way, even if you lose, you're likely to lose less, shortening the time needed to recover.

Passive vs. Active

I've spent a lot of years studying the perfect way to invest in stocks, including looking at momentum-driven markets in which large-cap stocks were dominant. During those times, indexing (buying index funds or exchange-traded funds) was superior. Called "passive management," this strategy mirrors a market index and doesn't try to beat the market by picking individual stocks.

I've also looked at secular bear markets and bull runs inside a secular bear market. In these types of markets, stock pickers usually beat index performance. Or small caps usually beat large caps. And weighting a portfolio differently sometimes produces superior results. Because it requires a human being to make such tactical moves, this is called "active management," meaning that the investor hires a money manager who seeks to deliver return in excess of a certain benchmark. But in the end, I concluded that there's really no way to know in advance which method—indexing or active management—will eventually prevail.

In truth, you shouldn't really care which method wins in the short run as long as *you* win in the long run. That's why you'll see that later I'll recommend to John and Chris, our hypothetical couple, a blend of indexing and active management. My recommendation to them and to you is: Manage your Bucket No. 3 by using both active and passive management styles. Employ an oversight manager experienced in money-manager selection, supervision, tax efficiency, and asset allocation. Then leave the portfolio alone, letting the money managers do what they get paid to do.

Pick Your Own Individual Stocks?

Some investors, of course, pick individual stocks themselves or use a broker to help them identify which ones to buy. Some have done so successfully and have saved on fees charged by mutual funds and investment advisors. That is, they saved *if* they consistently picked the right stocks and knew when to sell them. But as we've learned from more than one scientific study, individual investors don't have a great track record when it comes to picking stocks. Plus, most investors can't afford to buy enough stocks to achieve real diversification and thus, a comfortable risk level.

The bottom line? Buying a few individual stocks can work, but most of the time it doesn't unless they are ETFs allocated in a diversified manner. (An ETF is a tracking stock that invests in a basket of stocks within a specific index or sector. For example, if you want to own the S&P 500 index, you can buy the SPY on the American Stock Exchange. Hundreds of ETFs exist, mirroring every imaginable benchmark, such as NASDAQ or a total stock market index. Or a sector like gold, real estate, or biotech. Or even a country, such as Brazil or South Korea.) ETF fees are low because they require little or no management. And because there's very little trading, ETFs are more tax efficient than most mutual funds.

$ $ $

While you digest that, let's backtrack a little. Starting with the next chapter, let's make sure you understand some of the fundamental issues that the prospect of retirement poses for you.

$ $ $ $ $

CHAPTER TWO

The Six Keys to a
Comfortable Retirement

The decline of traditional pension plans has introduced a whole new piece to the retirement puzzle: longevity risk. That's the risk that you'll outlive your savings. It used to be that your pension lasted as long as you did. And often you only lasted a few years after you retired.

Now folks are retiring earlier, living much longer, and as a result, face 20, 30, and sometimes 40 years of retirement. And that change comes when the one traditional pillar of retirement income—the pension—is vanishing, and the other pillar—Social Security—is showing some cracks. Therein lies the problem.

In this chapter, I'm going to try to distill the longevity issue for you and then look at the basic elements of saving for retirement. Those elements entail six simple ideas. Being simple means they're relatively easy to explain but not necessarily easy to do. Still, if you can master them, you can definitely inject more freedom into your retirement.

Not an Exact Science

The first thing anyone must do is get a handle on how long he or she is likely to live. On one hand, you could live much longer than you expect, burn through all your retirement savings, and end up a pauper and a burden to your family and friends. That's not a pretty picture.

On the other hand, you could die earlier than anticipated, leave a lot of money behind, and forfeit the standard of living you should have enjoyed. That's not exactly heartening, either (except maybe for your heirs).

A baby born today can expect to live 77 years, up from 43 years in 1900. But life expectancy rises as we age. On the average, then, a 65-year-old today can expect to live to 83, according to the Centers for Disease Control and Prevention. But understand that "on average" means some of those 65-year-olds will live longer.

According to some research, there's a 66 percent chance that one member of a 65-year-old couple will reach age 85, and a 39 percent chance that one member will live to 90. So risk tolerance becomes an issue. If you want close to zero risk that you'll outlive your retirement plan, then you should set an age of at least 90, maybe 95 or 100.

Of course, simply assuming a long life expectancy has its downside: You either have to save more or live on less. Life and death is not an exact science, and guesswork is inevitable. But taking into account your current health, your family history, and mortality tables can be a start.

Lots of life-expectancy tools exist online and elsewhere, and the more data the calculator asks of you, the more accurate its projection is likely to be. But please understand that the estimates you get are based on statistical averages from a large number of people. Half the time you're going to outlive that number. Or to put it another way, chances are one in two that your nest egg will need to last longer than you think. Your life-expectancy calculation is more accurate than throwing a pair of dice, but you can't count on it to be precise.

Also, remember that longevity and inflation go hand in hand. The longer you live, the more inflation erodes your purchasing power. At an annual inflation rate of 3 percent, a $1 million nest egg will have the purchasing power of $737,000 after only ten years.

Some sites to check out: Northwestern Mutual Financial Network's "Longevity Game" is free at **www.nmfn.com** (click on "Learning Center"), and **www.livingto100.com** charges a small fee.

My suggestion: Take the time to fool around with one or more calculators. It can't hurt—and it may help put your situation in perspective. At least it's a start. Once you've got a handle on a reasonable expectation of longevity, you need to think about the six main factors within your control that will influence the financial aspects of your retirement.

1. The Amount You Save

In a world of disappearing company pensions, skimpy bond yields, rich stock valuations, and rising life expectancies, anybody interested in a comfortable retirement should be saving like crazy. Yet most folks aren't. And that spells trouble. As my friend Ben Stein says, "This is the greatest crisis facing the country that people can do something about."

For most people, living beneath their means is a major challenge. But trust me, trying to have a comfortable retirement without sufficient income will be an even bigger one. As Errol Flynn used to say, "My problem lies with reconciling my gross habits with my net income." But that's our challenge.

In 1999, the national savings rate dipped below 3 percent for the first time since 1959, according to the U.S. Department of Commerce. It's pretty much been declining since then, as I mentioned, and now is, charitably, at about 0 percent.

(Now, in all fairness, it must be said that there's a lot of criticism of the methodology used by Commerce Department's Bureau of Economic Analysis, which calculates this figure. Indeed, it may be flawed. But if it does understate savings today, then presumably it understated it in earlier years. So if the 8 percent to 10 percent of disposable income that was being saved in the 1960s through the 1980s was low, we're still being profligate. The overall conclusion, that Americans are saving a lot less than they used to, doesn't change.)

True, the savings rate doesn't include increases in household wealth due to soaring stock-and-bond prices. But capital gains don't regularly add to wealth the way regular savings do.

Of course, it's safe to say that many people figure that the equity in their homes will bail them out. And it's true that some home owners will be able to sell large homes and take cash out in their old age. But it's folly to rely on home prices rising ad infinitum. Something that can't go on forever is surely going to stop.

Nearly 37 percent of households do not own a retirement savings account of any kind. And among those who do, the median value of all such accounts was just $27,000, according to a 2004 report by the Congressional Research Service. This isn't just a problem for poor people. Even among households with incomes of $75,000 or more, 23 percent had no retirement savings or pension plan.

According to the AARP, households headed by baby boomers have median financial assets of just $50,700. Based on a 5 percent withdrawal rate, that would yield a meager $2,535 of annual retirement income.

So what should you do? To begin with, forget that old rule of thumb about socking away 10 percent of your pretax income every year. That probably stems from the days when most retirees had company pensions. The idea was that if you saved 10 percent and you augmented that with the pension and Social Security, you'd be okay. But as we've already seen, for most folks, the pension may be no more and Social Security is not likely to be what it has been. So that 10 percent rule is woefully insufficient.

If it's true that money talks, the only thing it says to many people is "good-bye." If you're one of them, then you really need to get into the savings habit. And the more you save, the better. But I'd suggest a minimum 20 percent of your pretax income. That hurts now, but it will feel much better later on.

2. How Long You Let Your Nest Egg Grow

This, of course, is a function of (a) when you start saving, and (b) when you retire.

When you start. Einstein famously said that compound interest was the eighth wonder of the world, and he was right. What's more, it's the safest road, and anybody can harness it. The catch is that it requires time. "Time," as noted investor Richard Russell, publisher of the *Dow Theory Letters,* has written, "is the single most valuable asset you can ever have in your investment arsenal. The problem is that none of us has enough of it."

But if you're savvy enough to start early squirreling away your pennies and allowing the miracle of compounding to do its work, you can do all right. Few investors ever have big sums handed to them via inheritances or gifts. Instead, they accumulate assets by working hard, by doing without, by managing well, and by accepting reasonable risks. All of us can learn from these poor but persistent savers.

And the first thing we can learn is: You can't start too soon. In fact, to start saving at an early age is the best way to ensure a comfortable retirement. When it comes to saving, sooner trumps later every time. Invest $500 a month at the age of 30, let it compound at 10 percent annually, and when you turn 65 you'll have about $1.9 million. Start doing the same thing at age 50 and you'll end up with less than $210,000.

When you retire. The answer here depends on lots of things, such as your health, how much you like your job, longevity, the amount you've saved, office politics (possibly), and how your firm fares. A lot of people who say that they'll work into their late 60s or even early 70s don't make it because of their health or company shake-ups.

In fact, many Americans begin dipping into their retirement savings at age 62 or thereabouts. Why? Two reasons: One, that's the age when they can first file for Social Security benefits; and two, that's the age at which many workers retire. (The average retirement age in the United States is 61.6 for men and 61 for women, according to Murray Gendell, an emeritus research professor at Georgetown University.)

But as appealing as early retirement might sound, it can really strain your savings, especially if you still have a mortgage and are on the hook for your own medical insurance. So waiting just a few years before tapping into your nest egg could make a real difference in retirement. Every extra year means that your money has an opportunity to grow.

My advice? Plan conservatively by expecting to retire at no earlier than 65. In fact, if possible, work a few more years and boost your standard of living in retirement. Workers who stay two years beyond the standard retirement age of 65 and increase their 401(k) contributions (for example, from 6 percent of salary to 8 percent) can significantly improve their retirement income, according to Hewitt Associates, a human-resources consulting firm. That study estimated that the average worker who retires at 65 without a pension or retiree medical coverage will replace only 57 percent of his or her preretirement income. But the average worker in the same situation who retires at 67 could replace more than 80 percent of his or her preretirement income, depending on how long the worker has been saving for retirement. Working longer can be a particularly important strategy for workers who won't receive a pension or company-provided medical benefits, Hewitt said.

And by the way, what's wrong with working a little longer than our parents or grandparents did? Remember, when Social Security was first enacted, we were supposed to be dead in three to five years after becoming eligible. Now, for those blessed with good health and maybe some money, too, retirement can be the start of a 20- to 30-year party.

3. How You Allocate Your Assets

Figuring out whether you've saved enough is just half the battle. The other half is creating an investment plan that will generate income without exhausting your stash.

You can't simply rely on the traditional advice for retirees: Put most of your savings into corporate bonds and dividend-paying stocks and then live off the income. For most people, especially those who've retired early, that's a recipe for disaster because you probably won't receive enough income. Then, forced to spend the principal, you'll risk using up your savings much too quickly, especially if there's an economic downturn.

Once you have enough set aside to retire on, you need to establish a reliable system that lets you invest in stocks and real estate for long-term growth, while holding enough in fixed income to mitigate the risk of owning equities. That way you'll have a reliable source of money to live on for years to come. This is called "asset allocation," and it can be a tricky balance to strike. If you put too much in fixed income, you won't get the growth you need. But if you put too much in stocks and you don't get the returns you're hoping for, you'll be in big trouble.

If you could spread your investments among noncorrelated assets (those that tend to move in opposite directions from one another), you could maintain higher returns while taking less risk. That's the Holy Grail of investing, akin to finding a nifty-looking sports car that seats six and can also pull your boat trailer. And that's what the Buckets of Money strategy, which I mentioned earlier, may be able to do for you. We'll soon get into that in more detail.

4. Your Annual Investment Returns

When it comes to investing, most investors can't simply hope to rely on interest from, say, municipal or corporate bonds or CDs. That's far too conservative for someone younger or someone who hasn't amassed a few million dollars or more or who can't live on just 2 or 3 percent of their assets.

That kind of portfolio would hurt your total return over time, and you'd risk using up your savings too quickly. In a very few years, you could end up scouring the job listings and circulating your résumé again. Far from getting out of the rat race, you'd become a rodent once more.

You have to assume the worst, such as a long, deep recession or maybe even several of them during your retirement. So don't make unrealistic assumptions about the returns your savings and investments will generate (or about how much you'll spend, which we'll discuss in the next chapter). It's important also to keep risk low by sticking to high-quality securities and diversifying broadly.

I concur with numerous experts who believe that in the future we'll be looking at modest stock-and-bond returns, especially after the heady gains of the past 25 years. The yield on the benchmark ten-year Treasury bond went from almost 16 percent in 1981 to about 5 percent today, driving up bond prices along the way. And the stock market rose from 8 times the most recent 12-month earnings in 1982 to something like 20 times recent earnings today. We aren't likely to see those gains repeated.

What kind of return should you project? Sure, you've read about stocks returning an average of 10 percent per year or more over the long term. But again, that's an average, not a gain that can be expected year in and year out. Remember the years 2000 to 2002? That's when more than a third of affluent investors lost 51 percent or more of the value of their portfolios. Another 39 percent lost up to 50 percent.

So what's a reasonable return to aim for? I'd say shoot for a 6 to 7 percent average annual return for a diversified portfolio. For example, if stocks earn 8 percent long term (that's less than their historic 10 percent, but realistic, I think, based on current valuations); and bonds earn 5 percent, a 60-40 mix of stocks and bonds would produce a 6.8 percent overall return.

There's much danger in overestimating your investment returns when preparing retirement income-and-expense projections. Of course, I hope you'll make more than 6 percent or 7 percent, but you don't want to bet your retirement ranch on that. Don't use a high investment-return assumption as a reason not to save enough money for retirement. And don't swallow any advisor's or salesman's claim that great returns can be projected out endlessly. Err on the conservative side. That way, if there *is* going to be a surprise, let it be a pleasant one.

5. The Investment Expenses You Incur

While I believe you'll probably do better working with an investment advisor (and several studies back up that belief), you still need to be sensitive to the fees you pay. That's because even small differences in expenses can make a big difference in your return. If a fund is returning 20 percent a year, should you even care that it's a bit pricey? *Yes.* You should also care about how much risk the fund took to get such a good return. There's a lot you need to know. For example:

Load vs. no-load. Every mutual fund is either "load" or "no-load", meaning that it does or doesn't charge a sales commission. The average load is close to 5 percent. Thus, on a $10,000 investment with a 5 percent load, only $9,500 would actually go to work for you. No-load funds, however, never charge a sales commission because they don't rely on brokers or commissioned financial planners to sell their funds.

So it comes down to this: If you can do your own financial planning and investing, you're probably better off saving the sales fee and choosing a no-load. Your investment will have a head start if no commission is deducted. On the other hand, if an advisor can keep you focused on the right things and help you stick with your asset allocation during good and bad times, the load may be worth paying.

Expense ratio. You can compare the ongoing management expenses of each fund by looking at its expense ratio. A fund is required by law to disclose that figure in its prospectus. Because those expenses are automatically deducted from your returns, they often go unnoticed by investors.

Adding to the murkiness is that different types of funds charge different expense ratios. A typical expense ratio for a domestic equity fund is about 1.4 percent. But index funds, which require less management, charge around 0.5 percent or less, and bond funds about 1.0 percent for managed accounts. More management-intensive funds include real estate (1.5 percent), precious metals (1.9 percent), and international or emerging-markets funds (1.8 percent).

Take the time to find out the expense ratios of the funds you may invest in. Multiply the amount of money you're going to invest by the fund's expense ratio to learn how much you would be paying for investment management.

Over the long run, shopping for the best deal can save you a ton of money. Obviously, a fund that combines low expenses with lousy performance isn't a great deal. But, believe it or not, top performance is often linked to lower expenses, especially with bond funds. Many times it's the cheap expenses—not the skill or intelligence of the fund manager—that vaults a fund to the top of its class.

An added complication is that a load fund may offer three classes of shares—A, B, and C—with widely varying fees and expenses. And it's important to make sure that you're getting the class that's cost-effective for you.

Classes A, B, and C all represent the same interest in the fund's portfolio. The only difference among them is how much you'll pay in fees and expenses and how your broker will be paid. Class A (called a "front-end" load) charges an up-front commission and lower annual fees. Class B ("back-end" load) imposes higher ongoing fees and a sales charge—not when you buy but when you sell—if you sell prior to six or eight years. Class C, or "level-load" shares, typically charge an ongoing fee of about 1 percent annually and may have a redemption fee if you bail out within the first 12 to 18 months. Class B and C shares don't offer a discount (known as a *breakpoint*) if you invest a lot of money (say, more than $25,000), but Class A does.

It's hard to make a good case for why you'd want to buy Class B shares, but a lot of people do because it galls them to pay front-end charges. But remember, some classes, though touted as being free of up-front fees, actually may end up costing you a lot more.

Usually, Class A is a better choice for a long-term, buy-and-hold investor because: (1) The impact of the initial commission will fade, and (2) the lower annual fees will improve the performance. But others may prefer C shares as a means to compensate a financial professional for working with them on multiple financial issues.

When deciding which class is best for you, consider how long you plan to hold the fund, the size of your investment, the expenses you'll pay for each class, and whether you qualify for any discounts. Always discuss this with your advisor before you invest, and determine what you get for the money you'll pay.

Be sure to read the fund's prospectus *before* you buy. Pay particular attention to the discussion of fund classes and fees. If you're considering a large purchase, make sure that you understand how the breakpoints work and if they apply to you. Don't be pressured into making an on-the-spot decision.

When you sit down with your broker or financial advisor, ask him or her to explain the loads in plain English and show you how they affect performance over several years. Some brokers pushing B shares argue that these are "no-load" (not true) or have no initial sales commission (true, but there's another shoe to drop). On big fund purchases, brokers can earn more from selling B shares than A shares.

My advice? If you use a financial advisor to help you select mutual funds, evaluate the merits of a purchase of A shares (for buy-and-hold, strategic investing) versus a C-shares purchase (a tactical portfolio requiring ongoing input from a financial professional).

6. The Taxes You Pay

As some wag once said, "Death and taxes may be life's only certainties . . . but at least death doesn't get worse every time the Congress convenes."

Tax efficiency is an oft-neglected issue. It's important that you tax-manage your investments. For instance, fully fund your IRA or 401(k). Hold your taxable investments 12 months or longer when possible to qualify for the lower long-term capital-gains rates.

Place your securities in the right kinds of accounts for maximum tax benefit. For example, keep high-yielding assets—bonds, REITs, and short-term investments that would be taxed at higher rates—in tax-advantaged retirement accounts. Put qualified dividend-paying stocks and longer-term investments in taxable accounts. And at year-end, offset realized gains with realized losses, if you have them.

Increasingly, too, larger investors seeking tax efficiency are gravitating to what are known as "privately managed accounts." Traditionally, these were available only to very wealthy investors who had, say, $1 million or more in assets. But now these accounts typically require minimums of $100,000 or more. At first glance, the privately managed accounts appear similar to a mutual fund because both are portfolios of securities managed by professional money managers. But they differ, in that investors in privately managed accounts can customize their holdings by instructing the manager to avoid certain types of stocks while mutual-fund investors have no say over which stocks the manager buys.

Most important, though, are the tax benefits. When you invest in a private account, you own each of the individual securities in that account and, thus, establish your own cost basis. By contrast, in a mutual fund you own a share of the pooled assets, not the actual stock, and are bound by the group's cost basis. That may mean that you're buying a fraction of the fund's tax liability on stock that may have appreciated before you bought the fund. Even though you weren't invested in the fund during the stock's rise in price, you'll pay part of the tax bill that gets passed on to the fund's shareholders.

So having their own stock with its own cost basis gives holders of privately managed accounts more control over their taxes. They only pay capital-gains taxes on the profits they realized while they owned the stock. This greater control also can create opportunities to harvest losses in their portfolios, further minimizing taxes.

Defying the Conventional Wisdom

No matter how much you save or how carefully you budget, two things will eat away at your retirement savings: inflation and taxes. Inflation is pretty much out of your control, but as we've seen, you can minimize the tax bite.

A bit of background: If you own mutual funds, stocks, and other investments outside of retirement plans, you're already paying taxes on dividends, interest, and capital gains. But on traditional IRAs, 401(k)s, and other employer-sponsored plans, you pay no taxes until you withdraw funds. But you can't leave them alone forever. Once you turn 70½, you're required to start taking what are called RMDs—required minimum distributions.

The conventional wisdom about taking withdrawals in retirement is to defer, defer, defer: Spend your taxable money first, and save your tax-deferred retirement accounts for last to give those accounts extra time to grow. A huge proportion of the population does that, apparently unaware of the big downsides.

Yes, their IRAs will grow tax deferred, but when it comes time to take those required minimum distributions at age 70½, they'll have to take out so much money that it may catapult them into the next tax bracket and possibly even increase the tax on their Social Security benefits. What's more, when the retiree dies with all that money in his or her tax-advantaged accounts, the heirs are taxed on it at ordinary-income rates, not a stepped-up basis as would be the case with securities inherited outside a retirement account.

So deferring the withdrawal of IRA money always makes sense *unless* you can take money out in a low tax bracket now instead of a higher tax bracket later. That's why the smart move in some situations is to defy the conventional wisdom and withdraw some money from taxable accounts and some from retirement accounts like IRAs.

For instance, you might first draw down some of the money from your traditional IRA, depending on your tax bracket. Remember, for a married couple, personal exemptions and the standard deduction alone will offset nearly $20,000. Plus, if you itemize deductions on Schedule A, your mortgage interest, property taxes, and charitable contributions can add up to even more. So by withdrawing taxable money from your IRA and offsetting it with an equal amount of deductions, you're withdrawing money that was probably once taxed in the 25 percent or higher bracket and taking it out in the 0 percent bracket.

Then you've still got the 10 percent tax bracket to use up, again depending on the size of your IRA. If you've got a big IRA, you'd be wise to use up the next $15,000 or so (for a married couple), which would exhaust your 10 percent bracket. Then, again depending on the size of the IRA, your advisor could help you determine whether to tap into a taxable account or continue to siphon off the IRA.

Thus, the order of priority is to use up your low brackets first: your 0 percent bracket, then your 10 percent bracket. Then make a further determination. If you have a $5 million IRA, for example, then you should draw it down all the way up to your 25 percent bracket. But if you're like most people and have, say, $200,000 to $400,000 in your IRA, you will probably want to withdraw some from both taxable accounts and tax-deferred accounts to get the most tax-efficient retirement income. You'll also want to look at such issues as step-up in basis at death, capital-gains-tax treatment, qualified dividends, and other factors affecting your taxes and retirement income.

Keep in mind that the Roth IRA, unlike the traditional IRA, allows tax-free withdrawals and doesn't require you to take minimum distributions at any time. So you may choose to let these savings continue to compound until you've exhausted your other sources of funds. Or blend some tax-free Roth money with taxable dollars from traditional IRAs to hold down your taxable income. Provided you've owned your Roth for at least five years and are 59½ or older, you'll never have to pay taxes on your withdrawals. That makes it an excellent planning tool.

So again, to keep your taxes down while you're working, fully fund your IRA or 401(k). Hold your taxable investments 12 months or longer when possible to qualify for the lower long-term capital-gains rate. (Or do your short-term trading in a tax-deferred account.) Pay close attention to brokerage commissions, mutual-fund expense ratios, and any loads you're being asked to pay. Keep high-yielding assets that would be taxed at higher rates—like bonds and REITs—in your qualified retirement plan. And rather than blindly postponing withdrawals from your tax-deferred retirement accounts, investigate whether you'd save on taxes by drawing down a mixture of some income from those and some from your taxable or tax-free accounts.

$ $ $

How much you save and for how long, your asset allocation, your return, your investment expenses, and your taxes are the six factors that—in addition to the vagaries of the market—will ultimately determine the value of your investment portfolio. If you save as much as you can, starting as soon as you can, allocate your assets properly, and minimize taxes and expenses, you will have done a lot of the heavy lifting. And you'll be on your way to retiring in comfort and safety.

So next, let's see how your situation shapes up.

$ $ $ $ $

CHAPTER THREE

A Self-Interview
about Your Future

Before you toss out the alarm clock, ditch the commute, and say a cheery "Good morning" to the idea of being retired, you need to ask yourself a bunch of questions. Answering them fully and honestly—*before* you even think about cracking open your nest egg—will boost your chances for a successful retirement.

It's tempting to want to jump in immediately to pick out specific investments. (And we'll soon do that, starting with the next chapter.) But first you need to do some thinking about where you are today, where you want to be in the future, and how you'll get there. Right now you don't need an investment vehicle as much as you need a road map. That's what this chapter is about.

After all, long-term investment success means different things to different people. You may need to fund college educations for your children or have a parent to look after. You may expect an inheritance that will ease your money challenges. Or you may plan to leave a legacy to your kids or to your favorite charity.

So your investment plan should be uniquely yours. Without a specific "end game" in mind, it's easy to become distracted and make poor financial decisions that will end up affecting your quality of life down the road. So your first task is to unearth your values and objectives. Then get down to the nitty-gritty of how best to make your retirement work.

Among your queries should be the following. (You might want to answer these questions in a notebook or on the blank Notes pages at the end of the book):

1. What do I want for my children? My spouse? Other family members?

2. Ideally, where would I like to be financially when I'm 60? 70? 80?

3. Could I live a rewarding, satisfying life on a reduced income? How?

4. When I think about money, what concerns, needs, or feelings come to mind?

5. How enjoyable is my job? My profession? Too enjoyable to give up entirely?

6. What nonfinancial benefits does my job/profession give me? Status? A sense of belonging? A place to be? A life's purpose?

7. How will I replace those benefits after I retire?

Those are big questions. Take some time to think about them, preferably writing down your answers . . . and then thinking about them some more. (Remember that old Jack Benny routine in which a mugger confronts him, demanding "Your money or your life"? Benny, the classic tightwad, is stony-faced and silent. The mugger repeats the demand. Benny, hand on chin, still says nothing. Agitated, the mugger shouts, "Your money *or* your life?" To which Benny finally replies, "I'm thinking it over.")

While you're thinking it over, add this to the mix: What is your investment horizon and your risk tolerance? They're related. Your investment horizon helps define your *ability* to take risk, while your risk tolerance involves your *willingness* to do so.

The closer you are to retirement—that is, the shorter the horizon—the more likely it is you wouldn't have time to recover from a severe bear market. Investors with a longer investment horizon have a greater ability to take risks, and thus can allocate a greater percentage of their portfolio to stocks.

But this is a highly personal matter based on your own risk tolerance. Here's my gauge for figuring out how much an investor should keep in stocks as he or she nears retirement:

- If you're super-aggressive . . . keep only five years of "safe" dollars in cash, money-market accounts, CDs, or other short-term securities.

- If you're moderately aggressive . . . ten years' worth of "safe" dollars should work.

- For most people . . . 15 years' worth of reasonably "safe" money is advisable.

- For the conservative-minded . . . aim for 20 years' worth.

- For the fainthearted . . . probably nothing less than 25 years of "safe" money will allow them to sleep well at night.

How do I arrive at those figures? Well, if you invest in the stock market for five years, you've got about an 85 percent chance of making money and a 15 percent chance of losing money, according to research by Ibbotson Associates, a major financial-research firm. And if you invest for 15 years, you've got (again, according to Ibbotson) a statistical 100 percent chance of at least breaking even. So if you want a statistical assurance (not the same as a real-world guarantee) that you wouldn't lose money on the stock portion of your portfolio, you'd invest for 15 years. Ibbotson also tells us that stocks have always beaten inflation over 20-year periods, and there hasn't been a 25-year period since 1950 in which stocks haven't produced at least a 7.94 percent return. Which benchmark will work for you depends solely on you. But my advice is to always err on the side of moderation.

That being done, the next big questions you need to ask involve the critical nuts and bolts of retirement:

- Am I starting at the right time?
- How much will I be spending?
- What assets will I have to work with?
- How can I ensure that my retirement income will outlast me?

Am I Starting at the Right Time?

Ideally, the answer to this ought to be the result of careful consideration over the course of several years. Okay, so much for theory. In practice, a lot of people peg their prospective retirement to the age at which they can collect Social Security benefits.

But Social Security is a lot more complicated than it used to be. In the old days, you just turned 65 and you drew your check. Now, you can get a reduced check as early as age 62. But the threshold for when you can draw the full benefit is rising, and tax complications abound.

The government is increasing the age people must reach to receive full benefits, raising it slowly from 65 to 67. And the percentage of benefits paid to those who apply at the earliest possible age is gradually being lowered, from 80 percent to 70 percent. These changes affect anyone born in 1938 or later.

For instance, a retired worker who is now 61 and earned $50,000 a year could begin receiving benefits a month after his or her next birthday. That would bring in approximately $1,015 monthly. (Benefits are based on a recipient's highest 35 years of inflation-indexed wages during a working lifetime.)

But if he or she opts to wait until full retirement age, which in this case would be 66, the benefit would be $1,401. Or if the worker waited until age 70, the check would be $1,940 a month. (The government sets each amount so that an average worker would receive roughly the same total benefit over a lifetime, regardless of which choice was made.)

So when is the best time to start tapping those benefits? People facing this issue fall into two groups: those who really need the money now to make ends meet, and those who have other retirement income.

If you really need the Social Security check to put food on the table, then you should grab it as early as possible—age 62. You'll get upwards of 20 percent less than you would if you waited a few years. But, hey, starving isn't an acceptable option. And taking benefits early is a lot better than going into debt just to live.

If, like most Americans, you have some other sources of retirement income, the choice is tougher, and it hinges on the issue of longevity. Live longer than expected and you get more than the government planned to pay. Die too soon and you get less than your share.

So if you expect to live long because of good health and family longevity, you may want to wait for your normal retirement age, or even longer, to collect a full or enhanced benefit for a very long time. Feeling poorly or have an adverse family history? Then perhaps you should start collecting your benefits as soon as possible. Of course, betting on a short life but living long is a wager you probably won't mind losing.

Let's take a closer look at some of the pluses and minuses for opting for early benefits:

The Advantages of Taking Social Security at Age 62

- You can get a monthly check for at least 36 months longer than you would otherwise. At, say, $1,000 per month, that's a pretty nice bird in the hand.

- A dollar now is worth more than a dollar three years from now because it can be invested and, potentially, can generate further income. Enough added income to make up for the decreased benefits? That will depend on market conditions, your investment skill, and how long you live.

- The Social Security check may delay the need to draw down your retirement portfolio, giving it a further chance to grow. Particularly if your portfolio is on a sharp upswing, this could be a big plus for your retirement.

- If you expect the government to tinker with Social Security and ultimately lower the benefits, you're taking action now to get what you can while you can.

- If you think you won't live longer than the average life expectancy, taking the check at 62 may help maximize your Social Security lifetime benefits.

Sound good? Maybe so. But especially if you plan to continue working, there are drawbacks to taking that check early.

The Disadvantages of Taking Social Security at Age 62

- You'll get about 80 percent of the check you'd receive if you waited until your full retirement age to start taking Social Security.

- If you continue to work between age 62 and your full retirement age, $1 in benefits will be deducted for each $2 earned above an annual limit. That limit is $12,000 in 2006. (Only wage income counts. Investment earnings, IRA or pension distributions, annuities, and capital gains are *not* included as income for this calculation.) The penalty decreases in the year you reach full retirement age, and there's no penalty, no matter how much you earn, once you reach full retirement age.

- Those making more than a certain amount of adjusted gross income (AGI) may have 50 to 85 percent of their Social Security benefits taxed. That AGI *does* include investment earnings and tax-free interest.

- By taking less at 62, you may think you're inoculating yourself against major policy changes to Social Security, but history suggests that such changes probably will be phased in over a long period anyway. (The inching up of the age for obtaining full benefits, for example, has only taken effect in the last few years, but it stems from legislation passed in 1983.) Thus, any future changes are unlikely to affect your check in the short to intermediate term.

What's the Trend?

In recent years, about 67 percent of men and 72 percent of women have claimed their Social Security benefits before reaching age 65. And that percentage is up sharply over the past 30 years. You might think it would be otherwise, what with life expectancies rising. And you might expect that especially to be the case with women. Because women generally live longer, wouldn't they be inclined to hold out until 65 or 66 and get the bigger check? Perhaps, but that's not the trend.

Why are folks rushing to take the benefits early? Probably too many do so without much thought. But many also think they can get high returns on their portfolios. It's true that your portfolio has the potential to grow more if you're living on your Social Security and not drawing down your investment savings. But how much return can you realistically expect? Investors are often overly optimistic.

Some take benefits early because that's the only way they can afford to retire. That's a good reason. But if your retirement funds are that scant, perhaps you should postpone retirement, work a few more years, and build up your nest egg.

And some take benefits early because they fear the Social Security system will collapse, or the benefits will be radically scaled back to prevent such a collapse. But, as mentioned, when and if the cutbacks occur, they will probably be aimed at folks some years from retirement. The lead time on systemic changes tends to be long.

Other Considerations

This is a highly individual decision you face. For those who expect to live into their 80s or beyond, delaying Social Security in favor of a larger monthly check for the years after 65 makes a lot of sense. But an argument can also be made that workers should take advantage of benefits earlier when they're still healthy enough to spend and enjoy the money.

Remember, events could happen after you decide to take the benefits that could make you wish you hadn't. For example, a market crash and/or some really bad decisions could decimate your savings. Or you could live a lot longer than you expect and outlive those savings. At that point, having delayed taking Social Security in order to get a bigger stipend might seem like one of the best decisions you've made.

How many elderly people do you know for whom 20 percent more in their Social Security check would greatly improve their lives and perhaps ease the burden on their kids? Probably quite a few.

And don't forget about inflation. It's been relatively benign recently, but if that changes, you might wish that you hadn't locked yourself into a smaller check. So put some thought into this. Don't make a quick decision that you might later regret.

As with so many other personal-finance questions, there's no one right answer. But the Social Security Administration's Website (**www. ssa.gov**) can help you sort through the options. It includes benefit calculators that use a worker's age and earnings history to show the monthly benefits he or she can expect under different scenarios.

Also take into account your tax situation. If, after you begin collecting Social Security, you have other taxable income, part of your Social Security benefit can be taxable. About 20 percent of recipients pay some tax on benefits.

Seniors also should monitor whether working will tip them into a higher tax bracket. It might help to fill out some worksheets or ask a financial advisor for guidance before making a decision about a post-retirement job.

When your annual Social Security statement comes in the mail (about three months before your birthday), check it carefully. It will show your lifetime earnings and what you can expect to get in Social Security benefits, assuming you keep earning at your current level. Those benefits will be adjusted each year to keep up with inflation.

Be sure to note the age at which you'll be eligible for full benefits. Understand that those benefits will increase if you postpone taking them until you're even older, say, at age 70. If you didn't get a statement or misplaced it, you can order a free replacement by phone (800-772-1213) or through the Website.

What We Say vs. What We Do

As people nervously eye the onset of retirement, there's a lot of talk about this generation of workers not retiring in the manner others have. Surveys show that many workers say they'll never retire or they'll work until they're 70, and by doing so they hope to make up the deficit in their retirement savings.

That may seem appealing from a distance, but be careful: Reality isn't always so kind. For example, the annual Retirement Confidence Survey a year or so ago found a gap between what respondents said and did. More than half of preretirees said they expected to work till at least 65, often longer. Yet the average retiree surveyed actually left work at 62, and 40 percent of those retirees stopped working earlier than expected, often because of health or job troubles.

The moral: Even though planning to work longer may be a good idea, a lot of people can't do that for one reason or another, such as failing health, office politics, or corporate restructuring. In fact, the average age at which workers claim Social Security benefits (usually a sure sign of someone retiring) has been virtually unchanged since 1985—about 63.5 years.

But let's stop predicting rain and instead start building arks. We'll do that by first seeing what materials we have.

How Much Will I Be Spending?

This is the first assignment almost every financial advisor gives to preretirees: Estimate your annual expenses. Because if you don't know what your bills might be each month or each year—for both essential and discretionary items—you won't know how much money you can safely withdraw from your nest egg.

Many people, though, are hesitant to take this step. There's something about reining oneself in that way that smacks of mortality and a tearful good-bye to youthful indulgence. But the truth is, you'll have a finite amount of resources with which to pursue infinite possibilities. Something has to give. This isn't easy, but it has to be done.

I know, I *know*. Unless you're already retired, it's tough to figure out what your expenses are going to be next month, let alone 5, 10, or 20 years from now. But it's important to start the process and give it a good shot.

The Typical Retiree

Some background: Conventional wisdom holds that you need to generate from 65 to 85 percent of your preretirement income to live comfortably in retirement. But that's off-the-rack wisdom. What you need is an estimate custom-designed for you.

Here's something with a little more meat on its bones: A study by The Boston College Center for Retirement Research showed that typical married adults aged 65 and older spend $14,792 a year. (Does that sound typical?) The top fifth in income have average expenses of $25,567, and the lowest fifth spend $10,111.

More statistically important are the percentages. For example, the typical retired couple devotes 29 percent of their budget to housing as well as 20 percent on health care, 13 percent on food, 2 percent on clothing, 12 percent on transportation, 10 percent on entertainment, 10 percent on gifts, and 4 percent on other stuff.

Researchers were especially surprised at the amount spent on housing. One in four retirees is a home owner still carrying a mortgage. If that doesn't apply to you, then factor that in the calculations that follow. But keep in mind that even if you own your home free and clear, you'll still be saddled with rising costs of utilities, property taxes, and maintenance. Of course, another option is to downsize. Emotions aside, that can free up money to pay for living expenses; as well as reduce the cost of utilities, taxes, and maintenance.

Health care is the other big-ticket item, and you'll probably have less latitude there. Retirees, on average, spend 8 percent of their income on health-insurance premiums, 6 percent on prescription drugs, 4 percent on health services, and 1 percent on medical supplies. But those numbers can change dramatically with changes in one's health. Those in poor health spend twice as much on prescription drugs, and those without employer-provided health insurance spend more on insurance premiums.

It may not be possible to trim health costs as one can with housing costs. So you should plan for the possibility of catastrophic costs. And keep in mind that even if you're covered by Medicare, it doesn't take care of all expenses.

Create a Cushion

The key is to be as precise as possible while keeping in mind that these expenses may change from year to year. For example, you may pay off your home mortgage or your children's education early in retirement. On the other hand, health-care and insurance costs may very well rise as you age. To protect against these variables, build a comfortable cushion into your estimates.

Also, make allowances for your dreams. Sure, you've got to figure in utilities, transportation, food, and the like, but you also may want to budget that trip to Tuscany you've dreamed about. When is that going to happen? And what is that going to cost?

Planning for expenses in retirement is tricky. In the end, it comes down to judging the value of a dollar spent today versus a dollar saved today. Online calculators can be very helpful, and many are free. For a couple good ones to check out, go to the Websites of mutual-fund firms T. Rowe Price (**www.troweprice.com**) and Vanguard (**www. vanguard.com**).

But, for now, let's get started the old-fashioned way: with paper and pencil.

Step 1: List Your Expenses

- *Food and clothing:* (Because you'll no longer be working, you probably won't spend as much on clothes. But not having an expense account might mean that you pay for more lunches yourself.)
  Expected monthly expense: $_____

- *Housing:* Rent or mortgage payments, property taxes, home owners insurance, property upkeep, and repairs. (Even if you pay off your mortgage, you'll still have taxes and the cost of maintenance, and they will likely go up.)
  Expected monthly expense: $_____

- *Utilities:* Gas, electric, water, telephone, cable TV.
  Expected monthly expense: $_____

- *Transportation:* Car payments, auto insurance, gas, maintenance and repairs, public transportation. (You will probably drive less because you'll no longer commute to work. But will you be taking more driving vacations?)
  Expected monthly expense: $_____

- *Insurance:* Medical, dental, life, disability, long-term care.
  Expected monthly expense: $_____

- *Health-care costs not covered by insurance:* Deductibles, co-payments, prescription drugs. (Figure on these increasing significantly as you age.)
  Expected monthly expense: $_____

- *Taxes:* Federal and state income tax, capital-gains tax.
  Expected monthly expense: $_____

- *Debts:* Personal loans, business loans, credit-card payments.
  Expected monthly expense: $_____

- *Education:* Children's or grandchildren's college expenses.
  Expected monthly expense: $_____

- *Gifts:* Charitable and personal.
  Expected monthly expense: $_____

- *Recreation:* Travel, dining out, hobbies, leisure activities. (These will probably increase greatly with your added free time.)
  Expected monthly expense: $_____

- *Care for yourself or others:* Costs for a nursing home, home health aide, or other types of assisted living.
  Expected monthly expense: $_____

- *Miscellaneous:* Personal grooming, pets, club memberships.
  Expected monthly expense: $_____

Step 2: Add Them Up to Get Total Monthly Expenses

Total *monthly* expenses: $ _____

Step 3: Multiply by 12 (months)
to Get Expected *Yearly* Expenses

Monthly expenses x 12: $ _____

Note: If you're already retired or about to retire, the above expense number is a good start. If you're five years away from retirement, multiply that number by 1.2 to produce an inflation-indexed (3 percent) number. If you're 10 years from retirement, multiply it by 1.3; 15 years by 1.6; and 20 years by 1.8. Also keep in mind some expenses like fixed-interest mortgages don't inflate. So that may give you a little fudge factor.

What Assets Will I Have to Work With?

Now you need to tally your assets. You'll be better off knowing where you stand, rather than just guessing or eyeballing it. Research suggests that those who have calculated their retirement savings are nearly twice as confident about their prospects as those who haven't.

Step 1: What Are My Retirement Assets?

Inventory what you've saved and what you can expect from other sources by using the checklist below.

Asset Amount
___ 401(k)/403(b)/457
___ Traditional IRAs
___ Roth IRAs
___ CDs
___ Bank accounts
___ Money-market funds
___ Stocks/mutual funds in nonretirement accounts
___ Bonds in nonretirement accounts
___Insurance (cash value)
___ REITs
___ Other investments

Total: _____ x .04* = _____ *(a)***

*Aim to draw down no more than 4 percent per year from the total assets. More on this subject later.

**If you'll be retiring in five years, multiply (a) times 1.3; if retiring in 10 years, multiply by 1.7; 15 years by 2.2; or in 20 years by 2.9. This assumes your portfolio will grow at 5.5 percent with no future contributions.

How much income do you expect from pensions? _____*(b)*

How much income from other sources, such as real estate investments? _____ *(c)*

Step 2: What Can I Expect from Social Security?

Get an estimate of your Social Security benefits by visiting the Social Security Administration Website (**www.ssa.gov**) and ordering a copy of your statement.

Social Security _____ *(d)*

Step 3: Do I Expect to Work Part-Time While Retired?
(Be cautious about this!)

Your job earnings, if any, will be another source of income. (Be sure to use net numbers because you'll still need to pay FICA, Medicare premiums, and state and federal taxes.)

Job _____ *(e)*

Step 4: Now, Calculate Your Total Expected Yearly Income

Add *a, b, c, d,* and *e* to get your total expected annual retirement income.

Total Expected Yearly Income: $ _____

Step 5: Compare Projected Income and Expenses

Expected Yearly Expenses: $_____

vs.

Expected Yearly Income: $_____

Now what? If your projected expenses exceed your projected income, your options are: (1) Reduce your spending; (2) increase your investment earnings; (3) work longer or part-time.

That first one is probably a good idea in any event, at least until you can see how your projections play out. (In fact, government statistics suggest that average annual spending by retirees tends to decrease in every area, except health care. In other words, the 65- to 74-year-old age-group spends less than the group who are 55 to 64, and the 75-plus age-group spends even less than that.)

To increase your investment earnings, you'll need to learn more about the kinds of investments that can improve your growth and yield. We'll get to that shortly. And in a later chapter, we'll explore in more detail how much you should expect to withdraw each year from your retirement savings.

How Can I Ensure That My Retirement Income Will Outlast Me?

If your projected income is less than what you'd like to be able to spend in retirement, you're going to need to make up the difference. To do that, you're going to need growth. That comes from investing wisely. How you should invest is the subject of the next several chapters.

But just to make sure we're all talking about the same apples and oranges, here's a quick rundown of some of the basic terms that will come up in succeeding chapters:

Stocks/bonds/mutual funds. A share of stock represents a unit of ownership in a company. If the company prospers or is perceived to have a good future, the value of that share may increase; thus, you can sell it for more than you paid for it. Of course, you may get back less than you paid, too. But many investors are willing to take that risk because the long-term trend—if you own stock in good companies—has been upward.

By contrast, if you own a bond, you have, in effect, lent money to a company or the government. Provided that the borrower remains solvent, it will pay you back a prescribed rate of interest—*and* give your principal back after a specified number of years.

Both bonds and stocks can be bought individually, but for most investors, owning them in a mutual fund is preferable because the fund professional picks the securities, manages the portfolio, handles the paperwork, and ensures diversification.

Annuities. These insurance products can provide several guarantees that traditional investments do not, such as guaranteed-floor interest payments and principal guarantees, while investing in stocklike accounts. In addition, with fixed annuities, you can, in effect, create a do-it-yourself "pension." In that case, the insurer takes the responsibility for investing your lump-sum cash, and in return, promises to send you monthly checks for life, or for a specified period of time, such as five to ten years. There are many kinds of annuities, and insurers are coming up with new ones all the time. One form that comes closest to a pension is an *immediate* annuity. You deposit cash into the investment, and your monthly payments start immediately. This can be ideal for someone retiring with, say, a 401(k) plan but who is uncertain how to invest it. But most immediate annuities don't come with inflation protection.

Insurance. The aim usually isn't to make money from life insurance; it's to protect against financial loss to you or your loved ones. The two basic types of life insurance are *term,* which insures your life for a specified number of years, and *permanent* insurance, which provides lifelong coverage and growth potential. If your kids have already been educated and are building up assets of their own, your life insurance needs should decrease . . . *with the exception* of those of you with a potentially hefty estate-tax bill, who might use life insurance to pay estate taxes.

However, there are some insurance strategies, which I'll explain later, that may create additional tax-free income at retirement through tax-free withdrawals and borrowing. But those are sophisticated vehicles that require careful consideration and thorough investigation before proceeding.

Having *long-term-care insurance* can help you avoid a terrible cash drain in your retirement years. It pays for nursing home and/or home-care expenses if the policyholder can no longer pay for him- or herself. And if you're not yet retired, you might want to consider *disability insurance,* which can protect you if you become seriously ill or injured and can't work.

Real estate. The best way for the average investor to own real estate is through a Real Estate Investment Trust (REIT), which provides income and appreciation potential without the hassles of owning individual pieces of property. Combining the stable cash flow of a bond with the appreciation potential of a stock, REITs are a particularly good long-term investment. As will be discussed later, REITs come in both traded and nontraded varieties. The nontraded REIT may produce a more stable share price and a potentially higher dividend, while a traded REIT or a REIT fund may have the greatest growth potential because of pricing anomalies and the use of leverage (borrowing).

Are You Willing to Do What It Takes?

That same Retirement Confidence Survey I cited (an annual study sponsored principally by the Employee Benefit Research Institute) found that 34 percent of those surveyed said they were "not too willing" or "not willing at all" to cut back on spending. Their reasoning included that they can't afford to save, that they are saving enough already, or that they have other priorities.

Of course, no one wants to hear a lecture about spending less and saving more. But the truth is, the essence of retirement planning often comes down to this: How much of your current lifestyle are you willing to sacrifice for the promise of a more secure future?

Making such sacrifices will hurt, of course. But will it hurt more than reaching retirement age and finding that you haven't saved or invested wisely enough? So what to do?

- First, understand that procrastination is the enemy. The longer that one waits to get serious about saving for retirement, the tougher it will be to set enough aside. Today is not too soon to start to plan and save in earnest.

- Use tax-deferred and tax-advantaged retirement accounts. Take advantage of any matching contributions and, if you're over 50, use catch-up provisions. Once you've maxed out these plans, shovel any extra money into taxable accounts.

- Plan for a wide variety of scenarios. Will you work until you're 70? You might, but you also may find yourself out of a job at 55.

- Talk to your financial planner. Juggle savings rates, asset allocations, expected rates of return, and spending needs. Ask about a Monte Carlo simulation, which mimics real-world stock-and-bond returns as opposed to using average annual returns.

- Study the next few chapters for financial strategies that could work for you.

$$$$

PART II

READY!

SET!

RETIRE!

CHAPTER FOUR

Facing Up to a Typical Couple's Challenges

Paper or plastic? Regular or premium? Debit or credit? Coke or Pepsi?

We're awash in daily decision-making. And of course, it's good to have lots of options. But as Yogi Berra *might* have said, "Decisions are difficult, especially when you have to make a choice."

In the investment arena, Americans are faced with choosing among 10,000 or so mutual funds—actively managed or indexed—and perhaps an equal number of stocks, not to mention countless bonds and bond funds, exchange-traded funds, options, certificates of deposit, real estate investment trusts, annuities, and other financial products that are being created almost daily. In fact, one writer calculated that if you keep up on financial news in newspapers, magazines, online, and on cable TV, you're exposed to at least 42,000 "tips" each year from ads and pundits.

Not only must the investor decide which of these ideas to act upon, but also whether to put the resulting purchases into an IRA (Roth or traditional), a 401(k), the new Roth 401(k), a 529 college-saving plan, or taxable accounts—some or all of which may be held at banks, brokerages (major and discount), credit unions, insurance companies, hedge funds, and who knows where else. What is the average person to make of all these choices?

Well, many become so flummoxed by the alternatives that they do nothing, or they choose the least complicated path—the passbook account, say, or the money-market fund—even though that's not in their best interest. Some, of course, go to the other extreme. They devour the financial magazines and news shows and can't wait to get in on the newest investment wrinkle. They jump on this week's hot stock or mutual fund, pour money into gold coins or pork bellies, jump at the chance to get into jojoba beans or nanotechnology—and end up shooting their portfolio in the foot as these once-hot fads and favorites ebb and flow.

My advice? Both of these groups of investors—and many of us belong to one or the other—should stop torturing themselves. If you find investment analysis boring or intimidating—or if you're one of those folks who checks your stocks 20 times a day, including weekends—I say: *Stop making this so difficult!*

Investing to get decent returns—maybe not astronomical, but decent—is not that difficult if you have a strategy and some patience. You're on your own as far as developing patience. But the strategy I can help you with.

The Buckets of Money Strategy

While saving for retirement can be difficult, the real challenge may be managing those savings wisely. And that's where my Buckets of Money strategy comes into play. Every investor dreams of achieving high levels of both income *and* growth. That's a great concept but tough to pull off.

The closest financial equivalent to that sort of perfection that I've been able to find is this strategy, which is a conservative but growth-oriented way to protect and grow your nest egg. In fact, in my more than 30 years as a financial planner and investment advisor, I haven't seen anything as simple—and as powerful—as this concept.

Unlike a lot of financial strategies, this one doesn't involve some high-wire act like futures trading, currency arbitrage, penny stocks, or dealing in distressed real estate. You don't have to predict the future and you won't need to raise chinchillas, or position yourself atop the crest of some so-called technological wave of the future.

All you need to do is know your financial goals, divvy up your money accordingly, and then invest intelligently under the model that I'm going to describe. Then you can:

- Live comfortably in retirement without having to work (though you may choose to)

- Sleep well at night without worrying about your money running out

In brief, here's how it works: You put your money into three piles, or "buckets," and invest each in a different way. (Sophisticated "Bucketeers" may ultimately have more than three buckets based upon taxable versus tax-deferred distributions.)

Bucket No. 1

You're going to need this money to live on, so you want to take near-*zero* risk. Thus, your Bucket No. 1 cash goes into very safe, low-growth but liquid vehicles such as CDs, money markets, Treasury instruments, fixed or immediate annuities, or short-term bonds or bond funds. Drawing down both principal and interest from Bucket No. 1 will provide a stable income stream that you can live off for a certain number of years, depending on your risk tolerance, how much of a stash you start with, and how great your expenses are.

You'll spend down this money, while the somewhat riskier and potentially higher-yielding assets in Buckets 2 and 3 are left to grow untouched for a number of years. *The result?* Even in the inevitable bear markets, retirees and preretirees can be assured that Bucket No. 1 will provide monthly income without worries about market volatility.

Bucket No. 2

Meanwhile, Bucket No. 2—invested slightly more aggressively—is also growing. In this bucket, you neither want nor need to take excessive risk. So the focus will be on medium-term investments with manageable risk—such as mid-term bonds; mortgage-backed securities; fixed, indexed, or certain variable annuities; and corporate bonds.

While still invested for a reasonable degree of safety, Bucket No. 2

investments also likely will earn a higher return than the Bucket No. 1 money. Thus, when Bucket No. 1 is depleted and you empty Bucket No. 2 into Bucket No. 1 for another specified number of years, you should be able to "pay" yourself a higher monthly income to keep abreast of inflation.

Bucket No. 3

This bucket was allowed to grow, while Buckets 1 and 2 provided you with income, and it's reserved for long-term investments, such as stocks and real estate.

By the time Bucket No. 1 is depleted for the second time (usually after 10 or 15 years), Bucket No. 3 will have had all that time to grow. With any kind of luck at all, by then you'll have a nice chunk of change in Bucket No. 3 to see you through your sunset years.

That's the principle: Because you bought time with the income from Buckets 1 and 2, your Bucket No. 3 will be able to grow for years without worry about market volatility. If the stock market meets its historical norms, your Bucket 3 investments should provide pretty decent returns. And as long as Bucket No. 3 grows faster than the other buckets are depleted, you're ahead of the game.

Yes, Bucket No. 3 *is* more risky—but that risk is mitigated by time. So if Buckets 1 and 2 last, say, 12 to 15 years, that should provide an ample cushion in the event the stock market takes a short-term dive requiring a few months or even a few years to recover. Also, including some conservative real estate investments in Bucket No. 3 may provide an extra margin of safety during a prolonged bear market for stocks. In addition, such REITs offer a relatively stable and high yield, which can provide additional income as well as be a buffer between safe accounts and riskier stocks.

The Short Course

That's the short course. Naturally, there are lots of variables, such as how much and what kinds of investments you put in each bucket and how long you let them grow. But one of the big pluses of this model is its simplicity. Even a rookie investor can understand and make use of the basic philosophy.

Another advantage is that the strategy is flexible enough for the more sophisticated investor, that person who likes to get every last quarter of a percentage point of return and who seemingly follows the financial markets with a magnifying glass. Further, you can modify your program as your situation changes. If you get a windfall, you need more cash to live on, or you want to increase or decrease your exposure to risk (which will change your expected return), this strategy is easy to alter.

I hasten to add that Buckets of Money is not a plan without risk—*no* investment is ever totally risk free. How the overall economy fares, the way the financial markets perform, and the ups and downs of your particular investments will affect the results you get. I don't predict any specific outcome. However, after almost two decades of overseeing such plans in good times and bad, I do have a high level of confidence in this strategy.

Against the Grain

Also, you should understand that in at least one sense, Buckets of Money goes solidly against the grain of conventional wisdom. "Never spend your principal" is sometimes cited as a cardinal rule of investing. The thought is that when you retire, you should live strictly on the interest income and dividends produced by your portfolio. But following this rule could prove to be quite foolish. That's because if a fixed-income investor never spent any principal, his or her income would be cut each year based on the annual inflation rate.

For example, take a $1 million portfolio invested in bonds or CDs that pay 4 percent. It produces $40,000 of income in the first year and all subsequent years until maturity. If interest rates never change and if inflation averages its historic 3.1 percent rate, 20 years from now the income from that same $1 million would only buy about $22,000 worth of goods and services. That's almost a 50 percent cut in pay!

On the other hand, an investor could skip such fixed-income

investments in favor of holding all stocks. That, however, would be exceptionally risky and ill advised. A prolonged market decline could cause a stock portfolio to run totally out of money in just a few years if, during a severe bear market, an investor needed to sell stock in order to produce an income.

For instance, in 2005, five years after the stock market peaked, most stock indexes were still underwater. The NASDAQ 100 was still down 60 percent from its 2000 high, and the Standard & Poor's 500-stock index remained 15 percent below its high point. If you'd retired in the year 2000 with the idea of living off a portfolio heavily laden with stocks represented by the NASDAQ and S&P 500, you would have been in serious trouble by 2005. You would have been getting income by selling stock for five years from a shrinking portfolio that by then would be only a fraction of what you started with in 2000.

That's why retirees need a strategy that will work in both good times and bad. Buckets of Money is such a strategy. It's not designed to make anyone rich, nor does it come with any guarantees. But it has stood up to numerous back tests representing some of the worst eras in past market history.

There's no way to *guarantee* a comfortable, inflation-indexed retirement income, but after many years of research—looking at bull and bear markets, market bubbles, and market crashes—I think this strategy is as close as anyone has come to finding the perfect solution to an age-old question: *What's the most efficient way to invest to last a lifetime?*

The premise behind the Buckets of Money strategy is to match your assets to your liabilities. If you need income tomorrow, you need an asset that's liquid tomorrow. If you need income 20 years from now, then long-term investments can be used to fund a bucket for that particular need. As I mentioned, the Buckets of Money strategy creates spendable income by depleting the principal and earnings from Bucket No. 1, while the other buckets are left to grow. Then, in order to produce an inflation-indexed income for another specified period, you fill Bucket No. 1 with the relatively safe investment assets from Bucket No. 2. Eventually you refill Buckets 1 and 2 with assets that had been left to grow in Bucket No. 3.

This refilling attempts to ensure that you will always have several years of relatively safe money set aside for income needs, while the money allocated for growth is left alone for an ample time period. Of course, once a Buckets of Money strategy is designed, then the hard work begins—such as deciding how much of your funds to invest for growth versus income, which REITs to buy, which investments fit best in which bucket, and when to refill and rebalance. That's where a competent financial advisor comes in.

But I believe—and have shown empirically—that this simple yet sophisticated concept reduces risk while still taking advantage of growth. But you don't have to believe me. Others, perhaps far smarter than I, have come to the same conclusion. One such guy is economist and market guru Ben Stein, who concurred, after I back-tested the strategy over several decades, that it works in good times and bad.

In fact, I back-tested it over several bear markets, including the dismal period beginning in 1966. Figuring 3 percent inflation, I found that drawing down $50,000 a year from a non-Bucketized, $1 million portfolio (60 percent stocks and 40 percent T-bills, with a pro rata distribution) would produce this result after 38 years:

Portfolio value: $30,000
Annual income: $0

By contrast, a similar $1 million portfolio from which the investor first takes the income from the T-bills (a partial Buckets of Money strategy) would conclude the period with:

Portfolio value: $1.2 million
Annual income: $150,000

Or try the complete Buckets of Money approach (assume 40 percent stocks, 20 percent real estate investment trusts, and 40 percent T-bills), and take income first from the T-bills and REIT dividends (assuming a 7 percent yield and no REIT growth), then spend the REIT principal before finally digging into the stock money. The results then become truly astonishing:

Portfolio value: $4.7 million
Annual income: $150,000

Meet John and Chris

I've talked to hundreds, perhaps thousands, of people, probably very much like you, who've used the Buckets of Money strategy to build and enjoy a financially comfortable retirement. And what I want to do over the next couple chapters is to talk about what kinds of investments might work best in those buckets.

Rather than just prattle on in typical book fashion, I'm going to let you sit in on a mock interview with a typical couple, John and Chris. I think it'll be easier for you to learn that way than with a traditional monologue. I think you'll come to like John and Chris. Unless I miss my guess, you'll also identify with some of their concerns. They ask some very direct and penetrating questions, the type you should ask when presented with retirement strategies and investment opportunities.

Here's their background: John and Chris, both 62, are about to retire. Their home is paid for, their health care is covered by John's former employer, and their current living expenses are a modest $40,000 per year. They want a comfortable, safe retirement income and would like to leave an inheritance for their two children. They want to know how they should allocate their assets so that they can have a decent retirement and still meet their goals.

They have an investment portfolio worth $700,000. They both claim to be conservative investors and are in a very low income-tax bracket. John expects to get $12,000 per year in Social Security benefits beginning this year, and Chris will get approximately $8,000.

Their current asset allocation consists of $500,000 in John's IRA—a rollover from his company-sponsored 401(k) and $200,000 in their personal portfolio (taxable account). So their combined asset allocation looks like this:

Personal (Taxable) $200,000

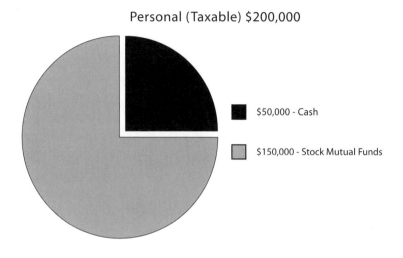

$50,000 - Cash

$150,000 - Stock Mutual Funds

IRA (Tax Deferred) $500,000

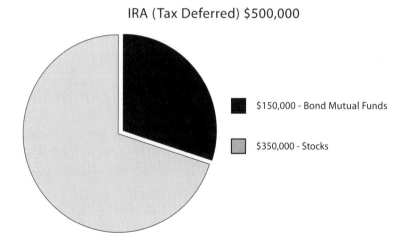

$150,000 - Bond Mutual Funds

$350,000 - Stocks

John and Chris's Asset Allocation

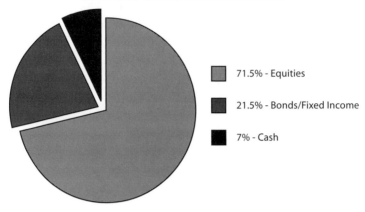

- 71.5% - Equities
- 21.5% - Bonds/Fixed Income
- 7% - Cash

With that in mind, let's eavesdrop on the interview.

$ $ $ $ $

CHAPTER FIVE

Designing a Stream of Current Income

Ray: John and Chris, welcome.

John: Thanks. We're glad to be here. We've been looking forward to this meeting because we know that our money I.Q. isn't as high as it should be. But the prospect of retirement certainly has our attention. So we're eager to learn.

Ray: Good. Now from our earlier conversation and the literature I gave you, you're pretty familiar with the Buckets of Money strategy, right?

Chris (nodding): Yes, we understand it. And I guess we're ready to start learning how to fill those buckets.

Ray: All right. Let's get to it. But, just to review, you consider yourselves conservative investors, not big risk-takers, correct? And you've got about $700,000 to invest?

John: That's right. But about $50,000 of that is in cash in our emergency fund, and we don't want to mess with that.

Ray: No problem. Tell me about your goals.

John: Well, we'd like to earn a reasonable return on our investments, decrease risk now that we're retiring, and, I guess, make our portfolio as efficient as possible. We think we can keep our expenses well below $40,000 a year, but that will increase with inflation.

Chris: And after we're gone, we'd like as much as possible to be left over so it can go to our kids and to charity.

John: Can we do all that with what we've got?

Ray: I certainly think so. Generating $40,000 to spend from your portfolio, including your Social Security, should be doable. Of course, we'll need to increase your income at the rate of inflation so you won't lose purchasing power during your retirement. For purposes of this discussion, let's use the historical inflation rate of about 3 percent and try to keep your income growing by that amount each year.

Chris: That sounds fine, but what about our $50,000 in cash? Can we hang on to that? Maybe we won't have an emergency, but we might need it to buy a car in a few years.

Ray: Sure. That $50,000 is a great rainy-day fund. You now have it in a bank savings account. But, as I'll explain, you might want to put it in a higher interest-bearing, liquid account instead, or maybe use it as a cushion in case one or both of you someday need an infusion of cash due to a long-term-care or home-health-care need. We can get into that a little later. But for now, no worries—that $50,000 will be on the sidelines for whatever comes along.

John: But how do you propose we get that $20,000 to live on over and above our $20,000 in Social Security?

Ray: Well, we'll get to that. But first I want to explain that based on your risk tolerance and need for income, I've revised your asset-allocation model.

Chris: What does that mean? I think I know, but could you go over it again?

Ray: Asset allocation just means how you divide your money up among broad categories or classes of assets, such as equities, real estate, bonds, and cash. You currently have $500,000, or 71.5 percent, in equities, which means in stocks. You also have $150,000, or 21.5 percent, in bonds and other fixed income; and $50,000, or 7 percent, in cash.

John: What's wrong with that?

Ray: Well, it's not necessarily wrong, but it is a tad aggressive, given your stated conservative nature and modest income needs. And I believe that we can do better by tailoring the mix a bit more precisely to your specific goals and risk tolerance. I'm recommending that you keep your $50,000 (7 percent) in cash and have $260,000 (37 percent) in fixed investments; $140,000 (20 percent) in REITs; and the rest—about $250,000—in equities (36 percent).

So I revised your pie chart to look like this:

John and Chris's Revised Asset Allocation

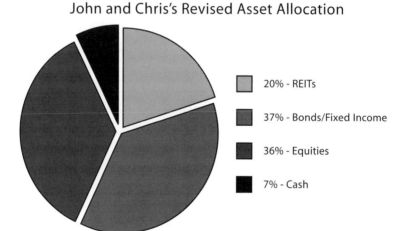

20% - REITs

37% - Bonds/Fixed Income

36% - Equities

7% - Cash

John: What's the biggest change? It looks as if you want us to sell some of our stock and buy more fixed income and those REIT things. What are those, anyway?

Ray: I reduced the stock allocation from 71.5 percent to 37 percent. I added about $110,000 to your fixed income and also added a 20 percent allocation (about $140,000) to REITs, or real estate investment trusts. I'll explain later what those are and why those moves will lower your portfolio's risk while still taking you where you want to go.

Chris: I read about Buckets of Money, and I bet this is all about buying time so that our investments in the stock market can grow without worrying about day-to-day volatility, right?

Ray: Right. That's the bedrock principle of Buckets of Money: getting you an inflation-indexed lifetime income stream and lowering risk so that you can enjoy retirement. So for starters, let's tackle the challenge of how you'll get that $40,000 in inflation-indexed income. According to Ibbotson Associates, a Chicago investment research firm, an investor has a statistical assurance of making money in the market if his or her stocks (as represented by the Standard & Poor's 500 index) are invested with a minimum 15-year time horizon, and the dividends and capital gains are reinvested. Does that make sense?

John: Sure. Time mitigates risk, right?

Ray: Yes. Also, historically speaking, such an investment in the stock market has beaten inflation 100 percent of the time over rolling 20-year time periods. Therefore, if you want to have a reasonable assurance that the money you invest in the stock market today will, at the very least, buy the same goods and services 20 years from now, then you should buy 20 years' worth of reasonably safe income by investing in fixed-income securities that can be spent down over 20 years.

Chris: So that's Bucket No. 1 and Bucket No. 2?

Ray: Hey, you really are good students! That's right. Your income needs will be covered by those relatively safe dollars. The balance of your funds can be invested for long-term growth in asset classes such as stocks and real estate with a 15- to 20-year time horizon. If you wanted to be more aggressive, you could reduce the amount invested in fixed income and buy just ten years' worth of relatively safe income. This would mean that more of your portfolio would be invested for growth. And that could produce a little higher return, especially if stocks grow at their historical 8 to 11 percent.

John: So how much money do we need to invest in Buckets 1 and 2 to provide the $20,000 inflation-indexed income we'll need from our portfolio?

Ray: That's the key question all right. And it depends on how long you want to allow your Bucket No. 3 stock portfolio to grow before having to tap into it. The preliminary asset allocation I'm proposing uses a 15-year time horizon for your stocks, but some investors are comfortable with 10 years of relatively safe income before tapping into their Bucket No. 3. Extremely risk-averse retirees may want as much as 25 years of safe money. By changing the number of years of safe income in Buckets 1 and 2, you change the overall asset allocation.

Chris: So a 10- to 15-year plan—versus, say, a 25-year plan—means buying more growth investments and fewer fixed-income investments? Sounds a bit more risky to me.

Ray: A 10- to 15-year plan is a bit more risky than a 20- or 25-year one, but I wouldn't say that it's over-the-top risky. Remember, we'll also have some real estate in the mix, and that should give us a buffer between fixed-income investments and stocks, as well as lower the risk in Bucket No. 3.

Chris: You're the CFP [certified financial planner]. So tell us, how many years should we plan for: 10, 15, or 20 years for Buckets 1 and 2?

Ray: Personally, I like a 15-year plan. And because it appears that, with Social Security, you'll have plenty of dollars with which to meet your goals, you may want to err conservatively and go with 15 to 20 years of safe income. So for purposes of our discussion, let's stick with a 15-year plan to fund the short- and mid-term buckets. After all, I can always adjust your buckets later.

John: Good. I like that. There's no reason to take on more risk than we need to. By the same token, though, we built up these accounts by being primarily invested in stocks.

Ray: That's true. In fact, some individuals take on more risk because they really want to grow their kids' inheritance or increase the amount they may be able to leave to their favorite charity. So they're willing to take on risk as long as it doesn't significantly affect their ability to reach their goals. Others who aren't in such a fortunate situation need to take on more risk in an attempt to increase their overall return in the hopes of enjoying even a modest retirement income.

Chris: I agree. Let's stick with the middle-of-the-road approach, a 15-year strategy. Whatever is left over is what the kids and charities will get.

Ray: Perfect. So based on your revised asset allocation, you'll have $50,000 of cash in your personal account for emergencies and opportunities. And $260,000 in fixed investments in your IRA, which we can work with in order to meet your income needs from Buckets 1 and 2.

Chris: You said earlier that we should put that 50 grand into a liquid, interest-bearing account. Any ideas about which kind?

Ray: Depositing your emergency stash in an interest-bearing money-market account instead of a checking or savings account may add to your income and not dramatically increase your risk. For example, some Internet banks offer FDIC-insured money-market funds paying 1 to 1½ percent higher interest than local banks.

Also, there are mutual funds that offer non-FDIC-insured money markets with check-writing privileges and competitive yields. And for those a tad more risk-tolerant, there are uninsured demand notes that are liquid and yield even more. These notes are offered by major corporations that use this money to finance everything from cars to receivables. They usually pay much higher yields than your typical bank account. They're by no means guaranteed, and their bond ratings sometimes border on junk status (usually BBB), but they may be worth considering for a portion of your liquid cash. By placing your $50,000 of emergency funds into accounts such as these, it's likely that you'll have an additional $1,500 to $2,000 per year of spendable income.

John: Sounds good. I'll check those out myself, and maybe we can compare notes later. Now what about the $260,000 in fixed income you recommended?

Ray: First, let's consider your tax situation. Money you withdraw from your IRA will be taxable. But you're in a very low tax bracket, so I think you'll be better off spending down IRA money and using up your personal exemptions, standard deduction, and, if need be, dip into the 10 percent income tax bracket. It's not likely at your income level that you'll even approach the 15 percent bracket, nor should your Social Security be taxed very much if at all.

By spending down IRA money while in the 0 and 10 percent income tax brackets, you're essentially tapping into money that was once deducted from your income while you were probably in the 15 or 25 percent bracket. This also allows your personal stock accounts to potentially grow at the lower capital-gains and dividend rates, which may be as low as 5 percent. It will also help later on when it comes time to take required minimum distributions at age 70½. If your IRA is smaller, your taxable distributions will be smaller. Meanwhile, your personal account is larger.

John: Wow, that's good!

Ray: And another advantage is that stock accounts that you hold personally will also receive a stepped-up tax basis upon death. This means that after you die, your heirs can sell appreciated stocks free of capital-gains tax. So under our current tax rates, withdrawing the amount of money you require from your IRA will produce little or no tax at all. Your standard deduction and personal exemptions enable you to earn almost $20,000 over and above your Social Security in the near-zero percent tax bracket. And as I said, it's likely that your Social Security will also be tax free or, if taxed at all, just marginally so. So tapping your IRA for income and allowing your taxable account to grow long term makes a lot of sense.

John: But we still haven't talked about how we'll split up money between Buckets 1 and 2. . . .

Ray: Not yet, but here goes: You need $40,000 to live on—$20,000 of which will come from Social Security, and $20,000 to come from your portfolio, preferably from your IRA.

Let's break your buckets down this way: Bucket No. 1 would be a seven-year bucket invested in relatively short-term assets that, let's say, will earn a projected 4.5 percent. Your Bucket No. 2 would last for eight years and be invested in more intermediate-term assets earning, say, 5.5 percent. You'll need about $260,000 to fill those two buckets.

Chris: You lost me there. How did you come up with that last number?

Ray: This is where my financial calculator really helps, so I'll work the numbers right in front of you to figure out how much you'll need in Buckets 1 and 2. If we need $20,000 from your portfolio paid out monthly at $1,666.60, we'll need to have about $133,000 set aside in Bucket No. 1 invested at 4.5 percent. I arrived at that by entering the income need of $1,666.60 per month, invested at a real rate of return of 1.5 percent (4.5 percent expected return minus 3 percent inflation), and then doing a present-value calculation over 84 months, which is seven years.

John: So you need about $133,000 invested today to produce a monthly inflation-indexed income of $1,666.60 for the next seven years?

Ray: Right. Then for Bucket No. 2, I did the same thing. For example, at 3 percent inflation, you'll need $2,050 per month inflation-indexed, beginning in the eighth year to buy what $1,666.66 buys today. And it will need to last eight years. The present value needed today using a real rate of return of 2.5 percent (5.5 percent expected return minus 3 percent inflation) is $122,000.

John: So $122,000 invested today will grow to enough money to provide $2,050 per month, indexed for 3 percent inflation, in years 8 through 15?

Ray: Correct.

Chris: Wait a minute. You're using a 1.5 percent return over the inflation rate for the first seven years, and a 2.5 percent real return for the next eight years. Isn't that a little too conservative?

Ray: Perhaps. Beating inflation by 1½ percent to 2½ percent is doable, but it's not a total layup. For example, you can invest your money in inflation-indexed government bonds such as TIPS or Series I-Bonds and probably receive a real rate of return of at least 1 percent, maybe more. You may be able to invest in other fixed-income investments and even do better. But I believe that it's always best to be conservative.

John: Aren't I-Bonds and TIPS pretty lackluster investments right now?

Ray: Maybe, but they do guarantee a core rate that's usually 1 percent or more, plus an inflation component based on the Consumer Price Index. I think using the 1½ percent margin over inflation for Bucket No. 1 is consistent with your conservative nature and illustrates that it's reasonable and realistic to achieve such a return. I'll be happy to suggest some alternative investments later. Because this is your money, you'll be able to choose from a myriad of fixed investments across the entire risk spectrum.

John: So if we add the $133,000 we'll need for Bucket No. 1 to the $122,000 for Bucket No. 2, that means we'll need about $255,000. But you've allocated $260,000 in your proposed model.

Ray: Right. That extra $5,000, along with the earnings from your personal account, will give us a little margin for error. Who knows what inflation and earnings rates will be in the future?

John: Let me repeat this once more to make sure I understand. For us to take $20,000 per year inflation-indexed, that will require about $133,000 to fund Bucket No. 1 to get us through the first seven years, and another $122,000 in today's dollars in Bucket No. 2 to get us through years 8 through 15. Adding those two figures tells us how much we should set aside in Buckets 1 and 2?

Ray: Right. That's how I came up with approximately $260,000 in fixed income for your asset allocation.

Chris: Does it really make a difference which account that $260,000 comes from?

Ray: Well, I would definitely allocate $260,000 of your IRA money to fixed-income investments. That means you'll have to sell some stock in the IRA.

John: So after you reallocate, we'll have about $260,000 in fixed investments inside our IRA for income to last several years. And we get to keep our $50,000 emergency fund in our personal account as a sort of slush fund.

Ray: Correct.

Chris: The bonds we have are actually bond funds, and they seem to go up one month and down the next. Aren't bond funds poor investments in a rising-interest-rate environment?

Ray: Good point. Yes, bond prices decline as interest rates rise, but if you're adding money regularly to your bond fund and reinvesting the dividends, they usually do fine over time even in a rising-interest-rate environment. Also, if all you need is current income and you won't be selling off any of the principal, bond funds can work well over the long haul. But in a Buckets of Money strategy, at some point you're probably going to need to sell principal in your bond funds to produce income. That's where the trouble starts, because you could be liquidating at a loss if you're selling in a rising-interest-rate world. That's why I recommend that we build a new fixed-income portfolio that works regardless of interest-rate moves.

John: How do we do that?

Ray: If you're adding new money to your bond funds and/or reinvesting the dividends, you're *dollar-cost averaging.* That means buying more fund shares at lower prices and fewer shares at higher prices. If interest rates go up, the bond funds' share price starts going down. That's okay over time because the money added to the fund, as well as the reinvested dividends, are buying more shares at cheaper prices. Eventually, this wound heals itself when interest rates settle down and the bond market ultimately recovers, but if you have to sell shares for income after the share price has declined, your loss is magnified. Once the shares are sold, they're gone forever, and there's no way to recover that loss even if rates decline in the future and the bond market recovers. So I typically recommend bond-fund-type investments for the longer time horizons like in Bucket No. 2 and when interest rates are high but likely to decline. For short-term accounts, it's usually better to stay with short-term assets that don't fluctuate.

John: Like what?

Ray: Well, that depends on where interest rates are and on your risk tolerance. But knowing that you're conservative, let me run through some of the appropriate fixed-income choices. I'll reserve the riskier stuff, such as junk bonds or complex derivatives like collateralized mortgage obligations or preferred stock, for a later discussion and perhaps for the longer side of a Bucket No. 2. While they can produce superior returns, they're best suited for very sophisticated investors who watch their portfolio daily or are willing to take on both market and/or interest-rate risk. If you decide that you want to roll the dice a bit, we can certainly consider a well-managed mutual fund that buys those types of investments for a portion of your Bucket No. 2 fixed-income portfolio. Meanwhile, I'd start with the more conservative fixed-income investments, especially for the first seven years.

John: We already went over TIPS and I-Bonds.

Ray: That's right. They're safe, and you pay no state income tax. They're boring, but sometimes boring is okay. Depending on the rate of inflation, these securities may under- or overperform other alternatives. Remember, with these types of government bonds, you're typically locking in a fixed or core rate for 10 to 30 years, and if inflation is low, your return is likely to be low. This is especially true if the core rate drops, and the core rate seems to hover between 1 percent and 2 percent for I-Bonds and TIPS. This means that you're guaranteed to earn 1 to 2 percent over the rate of inflation.

Keep in mind that in a Buckets of Money strategy, you're depleting both principal and earnings, usually on a monthly basis to support your income needs. This could make TIPS and I-Bonds a bit cumbersome. Many times you can shop for interest rates that are equal to or greater than these types of government bonds with more income flexibility, shorter maturities, and less potential interest-rate risk. But you may need to trade off some credit risk in return for a higher yield.

Incidentally, I do think that I-Bonds make a great short-term (more than one year) emergency fund. While I wouldn't recommend them for Bucket No. 1, perhaps you should consider I-Bonds as part of your $50,000 emergency stash. The earnings grow tax deferred, the rates are competitive, and if you need to liquidate them after one year but before five years, there's only a three-month interest penalty. TIPS, on the other hand, can represent an excellent choice for Bucket No. 2, especially if we have moderate-to-high inflation. However, like any other bond, they carry interest-rate risk if they must be liquidated before they mature.

Chris: So what do you normally recommend for Buckets 1 and 2 that's relatively safe yet returns a reasonable yield?

Ray: I like certain individual bonds such as zero-coupon, high-quality corporate bonds, CD ladders, and tax-free municipal bonds for individuals in high tax brackets. Also, I particularly like certain fixed annuities, managed bond portfolios, and strategic-income funds.

John: I understand how bond and CD ladders work, and as I said, we own some bond funds. But I'm not sure about fixed annuities. Why do you think they're good?

Ray: Well, annuities, while important, are a bit complicated. We've covered a fair amount of ground today. Let's set aside our next session to talk about annuities. Then we can get into the details when we're fresh. How does that sound?

Chris: We'll be here. You can count on it.

$$$$$

CHAPTER SIX

Deciphering Annuities

Few questions worry retirees more than "Will I outlive my money?"

Not only are Americans living longer, but the question is becoming more urgent as corporate pensions disappear for many, Social Security remains shaky, and the stock market, as always, is a roller coaster. One possible answer: an annuity.

An annuity is a contract between you and an insurance company, usually with the idea of generating potentially better returns than other short- and mid-term investments, or producing future retirement income. Though there are many annuity products and their names can be confusing, most fit into a small number of categories, so the choices are simpler than you might think.

Essentially, picking an annuity revolves around three key questions:

- How soon would I like annuity payments to begin? Now (an *immediate* annuity) . . . or later (a *deferred* annuity)?

- How would I like my money invested? At a fixed interest rate guaranteed by the insurer (a *fixed* annuity) . . . or invested in subaccounts that mirror the performance of the stock and bond markets (a *variable* annuity)?

- Do I want my returns tied to the performance of the stock market while protecting my principal (a *principal-protected* variable annuity or an *equity-indexed* annuity), or do I want a

guaranteed withdrawal rate while attempting to get potentially enhanced returns tied to the performance of the stock
market (a *guaranteed lifetime-withdrawal* annuity)?

Annuities work fine for pre-tax accounts, and an advantage of buying them with taxable dollars is the money you invest from a taxable
account grows tax-deferred until you take it out. With an immediate
annuity, for example, you deposit cash and tell the insurance company
when you want your monthly payments to begin. The insurance company assumes the responsibility for investing your savings. Because part
of the money you receive each month from a taxable-account annuity
is deemed to be a return of principal, that portion of the payment is
tax free.

Thus, taking retirement income from an immediate annuity may be
smarter taxwise than withdrawing money from, say, a money-market
fund, bond fund, or CD. Age, gender, and payment options affect how
big your monthly check will be. Women, for example, receive smaller
checks than men of the same age because they're expected to live
longer.

The insurance company also makes certain promises about the
safety of an annuity investment. For instance, with immediate life
annuities, the insurer promises the payments will continue as long as
you live—and even if the money you originally invested runs out.

Two Kinds of Investors

Annuities may make particular sense for two types of investors. The
first is retirees, or soon-to-be retirees who are conservative investors
and fear they haven't saved enough and risk outliving their modest
nest egg. They can create, in effect, a do-it-yourself pension. They can
attain the peace of mind that comes from knowing that no matter how
long they live, they'll have a guaranteed income. *Immediate annuities*
or guaranteed-withdrawl annuities would work best for them, especially if they have little confidence in their investing skills and/or lack a
company pension.

Another group for whom annuities may be right are those still saving for retirement but who want to save more than the maximum allowed in their IRAs and 401(k)s. These folks, who probably have many years before they retire, may choose to invest either a lump sum or add regularly to an annuity over a long period. *Deferred annuities* would work best for them.

With a deferred annuity as with a 401(k) or traditional IRA, the earnings grow tax-deferred, the cash is taxed when eventually withdrawn, and there's usually a penalty if you take out money before age 59½. Unlike a 401(k) or IRA, though, you can put as much money as you want into a tax-deferred annuity.

Whether you invest in an immediate or a deferred annuity, you can choose a conservative or more aggressive style. That's because both immediate and deferred annuities each come in two types, *fixed* or *variable.*

For retirees seeking a steady income without much risk, the fixed type may be attractive because you're guaranteed a set rate of return. The insurance company invests your money conservatively in government and corporate bonds. Interest rates and other factors will affect how much money builds up in your account, but the rate of return won't slip beneath the floor set at the time of purchase. While you're giving up the potentially higher returns of stocks, the trade-off may be worth it because you get the security of a guaranteed return.

A variable annuity, on the other hand, is a popular choice for those still saving for retirement because you have the option to direct your money into stocks and bonds. While it resembles a mutual fund, it's different in that it guarantees that you won't lose any of your original investment if you die. And some guarantee a lifetime withdrawal rate as previously discussed or actually guarantee your principal after a certain time period like 10 years.

Insurance companies have long been studying longevity, risk, and inflation. As a result, many offer guaranteed-withdrawal annuities as well as life-annuity contracts. The advantage of a guaranteed-withdrawal annuity is the initial withdrawal rate may start at 5 percent or 6 percent of the account value annually. But because these annuities are based on variable subaccounts usually linked to the stock and bond markets, that payment may increase over time if the variable accounts return rises more than the amount withdrawn.

You'll see that I also discuss with John and Chris a *principal-protected variable annuity* as well as a *fixed equity-indexed annuity.* These types offer certain guarantees and the potential of higher performance without exposing principal to market risk. Most equity-indexed annuities, for example, allow policyholders to receive a percentage of stock market index returns while guaranteeing at least a minimum rate of return—in other words, a combination of upside potential with limited downside risk. With an equity-indexed annuity, you pay little or nothing in fees but do not receive dividends. Certain variable annuities offer the full upside potential of the market along with principal protection; however, you pay a higher expense charge.

With that as background, let's see what John and Chris's questions are:

Chris: As we mentioned in our last session, we're fairly checked on stocks and bonds. But you briefly mentioned fixed annuities as a possibility for us. And I've got to tell you, we're pretty much in the dark about annuities, though we've heard bad things about them. Aren't they expensive? Don't many people say they should be avoided?

Ray: You're probably thinking about variable annuities, many of which do have high internal fees and lots of features that many investors may not need or want. Variable annuities are complex instruments that are often misunderstood by experts, let alone consumers. I'll give you more details later, and then you can decide for yourself.

But let's start by talking about fixed annuities. Fixed annuities are different from variables. Traditional fixed annuities are simple to understand. Most have no front-end costs and no ongoing management fees, so they're not expensive at all. Fixed annuities are priced just like bank CDs. There's typically no front-end "load" on a fixed annuity. Any commission paid to a broker is priced into the interest rate the insurance company credits. So if you're satisfied with the rates, terms, and security, how much the salesperson is paid is irrelevant because it comes from the insurance company and not directly from you.

In a potentially rising-interest-rate environment, though, I like the fixed annuity best of all. That's because a quality fixed annuity usually guarantees a competitive starting interest rate as well as a floor rate that's guaranteed for several years. Then each year on the anniversary date of the contract, the annuity credits a new rate that may reflect the current interest-rate environment.

For example, if short-term rates are low today, they may be significantly higher a couple years from now. Then the fixed annuity will most likely pay the higher rate on its annual anniversary date. But with a bond or CD, you usually have to lock in a rate for several years to get a high rate. If rates rise above your locked-in rate, you'll have to be satisfied with a lower rate of return until the bond or CD matures or you'll be forced to sell at a loss or incur a substantial penalty. Because the interest rates change annually on many fixed annuities, they tend to be a bit more competitive than many short-term bonds, bond funds, and CDs in a rising-interest-rate environment. All of this, of course, depends on the company you select and the yield curve at the time.

There also are more complex fixed annuities, like the equity-indexed annuity. While still guaranteeing a floor rate, the interest credited is based on the performance of a stock index, such as the S&P 500. Like a variable annuity with principal protection, these can offer more upside than a bond without the downsides of stock. But there *is* a cost to these types of guarantees.

Like CDs, fixed and indexed annuities usually have no ongoing management fees, although some fixed annuities charge a $5 to $30 annual contract fee. Interest is usually paid on 100 percent of the money you invest. If you shop for competitive fixed annuities, you can sometimes get a better rate of return than a bank CD and sometimes better than many government and high-quality corporate bonds with short- to mid-term maturities.

John: So what's the downside? There *must* be a downside.

Ray: Well, fixed annuities are not FDIC-insured like bank CDs, and not backed by the government, as is true of government bonds. Like corporate bonds, the underwriting company backs them. The insurance companies that sell fixed annuities are rated just like bond issuers and are held to very strict guidelines and reserve requirements. So if you select a highly rated company, your money is very safe in a fixed annuity. So long as the company stays in business, you're likely to get the interest rate promised and, upon maturity, your entire principal will be returned.

Also, as an added layer of protection, most states require insurance companies to participate in a state guarantee fund. This state insurance provides fixed annuities with a certain amount of principal protection if the insurance company fails.

Chris: Let's see. You say fixed annuities may have potentially better returns than CDs and may be better than some high-quality bonds. There are no loads, fees, or charges; and the investment is as safe as the major insurer, with some added insurance from the state. Still, isn't there a catch?

Ray: The only catch is that you buy into a fixed-annuity contract for a period of time . . . say, three, five, or seven years or more. While you can take a certain amount of money out each year at no cost, taking it all out would result in a substantial penalty.

Chris: So, just like a CD, there's a substantial penalty for early withdrawal.

Ray: Yes, but in my opinion, fixed annuities are superior to bank CDs most of the time.

John: Why?

Ray: Because not only do they only offer higher potential returns that keep pace with current market conditions, but they also offer several liquidity options. You can choose to just take the earnings like a CD, or let the interest grow inside the contract. And if you ever want to spend some of your fixed-annuity principal, in addition to the interest, you can do so by taking a penalty-free withdrawal of 10 to 20 percent of the total account value. Usually CDs only allow you to take out interest without a penalty, and with bonds you may be forced into selling the principal at a loss if you need to take out more than just the interest payments in a rising-interest-rate environment.

John: So if we decided to take the dividends from other invest-ments to live on—such as those REITs you mentioned—we could leave the interest to compound inside the fixed annuity?

Ray: That's right. But that would only make sense if the fixed annu-ity paid a higher rate than the REIT.

Chris: It's hard for me to believe that a fixed annuity is potentially better than a government bond or CD.

Ray: Don't think "better," think "different." In fact, using all of them—bonds, CDs, and fixed annuities as well as variable and indexed annuities—may actually offer you the best fixed-income portfolio.

Chris: Why is that?

Ray: That's because locking in rates in, say, a CD or a bond pro-tects you if interest rates decline, and a fixed annuity gives you some liquidity and a potentially higher rate if interest rates rise. Further, if the stock market rises, having income tied to its performance with an equity-indexed annuity or a variable annuity may offer an even better return.

John: Let's come back later to equity-indexed and variable annui-ties. Meanwhile, can you tell me again when it makes the most sense to buy a fixed annuity versus bonds or CDs?

Ray: Insurance companies usually offer higher guaranteed returns than government bonds or CDs when we have a normal yield curve—that is, when long-term rates exceed short-term rates and when the spread between government securities and corporate bonds is high. The reason why insurers can sometimes credit these higher returns is that they know they'll have at least some of your money locked up for several years, so they can go out longer on the yield curve and many times offer a better rate than that of short-term bonds or CDs. And because they're willing to accept the risk of buying higher-yielding securities, they can typically offer better returns to the consumer.

Sometimes the yield curve inverts, and short-term rates exceed long-term rates. When this occurs, CDs may offer better yields than fixed annuities, at least until the yield curve gets back to normal.

Chris: What's the reason fixed annuities look good relative to other short-term fixed investments?

Ray: Besides the yield curve that we discussed, there's this fact: If you bail out of a fixed annuity before the surrender period, there's usually a fee to pay.

Chris: A fee? That doesn't sound so good.

Ray: Actually, it's the surrender charge that makes the fixed annuity so competitive. For example, let's say you bought a seven-year bond or CD paying an interest rate of 5 percent. You might also find a seven-year fixed annuity that pays maybe 5.75 percent. The CD only allows you to withdraw the interest. But what if you need to spend more than the interest? With a CD, you'd get tagged with a "substantial" penalty if you withdrew more than just the interest. When you sell a bond before maturity, there's not only a commission paid, but there's also interest-rate risk—that is, as interest rates rise, bond prices fall. This means that if interest rates go to, say, 6 percent for comparable maturities (rather than 5 percent, where you started), your bond principal will be worth less if you had to sell it. And if interest rates continue to rise, the value of the bond would continue to fall if sold before maturity. If you were to take income by selling pieces of a bond or bond fund in a rising-interest-rate environment, by the time you depleted the account's principal over, say, a seven-year period, your return after commissions and interest-rate risk would be significantly less than 5 percent.

In that same interest-rate world, you may be able to find a fixed annuity that locks in a hypothetical 5.75 percent rate. That rate obviously would pay .75 percent more interest each year than the CD to start with. In this example, the fixed annuity would also allow a withdrawal of up to, say, 10 to 20 percent for spending, without penalty and without affecting the value of the principal. In short, then, you'd have a higher starting interest rate, no price volatility, and 10 to 20 percent annual liquidity with no loss of market value and no commissions or transaction costs for the withdrawal. You wouldn't get hit with a surrender charge on the fixed annuity as long as you didn't withdraw more than the 10 to 20 percent available for liquidity and you held the annuity for the seven-year term.

John: How sure are you that fixed annuities will always pay a higher yield than other short-term vehicles?

Ray: I'm not sure. That's why it's always wise to do comparison shopping, not only for the best fixed-income vehicles, but also for the highest-quality insurance companies with a long track record of competitive renewal rates. You want to look at fixed-annuity interest rates and terms compared to bank CDs and bonds with similar maturities.

Incidentally, in that example, I used the type of fixed-rate annuity with a guaranteed interest rate for a fixed period (seven years). Actually, when rates are low, I wouldn't want to lock in a rate for five to seven years. I'd rather buy a fixed annuity with a five- to seven-year contract period in which the interest rates change annually. That way, if rates are, say, 5 percent today, 6 percent next year, and 8 percent two years from now, the annuity would likely credit the current interest rate available at that time. So in the example cited, if interest rates rose, the annuity rate might start at 5.75 percent, then a year later move into the vicinity of 6 percent, then eventually up to a hypothetical rate of, say, 8 percent. Of course, if rates fell the next year, the fixed annuity rate would also fall, but never below the guaranteed minimum floor rate, which is usually 1.5 to 3 percent.

John: So how would we get the amount of money we need to live on out of a fixed annuity?

Ray: The contractual period for most fixed annuities is five to seven years. After that, the annuity is completely liquid. However, if money is needed prior to the end of the contract, many fixed annuities offer generous liquidity provisions.

Chris: What does that mean in plain English?

Ray: Usually, penalty-free withdrawals of 10 to 20 percent of the account value. So a five-year annuity with a penalty-free withdrawal of 20 percent annually would allow almost a complete refund by the end of the fifth year. The most competitive interest rates are typically tied to seven-year contracts with 10 to 15 percent free withdrawals annually.

John: I hate to sound cynical, but how do we know the insurance company won't pull a bait-and-switch on us when it comes to crediting rates in the future?

Ray: That's why you need to use a competent financial advisor who will not only shop current rates, but also the historical renewal rates. Because the advisor is the lifeblood of the insurance company, the last thing quality companies want to do is cause the broker to lose credibility with clients because the insurance company skimped on the renewal rate. Also, insurers desperately want to keep the investor's money during the contract period and long after the surrender period expires. If they have consistently credited lower, noncompetitive renewal rates, the investor will surely take the systematic free withdrawal each year and take his or her money elsewhere at the end of the surrender period.

Sometimes companies, especially those that deal directly with consumers, offer big signing bonuses for buyers of their annuities. Be very wary of that. If the insurer is offering a significant rate advantage in the first year or is crediting unusually high rates, it's likely that you'll pay for it later on. Still, it's logical that insurance companies can pay slightly higher rates than many other competitive sources but not unusually higher. The reason is, the advisor or agent selling fixed annuities provides the company with a consistent influx of new money. Thus, the company needn't worry as much about interest-rate risk because it usually has plenty of short-term capital coming from the new products being sold. The insurance company is further protected by the surrender penalty.

The bottom line? High-quality companies that offer competitive start rates as well as competitive renewal rates are likely to keep their brokers happy. Happy brokers keep the money flowing into the insurance company. Thus, the insurance company can usually afford to go out a little longer on the yield curve and offer the customer a slightly better return than shorter-term fixed-income securities and still allow 10 to 20 percent annual liquidity. In dealing with high-quality insurers for 30 years, I've found that many companies offer fair and reasonable products with competitive rates. The problem is that it's not always the same company. That's why it pays to have a relationship with a financial advisor who knows what's happening in the interest-rate world among bonds, CDs, and fixed annuities as well as indexed and variable annuities, and can recommend whichever is best for his or her client.

John: So are you saying we should buy a fixed annuity for our Buckets 1 and 2?

Ray: Not totally. I think fixed annuities are fine for part, but not all, of those buckets.

John: Why just part of them?

Ray: Remember, we said that you needed to rebuild your fixed-income portfolio. First, we have to match your need for income with the appropriate investments and the appropriate time horizon. You need $20,000 per year from your portfolio. Based on your risk tolerance, we decided on a seven-year Bucket No. 1 and an eight-year Bucket No. 2. We also determined that you'll need about $260,000 to fill those two buckets.

Because I'm not sure what will happen with interest rates in the future, I suggest that we design a portfolio of fixed-income investments that works whether rates go up, down, or pretty much stay the same. Because we have seven years before we'll need it, we might also want to shoot for a potentially higher return for Bucket No. 2, using different products that will respond well if stocks and bonds do well.

With that in mind, I think we should allocate some money to short-term, fixed investments such as money markets and laddered CDs. This will give you liquidity, lock in your rate, and protect you from future rate declines. Then we should place some of your money in annual-rate fixed annuities. That way, if interest rates rise, the annuity will likely follow suit. If they fall, the fixed annuity is protected by a floor return.

Then for the longer-term fixed income, we can choose between a managed bond fund or a strategic-income fund and equity-indexed or variable annuities. Or I might recommend that we use all three. The strategic-income fund invests in a myriad of bonds and income-producing stocks. These include government, corporate, high-yield, and international issues; and preferred stocks, utilities, and other high-dividend-yielding investments—all managed by an institutional money manager. The indexed annuity gives you a guaranteed floor rate, or a higher interest rate, based on the return of a stock index like the S&P 500, subject to certain participation rates and caps.

Certain variable annuities provide principal protection and/or guaranteed lifetime income for a fee but invest directly in the stock market through subaccounts. That way, if the stock market goes up, you get to participate in all of the upside without caps or participation rates. You can lock in your gains and possibly earn a better return than from other fixed-income vehicles. If the market goes down, you won't make much, but in some contracts your principal is still guaranteed. While I rarely recommend them, I think in your case a competitive variable annuity may make some sense.

John: Which do you think is better?

Ray: I can't predict which one will produce the best return. Because I like to diversify, I think I'd use all of the above. For example, because you're currently invested heavily in stocks and have done well in years past, I might build your fixed-income portfolio in such a way as to maximize your returns if the stock market does well, yet still minimize your risk.

For example:

Bucket No. 1—Short-Term Bucket (7 years): $140,000

- $20,000 money-market mutual fund (for Year 1)

- $20,000 one-year CD (for Year 2 income)

- $20,000 two-year CD (for Year 3 income)

- $20,000 three-year CD (for Year 4 income)

- $20,000 four-year CD (for Year 5 income)

- $40,000 fixed annuity (five-year contract)—use penalty-free withdrawal for added liquidity and inflation protection, and the balance to fund Years 6 and 7.

Bucket No. 2—Mid-term Bucket (Years 8–15): $120,000

- $30,000 equity-indexed annuity (7 years)

- $30,000 principal-protected variable annuity (7 years)— aggressive model with floor guarantee

- $60,000 strategic-income fund—dividends reinvested

Chris: Gee, it looks as if you've covered all the bases.

Ray: I think so. We have CDs, a money-market fund, and a fixed-rate annuity funding Bucket No. 1. And either indexed or principal-protected variable annuities, or both, along with a well-diversified income fund for Bucket No. 2. So if interest rates rise, the fixed annuity works well. If they fall, the bonds and CDs will do well. And if the stock market earns what it has historically earned, the indexed and variable annuities should perform best of all without the traditional stock-market risk. Each of these investments do different things at different times. Some are guaranteed; some are not. But we allow ample time and reinvest the dividends to help mitigate the risk while attempting to earn a decent return.

John: What's the difference between the indexed and variable annuities again?

Ray: The indexed annuity offers a floor return of about 3 percent to protect your downside. And you can lock in the annual market returns. But it usually caps your return at 7 or 8 percent per year. Some offer a participation rate, such as giving you 60 percent of whatever the S&P 500 does each year with no cap at all and no way to lose money. You don't receive dividends, but you don't pay ongoing fees either.

The variable annuity allows you full upside potential, including dividends, but the fees are high—about 3 percent annually. Some variable annuities, however, fully protect your principal by the end of the contract period, and you can lock in your gains annually. So if your portfolio goes way up one year, you can withdraw your gains. Or the contract will lock in a certain percentage of your gains, like, say, 80 percent of the high point in the contract. That high-water mark then becomes your floor-guaranteed return. So as long as you don't sur-render before the end of the contract period, there's no way to lose. It's just a question of how much you can win. (It's important to read the prospectus carefully, however.)

According to a study by Chris Lloyd of Lloyd Consulting in Scotts-dale, Arizona, since 1939 an equity-indexed annuity with a 60 percent participation rate produced a 6.4 percent average return. Variables have performed even better, depending on the allocation and time period measured, so you may like having both indexed and variable annuities as well as a myriad of bonds and other income-producing assets in your Bucket No. 2.

John: But everything in Buckets 1 and 2 is supposed to be guar-anteed, right?

Ray: Everything in Bucket No. 1 is usually guaranteed—so you can't lose money. The variable annuity's principal and the equity-indexed annuity floor rate in Bucket No. 2 are guaranteed. It's only the bond portfolio or the strategic-income fund that has no principal protection.

John: I follow you so far. But you're talking about investments I've never heard of, like equity-indexed and variable annuities.

Chris: Yeah, that makes me just a bit uncomfortable. Could you please explain all of these Bucket No. 2 investments again, including the risks?

Ray: Sure. The indexed annuity is a guaranteed contract, so it's not risky at all. It works just like the fixed annuity, except the interest that's credited is based on the return of a stock index like the S&P 500, with certain cap and participation rates. With a mid-term time horizon, it's feasible to have interest credited to your account based on stock-market performance (without dividends). If the market index does well, it might produce a better rate of return than traditional fixed investments, and you get a guaranteed floor rate of around 3 percent. However, there may be a cap, or maximum you can earn, of 7 percent or 8 percent annually.

I would expect an indexed annuity to earn 4 to 6 percent in an average stock-market environment. In a great stock-market environment you may earn 7 percent or 8 percent. And if stocks go straight down and never recover, you'd earn the guaranteed return of, say, 3 percent.

The principal-protected variable annuity also gives you the opportunity to earn stock-market performance (including dividends but subject to certain fees). Unlike the indexed annuity, there's no cap or ceiling on what you can earn. However, the floor return is not 3 percent; it's basically a return of principal. This type of variable annuity usually guarantees a return of your principal after several years as a floor on whatever the underlying portfolio does. Some variable annuities even allow you to withdraw your gains or lock in a percentage of your gains annually, and that becomes your new floor return. You do have to pay for these benefits, so this type of a product is best to compete for Bucket No. 2 money, not Bucket No. 3.

But the bottom line is if the stock market does very well, the variable annuity may produce the best return of any mid-term investment, perhaps in the 6 to 9 percent range. But due to the fees, it will probably never do as well as the overall market. In other words, you're paying for the guaranteed-principal protection. If the market performs only in average fashion, the variable annuity probably will produce bondlike returns. And if the market tanks, you still have your principal guaranteed. Another major advantage of a variable annuity is that you can protect against liquidity risk by taking a guaranteed-lifetime withdrawal of, say, 6 percent; and if the underlying account grows beyond 6 percent, your income goes up for life.

The strategic-income fund or managed bond portfolio is a little more risky than the indexed and principal-protected variable annuities in the short run because there's no principal guaranteed. But that's probably an acceptable level of risk based on the time horizon we're discussing. A strategic-income fund is a diversified portfolio of fixed-income securities and dividend-paying and preferred stocks.

John: What exactly is a preferred stock?

Ray: A preferred stock is a bondlike investment that pays interest, usually higher interest than many quality bonds pay. Technically, they're stocks that receive a preferred dividend. Such funds have two major risks. First, there's market risk. In the event of a bankruptcy, preferred stockholders get paid off before common stockholders but after bondholders. Also, most preferred stocks have no maturity date. So, unlike a bond, many never get paid off at all. Their share price fluctuates daily based on interest-rate movements as well as the projected financial well-being of the company.

In a rising-interest-rate environment, preferred stocks are also subject to interest-rate risk and may decline in value. As a general rule, if interest rates increase 1 percent, the preferred-stock fund will most likely lose between 5 and 10 percent of its principal value. On the other hand, you're handsomely rewarded for buying preferred stocks if the issuing company remains solid and interest rates don't move, or if they move lower. Preferreds typically pay out 1 to 3 percent per year more in interest than government bonds, and reinvesting the dividends inside a mutual fund tends to smooth out the volatility. However, all of the securities in a strategic-income fund or managed bond fund are selected and managed by a professional. So you don't have to be a fixed-income expert.

Chris: So what else goes into a strategic-income fund?

Ray: The strategic-income fund also acquires bonds—government, corporate, high-yield, and international bonds and maybe even some dividend-paying stocks if that's what the fund manager wants. Which type of securities and how much will depend on the fund manager. The high-yield and international bonds are riskier than government and high-quality corporate bonds but typically earn more interest. Remember, a bond is a loan. A loan to a company that may not have the ability to repay the debt is referred to as a high-yield or junk bond. Those pay higher yields because there's a greater chance of default. International bonds carry the similar market and interest-rate risk as any other bond, but they're also subject to currency risk. If you make a loan to a foreign entity, you must convert U.S. dollars into euros, yen, or whatever currency is used in that country. When it's time to repay the loan, the foreign currency must be converted back to dollars. If the dollar strengthens, the foreign currency will buy fewer dollars when repatriated and you may lose money on your bond investment. If the dollar weakens, you may receive an enhanced return.

The government and corporate bonds are less risky. The yields are usually less than riskier bonds. Typically, they pay better than CDs, except when the yield curve inverts. Over the long haul, it's likely that strategic-income funds will produce the best fixed-income returns, especially if dividends are reinvested. However, that's by no means guaranteed. Keep in mind that the strategic-income fund is for the latter part of your Bucket No. 2. I believe that there's ample time for it to work through any downturn. And because we'd be reinvesting the dividends and dollar-cost averaging, it's likely that the strategic-income fund would grow to a nice sum of money by the time it's needed.

John: Will the indexed or variable annuity produce returns close to that of a strategic-income fund?

Ray: That depends on how the stock market does. Let's say you put $20,000 into a seven-year equity-indexed annuity contract. It will usually offer a guaranteed return of, say, 3 percent. So at the end of seven years, the worst-case scenario is that your $20,000 will be worth $24,597, guaranteed. That guarantee is certainly not true of a strategic-income fund. Each year, or on a cumulative basis, the actual interest rate credited on an equity-indexed fund will mirror the performance of a stock index like the S&P 500.

Chris: So if the stock market earns higher than 3 percent, you'd get that amount credited to your account?

Ray: Yes, but there are several moving parts to an equity-indexed annuity that you need to know about before you invest. Usually when the company resets the earnings rate annually, there's a cap on how much your equity-indexed annuity can earn. Caps vary from a low of, say, 5 to 6 percent, to as high as 8 to 11 percent.

John: So if stocks go up at their normal 10 percent per year, and I buy an indexed annuity with an 8 percent cap, I get 8 percent in a year in which the stock market does 10 percent, right?

Ray: Well, yes and no. Equity-indexed annuities (EIAs) don't credit the dividend as part of the total return. Stocks have historically earned 6.8 percent exclusive of dividends. So you might expect a return somewhere between the guaranteed rate of, say, 3 and 6.8 percent. So if the market grows at, say, 10 percent in any one year, and dividends (on the S&P 500) are paying 2 percent, you may earn 8 percent. That's if the company offers a 100 percent participation rate. Some companies only allow you to participate in a percentage of the gain in the S&P 500 or other indexes. Others may remove the cap and average the returns on a monthly, or even a daily, basis.

So, as you can see, annuities can be very complex, and we'll need to spend a lot of time discussing them before moving forward. This is why you need to work with someone who knows which products fit best in each bucket and will take the time to compare annuities with other fixed-income alternatives.

Chris: So how much of the recent performance of the stock market is attributable to dividends?

Ray: Currently, about 2 percent on the S&P 500.

John: So if the stock market earns 7 percent before dividends, we get all 7 percent in an EIA?

Ray: That's right, subject to a cap or participation rate. If the cap is 8 percent, then you'd get the full 7 percent. If the cap were 5 percent, you'd only earn 5 percent.

Chris: That doesn't sound bad. Safety and a decent potential return.

Ray: It's a reasonable deal, but indexed annuities shouldn't be compared with the stock market because stocks move in fits and starts. Some years they go up 20 to 30 percent, and others may fall by that much or more. In the years when the market goes up substantially, you'll only be credited the cap rate of, say, 5 to 8 percent or, say, 60 percent of the market's performance. But in years when the market tanks, you get credited with a 0 percent return. So you limit your upside and eliminate any downside losses.

That's why I'm also recommending a variable annuity with principal protection. Here you get 100 percent of the stock-market returns, plus you get all of the dividends, and after, say, nine or ten years, if your portfolio is in the negative, you get a complete return of principal. Also, if you have a big year, you can lock in those gains forever by taking a cash withdrawal. The downside is that you pay handsomely for these features. But it's okay because what you're attempting to do with annuity contracts is get a potentially better return than bonds and CDs. If stocks perform well, you should get the result you're looking for without the risk of loss.

John: I think I asked this before, but I'm still a little unclear: How does a competitive EIA or variable annuity compare to a strategic-income fund?

Ray: If the stock market continues to produce returns anywhere near 7 to 8 percent per year before dividends, I suspect that it would be about a wash, depending on what happens to interest rates and the bond market. If the stock market does better than that, both the EIA and the variable annuity will most likely do better than the strategic-income fund. If the market is just average or lackluster, the strategic-income fund will likely outperform both of them.

Keep in mind that EIAs are fixed contracts with a guaranteed floor, and some variable annuities are variable contracts with a floor. Mutual funds don't come with that guarantee. You get few, if any, guarantees with a stock-and-bond portfolio. But remember, time tends to mitigate risk for both stock and bond funds.

John: It sounds as if EIAs and variable annuities are more conservative than mutual funds. And it's possible that they'll beat regular fixed accounts over time if the stock market does well.

Ray: That's a reasonable expectation, but that's not guaranteed.

John: But didn't you say that variable annuities have high fees?

Ray: That's right. They do. That's why I wouldn't recommend them for your Bucket 3's long-term growth portfolio. Instead, I suggested them as a competitive vehicle to potentially help juice up your fixed-income portfolio. For example, if the fees add up to 2 or 3 percent annually and the market performs at its historic 10 percent annually, you'd net about 7 percent. The historic return for bonds is 5 to 6 percent.

Chris: So getting back to our fixed-income portfolio, what do you recommend?

Ray: As you can see, I like diversification. So here's what I propose for you:

Bucket No. 1

1. You need an emergency fund, so we'll take the $50,000 you have in personal savings and invest some in a money-market mutual fund and the balance in Series I-Bonds.

2. Invest $20,000 of your IRA money into a money-market mutual fund. This will cover your income needs in Year 1.

3. Invest $80,000 of your IRA money in laddered CDs in the amount of approximately $20,000 per year for Years 2 through 5. This will cover your income needs during that period.

4. Invest $40,000 of your IRA money in a fixed annuity to cover the income needed for Years 6 and 7.

Bucket No. 2

5. Invest $30,000 of your IRA money in an equity-indexed annuity. This should take care of Years 8 through 9.

6. Invest $30,000 in a principal-protected variable annuity. That should handle Years 10 and 11.

7. Invest $60,000 in a strategic-income fund. This should give you the balance of the income needed through Year 15.

Of course, if the strategic-income fund does very well, we can always tap into it early and allow the funds tied to the stock market more time to grow.

So your $310,000 fixed-income portfolio, which includes your $50,000 emergency stash, would look like this:

Fixed-Income Portfolio

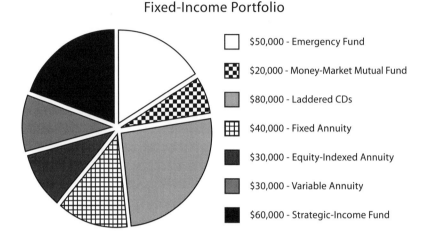

☐ $50,000 - Emergency Fund

▨ $20,000 - Money-Market Mutual Fund

▨ $80,000 - Laddered CDs

▦ $40,000 - Fixed Annuity

■ $30,000 - Equity-Indexed Annuity

■ $30,000 - Variable Annuity

■ $60,000 - Strategic-Income Fund

John: Looks really good. I like the diversification. But just to double-check, you're recommending that we use IRA money for the fixed-income portfolio?

Ray: Absolutely, except for your emergency money. You're in, and will most likely remain in, the lowest of tax brackets. Thus, it's better to spend your IRA money using up your 0 and 10 percent tax brackets and invest your personal money in the stock market for long-term growth. This way you'll get the favorable tax treatment on long-term capital gains and dividends in your personal account. Also, if either one of you were to die (in a community-property state), there would likely be a complete step-up in tax basis on your personal stock portfolio. This means that your beneficiaries will receive your assets totally free from capital-gains tax.

John: Okay, just a couple more questions. Wouldn't we be better buying longer-term corporate bonds instead of fixed and variable annuities?

Ray: Maybe, but maybe not. Remember, you'll have plenty of bonds in the strategic-income fund and a manager watching over it. It's really a matter of how aggressive you want to be and how much faith you place in the stock-and-bond markets. Your current allocation to stocks is more than 70 percent, so you must feel pretty good about the long-term prospects for the stock market. That's one of the reasons why I'm recommending the EIAs and the variable annuities.

If the stock market does in the future what it's done in the past, the EIAs and variable annuities should be very competitive and may outpace the income fund. If not, the strategic-income fund invests in all sorts of bonds—some long-term, some short-term, some high-yield, some international, and some income-producing stocks as well. We'd be committing an equal amount in Bucket No. 2 to bonds and annuities, so I think all the bases are covered.

Also keep in mind that we need a current income of approximately $20,000 per year from your fixed-income portfolio. If you only needed interest from your portfolio (or about $13,000 per year instead of $20,000), longer-term corporate bonds may work great. But at the point where you need to sell bonds to create income, problems can arise. Keep in mind that for every 1 percent increase in interest rates, longer-term bonds will lose between 5 and 10 percent. If you have to sell then, you've lost. So if you need more income than is generated by the bond's interest—and certainly with inflation protection, you will—you'll have to sell.

Because many fixed annuities offer annual liquidity of between 10 and 20 percent, you don't have to worry about selling at a loss as you might if you bought a longer-term bond at a time when interest rates are rising. As long as the income needed doesn't exceed the amount of liquidity available from the fixed annuity, you needn't worry about interest-rate fluctuations or the potential loss of principal. This is why the strategic-income fund and the indexed and variable annuities are recommended for the longer side of your income needs. And the CDs and fixed annuities are there for income needs during the first five to seven years.

John: Good. I don't want to sound like Columbo, but just one more question: Couldn't we just buy a bond ladder or higher-yielding bond portfolio and live off our income and never spend our principal?

Ray: You could, but you'd have difficulty keeping pace with inflation in the long term. There's no doubt that if interest rates are high relative to the rates offered by fixed annuities and likely to move lower, bonds typically make the most sense. That's because with a bond, you lock in the interest rate until it matures. But locking in low, longer-term bond yields in a rising-interest-rate environment seldom makes sense.

We'll have to meet from time to time to further refine your port-folio and make decisions along the way on bond ladders, CDs, and annuities. The key here is to build a portfolio limber enough to adapt to changing interest rates and market conditions.

As you can tell, I'm a fan of diversifying among a number of invest-ments in Buckets 1 and 2. Therefore, if interest rates go up, you're protected. If interest rates go down, you're protected. And if the stock market goes up, you win. If it goes down, at least you don't lose.

Chris: Well, what about investing in tax-free municipal bonds?

Ray: Good point. Taxes are critically important, and many times I recommend municipal bonds for the best after-tax returns on the fixed-income buckets. But you're in a very low (almost nonexistent) income-tax bracket. So it's better for you to take your income from your IRA and invest your personal money for growth in assets like stocks. That way you take advantage of the 0, 5, and 15 percent tax brackets and the low capital-gains and dividend tax rates, as well as the step-up in tax basis if one of you dies. ("Step-up basis" means that your spouse or heirs inherit stock at its market value the day you die. Thus, there's no capital-gains tax on its appreciation.)

Individuals investing taxable money for income and safety usually do well in municipal bonds when their income-tax bracket is expected to exceed 25 percent. Even then, when you have both personal and IRA money, it's usually best to invest your IRA in income-type investments and your personal money in growth-type investments.

Sometimes it makes sense to have liquid money in a taxable account in order to blend your buckets. By doing so, you can better manage taxes. However, during the accumulation phase, it's almost always better to invest in bonds inside your IRAs and qualified plans. Having said that, if you do end up with some of your taxable money needing to be invested in fixed accounts and for some reason tax rates change or you find yourself in a 25 percent bracket, munis are worth considering.

Retirees do need to be careful, however, when considering municipal bonds. Remember, muni-bond interest is included in your modified adjusted gross income (MAGI) calculation and may trigger tax on your Social Security. In your case, your income-tax bracket is very low, but you're nearing the amount of MAGI that would cause your Social Security to be taxed. So I would definitely not recommend tax-free municipal bonds for you.

Chris: Speaking of taxes, can you tell us how much income tax we'll be paying?

Ray: Not much. You can expect to take between $17,000 and $18,000 out of your IRA in the 0 percent tax bracket. You need a total of $40,000 to spend, $20,000 of which will come from Social Security. At those levels, the tax on your Social Security would be minimal, if any.

Your personal exemptions and standard deduction is about $17,000, so only about $3,000 of the $20,000 you take out of your IRA will be taxed. And the rate at that level is only 10 percent. That's a federal tax bill of about $300 on $20,000 of income today; and as brackets creep up, it's probably a tax of near zero later on. That's a 1.5 percent tax rate. In other words, very, very good. And as I said, in your case your Social Security probably won't be taxed much. So you got a tax deduction for all of the money you put into your IRA, and you'll be withdrawing that same money pretty much tax free.

John: Great. I like this bucketizing idea when it saves me money on taxes.

Ray: Meanwhile, your personal account is invested for long-term capital gains and a step-up in basis.

Chris: I like the low taxes, too. But something's been bugging me. I know this goes against the point of this whole discussion, but help me understand: Why shouldn't we just buy a balanced mutual fund or a totally diversified portfolio and then not worry at all about this whole buckets thing? Wouldn't that be much simpler and yield the same result?

Ray: Simpler? Yes. But the same result? Not if your timing is wrong. A balanced portfolio, where you routinely withdraw a pro rata amount for income, can prove financially devastating if your timing is wrong. Let me give you an example.

Take the period 1966 to1982. Let's say you had $1 million invested in a 60-40 mix of stocks and T-Bills, and you wanted to withdraw 5 percent annually ($50,000 per year), plus 3 percent for inflation. You would've been able to that for a number of years. But by the end of 2003, there would've been virtually no money left in the account ($30,000, to be exact).

If the same individual bucketized—investing 40 percent in T-bills, 20 percent in a 7 percent yielding REIT (assuming no future growth), and 40 percent in stocks—he or she would have been significantly better off. That person would've taken the REIT earnings (7 percent) and fully depleted the T-bill portfolio for income over the first several years, then began selling off the REITs, and then finally sold the stocks (S&P 500). The result, if that hypothetical strategy had been adopted in 1966, would have given the investor an income of about $150,000 in calendar year 2003. And his/her investments would have grown to the astonishing sum of $4.7 million.

Chris: *Wow!* Is that possible? A $50,000 income stream in 1966 growing to $150,000 by 2003? Meanwhile, the portfolio rising to $4.7 million compared to $30,000 using the simpler, mutual-fund strategy?

Ray: It's true. And the key was to spend down the T-bills first just like a Bucket 1 or 2, then the REITs, then the stocks. That's the Buckets of Money strategy in action.

John: That was a pretty bad time for the stock market.

Ray: Sure was. Remember, in 1966 the Dow stood at about 1,000; and by 1982, it was still around 1,000. While there were dividends paid, the market hadn't appreciated for 16 years. Those were devastating times, especially for retirees needing income from their portfolio.

Chris: Thanks, Ray. That's a great example. I now see the logic of the Buckets of Money strategy: Spend your short-term assets, while you leave the long-term assets alone to get you through the tough bear markets.

Ray: That's right. And sometimes it can take years to recover. So you need an adequate time horizon for your Bucket No. 3, and ample money for Buckets 1 and 2 to backfill the need for income during that period.

John and Chris, you're good people and quick learners. Thanks for your interest. You asked a lot of the tough questions that needed to be asked. Next time we meet we'll delve into long-term investments for Bucket No. 3.

$ $ $ $ $

CHAPTER SEVEN

Exploring the Ins and Outs of REITs

Everywhere we look we see real estate—homes, office buildings, malls, shops, factories, hotels, golf courses. But when it comes to investing, many of us think of real estate as too pricey . . . or too risky . . . or too hassle prone. And we think of real estate investors as just the big guys, the Donald Trumps of the world.

But the truth is, real estate should be part of every investor's diversified portfolio. One of the best ways to own real estate is through what are called real estate investment trusts, or REITs (pronounced *reets*). These are versatile investments because, like bonds, they produce income; and like stocks, they offer the potential of price appreciation. They also provide a:

- Possible dividend growth that can create a hedge against inflation

- Professional property management that frees you of the hassles of being a landlord

- Complement to stocks and bonds because REIT prices usually move in an opposite direction

A broad range of investors, from huge pension funds to retired schoolteachers, use REITs to help solve an age-old investment problem: *How can I increase my return without taking on more overall risk?*

A REIT is usually a company that owns, and in most cases, operates real estate that produces rent. Almost any type of real estate holding —apartment buildings, shopping centers, office towers, hotels, warehouses, health-care facilities, golf course, even prisons and race tracks—can be owned by a REIT, although most specialize in just one or another of these categories. Some REITs invest in real estate-related loans, yet others own a combination of real properties and mortgages.

But here is what is common to all of them: They collect capital from investors and use it to buy income-producing properties. The REIT shareholder then owns a pro rata share of each separate property. The REITs collect the income (usually rent) and then pass on the earnings to the investor in the form of dividends. A REIT may also produce gains when the property it owns is sold at a profit.

REITs can be especially attractive because owning one is simpler, less risky, cheaper, and more diversified than buying property yourself. You get fewer hassles, less risk, and lower costs than actually owning your own income property. There are no calls in the middle of the night because the toilet is stopped up or the ceiling's leaking . . . no real estate commissions or title fees that you pay directly . . . no property taxes directly out of your pocket . . . and minimal risk that a governmental change, like the closing of a military base, will adversely affect all your holdings. Also, while most of us can't afford to buy more than a few properties in our lifetimes, a REIT can own hundreds, resulting in much greater diversification.

Another plus for REITs is that investors can expect reliable and significant quarterly dividends, averaging 4 to 6 percent annually for traded REITs. Many nontraded REITs pay even more, and in either case, that's usually much more than you can expect from even the bluest of blue-chip stocks. Because rents tend to increase along with inflation, REIT dividends can offer protection during periods of rising prices.

REITs also provide an element of safety that some other investments don't. If you own stock or a bond in a company that goes bankrupt, you'll probably lose everything. But if you own a building through your REIT and your tenant goes bankrupt, you still have a building. Thus, even in the worst of situations, REITs have some advantages over stocks, bonds, and other forms of real estate.

Among the most important questions when shopping for a REIT are:

- Do you like the properties?

- Do you like the quality and creditworthiness of the tenants?

- Do you like the dividend yield?

- Are you willing to invest your money for a long enough period—at least four or five years—to spread out the acquisition costs and smooth out the volatility?

Diversification is key. Thus, average investors should try to construct their REITs with an eye toward achieving diversity in:

- **Geography.** Avoid being concentrated. For instance, you wouldn't want to have owned properties only in the Silicon Valley before the "tech wreck" of 2000 to 2002.

- **Industry.** Spread your investment over several industries. And within any particular industry—say, hotel, retail, industrial, or office REITs—try to own a variety of properties.

- **Tenants.** Seek REITs with diversified tenants, but with a bias toward "substantial," high-quality tenants as opposed to small or fledgling firms.

- **Lease terms.** Avoid REITs where the majority of the underlying leases all expire at or near the same time. That way the REIT will have time to replace a tenant or two, something that would be very difficult if all the tenants moved out at the same time.

Every REIT is unique as far as acquisition costs, liquidity, and dividend policies. So you'll probably need help in evaluating which REITs may be right for you. As you'll see as we rejoin John and Chris, many of these differences loom large as you plan for your retirement income.

Ray: Welcome back! Ready for more punishment?

John (chuckling): No, it wasn't punishment at all. We enjoyed it and learned a lot.

Ray: Are you both feeling okay about what we came up with for your Buckets 1 and 2?

Chris: Yes. We talked about it some more, and diversifying makes perfect sense, especially because it's really hard to predict the future of interest rates and the stock market. I do have one question, though.

Ray: Okay, what's that?

Chris: Do you actually deplete Bucket No. 1, then Bucket No. 2, and then tap into Bucket No. 3?

Ray: Not really. I said that by way of explanation. While that certainly can work for you, what I actually recommend is that you rebalance your buckets from time to time. But let me come back to that after we've had a chance to discuss your Bucket No. 3.

John: Good. I'm eager to see what you suggest for the $140,000 going into REITs and the $250,000 that's to be invested for growth.

Ray: I want to make the growth portion of your portfolio more efficient and potentially less risky, so my first recommendation is to sell approximately $250,000 of the stocks in John's IRA. As previously discussed, we'll need an additional $110,000 to complete the funding of Buckets 1 and 2. And the balance of $140,000, or 20 percent of the entire portfolio, should be invested in real estate investment trusts. Those are the REITs that we briefly mentioned earlier.

John: Why is that a good idea?

Ray: Well, because of some pretty good data. Research by Ibbotson Associates, a Chicago investment firm, and a white paper on REITs (prepared for Wells Real Estate Funds) by Roy Black, a prominent real estate lawyer, show that a 10 to 20 percent allocation to REITs increases the potential for return while decreasing the potential risk in a diversified portfolio. Based on this information, my revised asset-allocation model for you would look like this:

Personal (Taxable) $200,000

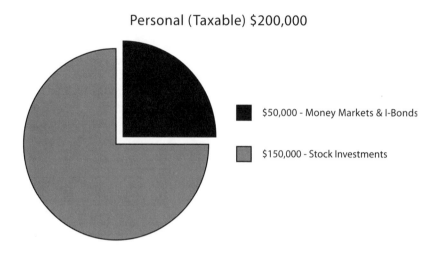

$50,000 - Money Markets & I-Bonds

$150,000 - Stock Investments

IRA (Tax Deferred) $500,000

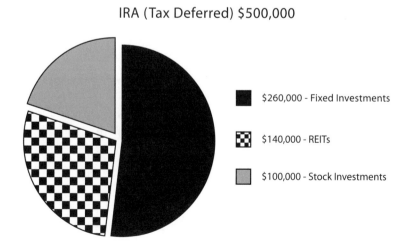

$260,000 - Fixed Investments

$140,000 - REITs

$100,000 - Stock Investments

John and Chris's Revised Asset Allocation

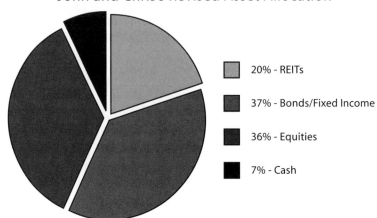

20% - REITs

37% - Bonds/Fixed Income

36% - Equities

7% - Cash

Chris: Potentially better returns while lowering risk? I like that. Which REITs do you recommend?

Ray: I suggest that you consider a REIT mutual fund for broad diversification in conjunction with low-leveraged, nontraded REITs.

John: We pretty much know how mutual funds work, but what are these nontraded REITs? And that $140,000 investment sounds like a lot. So we'll probably have a bunch of questions before we agree to move forward on that.

Ray: That's fine. That's why I'm here. So let's get started. First, I'm glad you see the point of the Ibbotson and Roy Black research and why I'm recommending that you allocate REITs for about 20 percent of your portfolio. Second, while you do have experience with mutual funds, I still want you to review the prospectus because REIT mutual funds are a little different from regular stock mutual funds. Meanwhile, let me go into some details about the nontraded REITs.

Chris: Please do. I must tell you that we're a bit skeptical. We remember the '80s and the big problems with limited partnerships back then.

Ray: Good point. And you're right to be skeptical. Don't invest until you have all the facts, including the risks. All that is covered in any REIT prospectus, which, as I say, you should read carefully before you invest. Some similarities exist between REITs and limited partnerships. In both cases, money is raised from a pool of investors and then the general partner or REIT management buys property or several properties. But that's pretty much where the likeness ends.

John: How so?

Ray: In a limited partnership, the general partner has total control over your investment, so you're really entrusting the general partner with all of the oversight and all of the decisions. As a limited partner, you have no one watching out for you other than the general partner and, practically speaking, there's no one watching over the general partner.

This doesn't mean that all limited partnerships are bad. It just means that they lack the type of oversight you find in a public company. Limited partnerships aren't public entities; therefore, they don't need to live by the same rules and governance as REITs, which are public C-type corporations. Very strict requirements are placed upon all public corporations, including REITs. I'll review many of the key points affecting REITs and answer any of your questions. I believe in full disclosure, so feel free to ask me anything.

John: Well, for starters, you mentioned *nontraded* REITs. I guess those differ from traded REITs. But how? And why?

Ray: Yes, there are both traded REITs and nontraded REITs. First, their similarities. Both traded and nontraded REITs are public C corporations. However, REITs are taxed differently than regular C corporations. Under REIT tax law, at least 90 percent of the pretax income generated from the rents collected on the properties the REIT owns must be distributed to the shareholders. As public companies, both traded and nontraded REITs are governed by state and federal regulators and must file the appropriate documents with the Securities and Exchange Commission. Both are subject to the same disclosures and government oversight as other public companies, including the Patriot Act and Sarbanes-Oxley legislation.

Both traded and nontraded REITs must have an independent board of directors that's responsible to the shareholders. That's a huge difference right there from a limited partnership, where the general partner has total control. With REITs, the independent board is ultimately responsible for all decisions and must always act in the best interest of the shareholders.

Chris: Sounds good so far. I see how REITs differ from limited partnerships. But how do traded or nontraded ones differ?

Ray: The one factor that really sets traded and nontraded REITs apart is the share-price volatility. Traded REITs are stocks that trade on the exchanges, and their prices fluctuate during the day based on supply and demand, just like the prices of any other stock. The price moves up and down as buyers and sellers bid on the REIT stock. Most of the time the price moves up or down only pennies per share. Sometimes, however, the share price on traded REITs can be quite volatile. For example, in April 2004, the threat of inflation and higher interest rates caused most traded REIT shares to drop 10 to 20 percent in just a day or two. Bear in mind, I said the *threat* of inflation and higher interest rates. There really was no inflation to speak of, nor did interest rates rise substantially. So the REITs recovered and prospered in 2004 and 2005, although the threat that caused the temporary sell-off could have spooked some investors into selling prematurely.

By contrast, nontraded REITs don't trade on the exchanges and, thus, their share prices don't usually change from minute to minute or from day to day. They typically remain stable until the nontraded REIT either goes public, the REIT is priced for sale in the secondary market, or it begins to liquidate and sells its property. Also, because many traded REIT prices have increased substantially in the past few years, their dividends, relative to that higher price, have trended lower. Dividend yields on traded REITs that buy the same types of properties as nontraded REITs currently tend to be a bit lower than dividend yields on nontraded REITS. The nontraded REITs might yield about 1 or 1.5 percent higher than most of their traded-REIT counterparts.

John: Sounds too good to be true—higher potential yield and no price volatility. What's the catch?

Ray: Remember how I said traded REITs have enjoyed substantial gains over the past few years? Well, nontraded REITs usually have a stable share price until they either liquidate the underlying real estate, the REIT buys back the shares at market value, or the REIT actually goes public, at which time they trade on the stock exchanges just like other REIT stocks. While most traded REIT shares enjoyed healthy double-digit gains in recent years, most nontraded REIT prices didn't move at all. All investors received was the stable dividend.

Chris: So there's *no* upside in a nontraded REIT?

Ray: I didn't say that. If the real estate is liquidated (or the shares are bought back) someday for more than the REIT originally paid for the properties, at least 90 percent of that additional equity is distributed to the shareholders. So there's some upside if the properties appreciate in value. But that potential gain is deferred until after all the real estate is sold or the nontraded REIT goes public, or is valued at a price higher than your initial cost, then subsequently sold or redeemed. If the share price is more than you paid, you'd have a gain upon sale. If it's less, you'd incur a loss, just as with any other stock. But remember, the main reason you buy nontraded REITs is for stable cash flow and a stable share price. So to keep it simple, assume for purposes of your planning that your nontraded REITs will, it's hoped, return your principal sometime in the future and pay you a current dividend of approximately 6 to 7 percent. If you happen to get appreciation, too, that's an added bonus.

Also, some nontraded REITs subordinate to a preferred return to the investor of, say, 8 percent annually. This means that before the REIT could take any of the profits from the sale of the real estate, investors would receive a return of their capital plus 8 percent simple interest per year dating back to when the original investment was made. This is not true of all nontraded REITs, so you'll have to review the prospectus of the particular one or ones you're considering. But if a REIT subordinates to an annual return of 8 percent to the investor before the REIT participates in the profits, it clearly has confidence in the underlying investment and its ability to manage it.

Chris: Could we earn less or even lose money on a REIT?

Ray: There's no telling what the future market will be for real estate. We hope that prices will go higher and the dividend will increase as the rents increase, but there's certainly no guarantee. Incidentally, this building containing my office is owned by a REIT. Every year my rent goes up, and if I don't pay the increase, I'll get kicked out of my space and won't have any place to conduct my business. As long as the expense of operating my space isn't more than my increased rent, the building owner is pocketing the difference. I've signed a triple-net lease, and most REITs require their tenants to do the same. This means that the tenant is responsible for most of the annual expense increases, like utilities and maintenance. So my REIT landlord obviously benefits by my paying a higher rent each year. Ninety percent of the increased rent beyond any expenses will end up in some REIT shareholder's pocket, financed by myself and the other tenants occupying the building.

An important way to potentially mitigate some of the downside risk in a REIT is to diversify—that is, own multiple properties in numerous cities with varying lease maturities. Another way to reduce the risk is to purchase low-leveraged REITs for at least a portion of your real estate portfolio. Clearly, if you own a lot of diversified real estate and owe very little, your risk is greatly minimized.

But no real estate purchase comes with a guarantee. If the property sells or goes public at less than you paid for it or you redeem your REIT shares while its price is down, you could lose some of the principal you put into a nontraded REIT. Of course, if a traded REIT stock or REIT mutual fund goes down in value and you sell your stock or fund shares, you can also lose money.

Chris: Earlier, you used the phrase *low-leveraged* in describing some nontraded REITs. What exactly does that mean?

Ray: Low leverage refers to the amount of debt placed on the real estate. The lower the debt (leverage), the less interest cost the REIT has to pay on its debt. If there's no debt on a property, it may take, say, 20 percent occupancy to cover the expenses of maintaining and operating a building. So if a REIT has several geographically diversified buildings with little debt, it might be able to survive even if, say, 50 percent of its tenants moved out. A REIT with 50 to 60 percent leverage or more might run the risk of serious negative cash flow if several of its tenants moved out at the same time. It's not likely that would happen all at once, but more conservative investors can take comfort in knowing that their REIT's survivability increases as the amount of debt decreases.

Chris: So how much debt is advisable in a REIT?

Ray: For reasonably conservative investors like yourselves, I'd recommend that you consider at least one REIT with as little debt as possible. But how many different REITs you acquire and how much debt you're willing to accept really depends on you. Remember, while little or no debt makes the REIT safer, it can also negatively affect the overall rate of return. For example, if you were to buy a rental property for $100,000 cash and rent it for $600 per month, your annualized yield would be 7.2 percent, assuming no expenses.

If you bought a $100,000 rental property with 20 percent down (80 percent leveraged) and borrowed $80,000 at 6 percent interest only, your debt service would be $4,800 per year. With an income of $7,200 per year and a debt service of $4,800, you'd be left with $2,400 per year in positive cash flow on an investment of $20,000. That's a 12 percent annualized yield (again, assuming no expenses). Plus, you could own five times more real estate using 80 percent leverage and 20 percent equity. So leverage creates the potential for a significantly higher return. But, of course, there's significantly more risk as well.

Or another example: Let's say you have $100,000 to invest. So you put $20,000 down on five $100,000 properties and borrow a total of $400,000 at, say, 6.25 percent and pay interest only. Now you have five properties, five $80,000 mortgages, and a total equity of $100,000. If your five tenants were to all move out at the same time, you'd have to make the payments on the $400,000 in loans. Thus, on an annualized basis, your negative cash flow would be approximately $25,000, or a minus 25 percent return on your $100,000 investment. This compares to a zero negative cash flow if you owned just one $100,000 property free and clear (assuming no other expenses). Of course, if your five properties (worth a total of $500,000) appreciate by 5 percent, you'd gain $25,000 of equity. That's a 25 percent return on the amount of capital you invested. If your one $100,000 property appreciates by 5 percent, you gain just $5,000 in equity for a 5 percent return.

In other words, if your goal is maximum gain for maximum risk, buying highly leveraged real estate may be okay in modest amounts. If your goal is to produce a reasonable, stable income and modest potential growth with a reduced risk, then lower-leveraged real estate may make more sense. Both can work in your portfolio, but you must weigh the risks versus the rewards.

Chris: As you know, we're about to retire, so what we want is a steady flow of income that we hope will keep pace with inflation. We don't mind giving up the potential of huge gains in return for being able to sleep a little better at night.

Ray: So let's say you own a low-leveraged REIT that pays a consistent dividend of 6 to 7 percent over its life of 5 to 15 years. Let's also assume that your REIT share price didn't increase a penny. When it was all said and done, you got back just the money you invested, maybe a little more, maybe a little less. Would you be okay with that?

John: Gee, 6 to 7 percent sounds pretty good these days.

Ray: Remember, neither I nor any REIT can guarantee you'll get 6 to 7 percent, nor can anyone guarantee that you'll get all of your principal back. But that's also true with stocks and even some bonds. However, I think you'd agree that if you buy quality real estate, have good tenants, and diversify not only geographically but also among industries, types of tenants, and lease maturities, you will have gone a long way toward mitigating the risk. And if you buy the properties with only a moderate amount of debt, you're further protected.

John: Agreed! So let's see if I understand this. You recommend that we invest a portion of the $140,000 (20 percent) allocated to real estate of our IRA money in REITs, some of it in low-leveraged, nontraded REITs and perhaps a REIT mutual fund. The nontraded REITs buy real estate, like big office buildings, for mostly cash and low debt. By today's standards, we could expect to receive a dividend of approximately 6 to 7 percent in annual cash flow; and someday, if all goes well, the properties will either be sold at a profit, or the REIT will go public. If the real estate gods are with us, we will most likely get our money back, but that's not guaranteed. And if this real estate appreciates in value, we may even get back a little more than we invested, again not guaranteed. Because we're buying modestly leveraged REITs and because eventually there will be dozens of properties rented to dozens of tenants, it's likely that the cash flow will be relatively stable.

If we also opt for a REIT mutual fund consisting of dozens of publicly traded REIT stocks, it will probably be somewhat volatile, just like any other stock fund, but it will provide a reasonable dividend and good diversification when added to a portfolio of other stocks and bonds. Did I get that right? If so, that sounds pretty attractive for at least a portion of our investment portfolio.

Ray: You nailed it, but there are a few other things you must know. Real estate—especially a nontraded REIT—is a long-term proposition, like any other stock investment. So you shouldn't plan on touching your principal for a long time, say, five to ten years or longer.

Chris: Why so long?

Ray: Two reasons. First, to offset the fees associated with raising funds and the costs of finding the properties and checking them out, the REIT will need some time to collect rents and eventually begin to increase them. Over time, it should be able to recover those up-front expenses. Second, from a pure investment standpoint, stocks and real estate need time to smooth out their volatility. Even though a nontraded REIT has a stable share price, it's still real estate; and real estate goes through up-and-down cycles. If, when you want out, the real estate market is in a down cycle, it may not be an opportune time to sell. Time allows the real estate cycles to run their course. Thus, any real estate investment needs a long time horizon.

That's why, in addition to the stocks in your portfolio, I've recommended $260,000 in fixed-income investments and $50,000 in cash. By spending the principal and interest from a relatively safe account with little volatility, you'll get inflation-indexed retirement income to live on for at least the next 15 years, perhaps even longer if you decide to also tap the REIT dividends. That should be an adequate holding period for both stocks and real estate.

John: That sounds good, but one thing worries me. Since we last talked, I read a little about REITs. And I remember something about high fees—maybe as much as 10 percent or more in up-front costs on these nontraded REITs. Isn't that a problem?

Ray: Having purchased a lot of real estate myself, I can tell you that on a relative basis these costs aren't particularly high. Keep in mind that all of those fees are priced into the current dividend yield. What that means is that the assumed 6 to 7 percent dividend is actually paid on 100 percent of the money you invest, not 90 percent. So if you invest $100,000 and the dividend yield is 6 percent, you'll receive $6,000 per year, usually paid quarterly. Also, remember that nontraded REITs are acquiring new properties all the time. To do that they need capital for expenses and due diligence. But even after taking a 10 percent-plus "haircut" off the top, leaving the REIT 90 percent or so to invest in bricks and mortar, the REIT still produces an assumed 6 to 7 percent dividend on 100 percent of your money.

As long as that dividend comes straight from the rental income and isn't subsidized by borrowing money or selling assets, the investor can feel secure in knowing that the underlying real estate is producing sufficient rent to cover all of the up-front and ongoing expenses and still provide investors a 6 to 7 percent positive cash flow. The hope is that the REIT will continue to generate a relatively high, nonsubsidized dividend, and that over time the dividend will increase as the rents increase.

Chris: So 10 percent or more off the top? Does it really cost that much to buy real estate?

Ray: Well, let's assume that you and I want to buy some real estate. What's the first thing we need?

Chris: Money.

Ray: Right. So we decide to raise some money so we can put 20 to 30 percent down on some property. If we have the cash personally, great. But most of us can't write a check for a couple of billion dollars. Therefore, we may need to pay a firm or someone experienced to raise the money. Raising funds is a profession unto itself. Churches and charities raise money all the time through auctions and fund-raising campaigns. The firms spearheading the campaign usually charge a percentage fee on the money raised, right off the top. That could be as high as 10 percent or more.

Then the next thing we'd need to do is hire a lawyer to put together all of the appropriate documentation to protect the investors and keep us in legal compliance. We'll also need an accountant to advise us on all of the tax and accounting issues and assemble a due-diligence team to check out the property in great detail. All that will cost some up-front money, right?

John: Right. But more than 10 percent?

Ray: I don't know, but I know that it costs something. Next, we'll need to find some properties that meet our strict criteria for cash flow and tenant strength. So we hire a real estate professional who works on a commission basis (usually 2 to 5 percent). Let's say that he brings us ten potential properties—two in California, one in Utah, three in Chicago, one in Houston, and three in New York. So we need to pay our lawyers to review the terms of all the leases and pay the CPA to look at the cash-flow projections and the tenants. We jump on an airplane to visit all of these properties and do on-site inspections. After the trip—and much research and money expended—we narrow the list down to three properties that we're willing to make an offer on. What do we need in order to make an offer?

Chris: More money.

Ray: Yes, for a variety of reasons. For starters, because you and I are probably raising only 30 percent of the money, we'll need to contact lenders and find out how we'll be able to arrange financing for the other 70 percent to buy the property. The cost for the loan will usually be at least 2 percent plus some other junk fees. Because these are great properties and we don't want to risk losing them, we make an offer on all three properties contingent on obtaining financing and completing the due-diligence process. We put some earnest money down and take the next 60 days to evaluate the merits of all three properties.

Let's say we're unlucky and the property we like most falls out of escrow because another firm also makes an offer—a cash offer with the ability to close in 14 days. (That's an advantage when you have the cash available to move quickly.) It's likely that our lender told us it would take at least 60 days or longer to close on our loan. Because we don't have the money to make a noncontingent offer, if somebody else comes up with the cash first, we lose.

Now assume that there are two properties left, one in New York and one in Chicago. We begin our due-diligence process by hiring local lawyers to review laws affecting our purchase in those states, local CPAs to review any city or state tax issues, structural engineers to check the building for defects, soil engineers to check the ground, and numerous other contractors and consultants. This is a major purchase; the stakes are high, and the work doesn't come cheap.

We love the Chicago property, but our soil engineer finds oil 15 feet below the ground. It's from a gas station that was on this property 40 years ago. Because the risk of oil seeping into the water table could be costly to remove and potentially an environmental disaster, our attorney advises against the purchase. After exhausting countless hours and tens of thousands of dollars in expenses evaluating multiple deals, we're now down to just one property left to buy.

We go to the bank, pay a few points, and get our loan. It's a secured loan with a stiff prepayment penalty and a balloon payment in seven years. At that time we'll need to shop around for a new loan, pay points again, and pray that interest rates haven't gone up. If they have, our cash flow goes down. The lender also requires that we reserve a healthy percentage of our cash flow for maintenance and repairs in a side fund. That reduces our cash flow a bit, but at least we own a great building. In the end, we paid for travel, legal, accounting, due diligence, commissions, loan discount points, and we exhausted a lot of labor. The real estate is great, but our cash-on-cash return is probably nowhere near 6 to 7 percent.

John: So basically you're saying that this all adds up to 10 percent?

Ray: I don't know for sure, but I expect that by the time all of the hours and energy spent are totaled, as well as the other costs like raising the initial capital, it might even exceed 10 percent. It could even be 15 percent or more.

John: Okay, I see your point. But isn't that an argument for buying a traded REIT? They don't charge 10 to 15 percent up front. And don't they enjoy the same economies of scale?

Ray: Absolutely—and as I mentioned, if you're okay with a fluctuating share price, traded REITs are fine. Remember, I'm recommending both traded and nontraded REITs.

Chris: Not having to pay that 10 to 15 percent load sure appeals to me.

Ray: By the time they're publicly traded, these REITs have already acquired most of their properties. They incurred acquisition and due-diligence costs when the properties were first purchased. How much, I don't know. However, all costs ultimately are reflected in the dividend yield. So the current dividend paid on traded REITs takes into account all of the prior acquisition costs as well as any premium investors are currently willing to pay to buy that particular stock.

As I mentioned, most traded REIT dividends for similar-type properties now yield about 1 percent to 1.5 percent less than nontraded REITs. (These traded REITs, it's hoped, aren't borrowing or selling assets to support that dividend. Many *do!*) Nonetheless, if you believe that real estate is a long-term investment and you hold on to your traded REITs for 10 to 15 years, that 1 to 1.5 percent lower dividend represents 10 percent to 15 percent in potential lost future cash flow. I guess that's like a 10 to 15 percent load being levied on traded REITs over time. Also keep in mind that if a traded REIT decides to raise capital to buy property, it must do an underwriting, which means issuing stock and paying an investment banker or a brokerage to set up the deal.

Investment bankers and brokerages charge big bucks for that, and in addition, usually the share price of the REIT stock takes a hit when the shares are diluted. That could be 5 or 10 percent, maybe more. So traded REITs, when in the acquisition mode, also have pseudo "loads" if they're going to grow. However, the investor rarely sees them except in the stock's share price.

Having said all that, I must emphasize that traded REITs are stocks and perform like stocks, both in good and bad ways. Nontraded REITs are more like bonds with an upside. Both have merit, and both should be in your portfolio.

Chris: But when you buy a traded REIT, at least you don't have to pay a load to a broker, right?

Ray: That's true. But it's not the most important factor. The most important one is acquiring quality properties that attract quality tenants. The best way to do that is by having the cash available when you need it most. Brokers get paid to raise the capital so that the nontraded REIT can act decisively on a property, securing the best price and the best terms. Thus, nontraded REITs, knowing they have a constant inflow of capital, can sometimes move more quickly than traded REITs to make offers and close quickly on the desired property. Furthermore, a cash buyer, or one with substantial wherewithal who can write a check for the total purchase price, may be able to negotiate a price that more than offsets the cost of fund-raising. Or, at the very least, having the cash allows the nontraded REIT to compete favorably against other potential buyers who require more time to close because they need to secure financing.

Also, keep in mind that most nontraded REITS are very large—in the billions of dollars. This enables them to be more diversified. They can buy bigger and better buildings to attract bigger and better tenants. It may sound a little funny, but even a billion-dollar REIT would be small by nontraded REIT standards today.

And remember, it's the load or commission that gives the non-traded REIT the cash to act swiftly. Some of the largest buyers of institutional commercial real estate today are nontraded REITs because they have access to cash when they need it and thus can negotiate hard and close quickly. And don't forget, if a nontraded REIT yields 1 percent or more higher than the average traded REIT owning similar properties without borrowing and you plan on a 10- to 15-year time horizon, it doesn't take long to mitigate the cost of raising the money.

John: So what are you recommending?

Ray: I recommend that you fill a portion of your REIT allocation with nontraded REITs for stability and high yield and a portion with traded REITs or a REIT mutual fund to provide added diversification, additional upside potential, and perhaps a slightly lower but still very competitive yield.

Chris: Do we really need both?

Ray: I think so. It's the most efficient mix of real estate in your portfolio. Why? Because traded REITs give you higher volatility but also a better short-term upside potential, with a little closer correlation to the stock market. Nontraded REITs have lower volatility and less stock-market correlation. The upside is usually on the back end. Also traded and nontraded REITs aren't positively correlated. Thus, you add to your diversification and your overall return when you have both.

Chris: Sounds good, but I also read where it might be best to hire a "fee-only" planner. Is that a better way to buy the REITs?

Ray: You certainly could pay an annual advisory fee instead of an up-front commission. Such a fee typically ranges from 1 to 2 percent a year. That arrangement is usually great for the advisor, but in the long run may be more costly for you. Because this is a long-term investment of 10 to 15 years, you'll probably end up paying far more. Remember that 6 to 7 percent dividend already accounts for all of the up-front costs, including any commissions paid. By paying an advisor 1 to 2 percent annually, the yield on the REIT is effectively lowered by at least .5 to 1.5 percent per year. And that fee exists as long as the REIT exists, which could be 10 to 15 years or more. In that case, you could be paying significantly more than if you simply paid up front.

So most investors opt to pay the load rather than have a lower-yielding investment. In my experience, it's best to pay an ongoing management or advisory fee when the advisor is spending considerable time managing the portfolio, as he or she would with the stock allocation. But in a case of, say, bonds or nontraded REITs, where there's no need for a lot of active management, you're probably better off paying up front.

Chris: Okay, that makes sense. But what if we need to get out of this investment? How liquid is it?

Ray: If you can't commit this relatively small allocation (10 to 20 percent) of your total portfolio for a 10- to 15-year period, then you probably shouldn't invest in REITs, or any stocks for that matter. However, if faced with an emergency and you need to get out of a nontraded REIT, there are usually a couple of ways to do it. You'll need to review each REIT's prospectus for the specifics. But, for instance, in the case of death, most nontraded REITs allow the heirs to redeem the REIT shares at their full market value.

Also, if you must get your money out for reasons other than death (or, in some cases, disability or illness), nontraded REITs typically have a share-redemption plan. There may be a cost to get out of a nontraded REIT early, especially in the first three to five years. Some REITs will actually buy back your shares at 100 percent of fair market value; others may charge a fee of 5 to 8 percent.

That fee is usually accretive to the remaining investors. In other words, those that stay in end up sharing in the redemption fee paid by those who exit. Thus, their profits go up each time someone else bails out.

But again, you absolutely shouldn't look at your nontraded REIT investment as even remotely liquid. My experience suggests that it commonly takes a few months to do redemptions. Even then you should expect to get back less than you paid if you redeem in the first

few years. This, of course, depends on the REIT you buy, and the prospectus will provide the details. But remember, nontraded REITs aren't
liquid investments. As a general rule, they can't be sold in a primary
market for several years. But that's what makes them good. Investors
can't openly trade them, so REIT investors can't make the wrong moves
at the wrong time.

John: Earlier you said something about how we could use the REIT
income.

Ray: If you don't currently need the dividends, you can reinvest
them and buy more nontraded REIT shares. Or you can direct your
dividends to a traded REIT mutual fund or an investment of your choosing. If you select a mutual fund, you'll be dollar-cost averaging into a
potentially more volatile portfolio. Doing so could smooth out some
of that volatility, buying more shares when prices are lower and fewer
shares when prices are higher. This may also help create more liquidity
over time, although REIT mutual funds are still stocks and should be
looked at as long-term investments.

Chris: But if we already own a house or other rental property, do
we still need a 10 to 20 percent allocation to REITs?

Ray: While there may be some correlation between REITs and your
privately owned real estate, it's not advisable to replace a critical asset
in your portfolio—in this case, broadly diversified real estate—with one
or two properties in your local area. So for purposes of asset allocation,
I've left personal real estate out of the asset-allocation model.
Remember, real estate is regional. One region can be on fire
and another may have already burned out. So we need broad
diversification.

John: So we should have a 10 to 20 percent allocation to REITs?

Ray: That depends on your personal comfort level. The Ibbotson
data, you'll recall, suggests that a 10 to 20 percent allocation produces
a higher potential return with a lower potential risk. So I would stay

within those parameters. How much are you comfortable investing in nontraded and traded REITs?

John (getting a nod from Chris): Let's do the recommended 20 percent. Divide it up 15 percent to nontraded and 5 percent to the REIT mutual fund. And let's send the nontraded REIT dividends to the mutual fund to increase our future liquidity, and dollar-cost average into the more volatile portfolio.

Chris: I hate to be repetitive, but should we use personal money to fund the REIT investment, or should we buy it with the IRA?

Ray: In your situation, I'd buy REITs in your IRA and leave your personal money to be invested in tax-managed equities. That's because the REIT dividends are taxable at mostly ordinary-income rates. REIT dividends don't qualify for the 15 percent maximum tax rate on dividends, as do traditional stock dividends. Although REITs bought in a taxable account receive some tax shelter due to the depreciation of the real estate, the bulk of your return comes from taxable dividends.

So for you, it's better to have your personal money invested in stocks and buy your REITs in your IRA. (Remember, stocks receive favorable dividend tax treatment and the potential of long-term capital-gains rates maxing out at 15 percent. But those rates could be as low as 5 percent.) For some people, the nontraded REITs may be more attractive than taxable bonds in a personal portfolio because of higher potential yields and the depreciation write-off. But for you, it's probably better to own the REITs in your IRA. How does that sound to you?

Chris: Sounds great. I think we're okay with putting REITs in our portfolio. So are we all set on the real estate part of our Bucket No. 3?

John: It makes sense to me. But we haven't yet talked about other kinds of stocks, have we?

Ray: That's right. And that will bring us to most fun part of our discussion.

$$$$

CHAPTER EIGHT

Straddling the Divide:
Passive vs. Active Stock Investing

Stocks over the long run will give you the biggest bang for your investment buck.

That's not just my opinion. It's been proven time and again that stocks (and real estate) are the only major kinds of assets that consistently have provided over the long term a real rate of return—that is, a gain above and beyond the rate of inflation.

But not just *any* stock investing does that. As we've seen, becoming a successful stock investor depends on how long you invest for; how diverse your portfolio is; and how you spread your wealth among stocks, bonds, and cash. But once you've got your time horizon, diversification, and asset allocation in hand, you're faced with another dilemma: Do you concentrate on picking individual funds and stocks or invest in the broad stock indexes?

This is known as the active versus the passive approach, and each has its ardent advocates. A head-to-head comparison between the two produces mixed results: Sometimes active managers beat their respective index or benchmark, and sometimes they don't. While it's easy to determine which methodology is better in hindsight, trying to figure out which will perform better in the future is another story.

When the markets are more volatile and smaller stocks tend to be in favor, the stock pickers or active managers usually win. That's because they can buy and sell stocks when they believe them to be under- or overvalued. But when momentum and demand in the market causes most stocks to rise, indexing typically wins out over active management.

During most of the '90s, it was very difficult for active managers to beat index funds because large stocks kept getting larger. But after the bottom fell out of the market in 2000, active money managers were often able to beat the indexes because they were able to tilt their portfolios toward value or small-cap stocks, or even moved some money to cash, while the mostly tech- and large-cap-laden indexes declined.

Such adjustments are rarely made in index funds. That's because there's no management necessary. A computer or a group of individuals pick the stocks for the index, then occasionally reshuffle the stocks within the funds. So if the market is heading south, the index fund will likely follow suit. But active managers can adjust their holdings based on current market conditions, and many do so effectively. However, some do not, which explains why the debate over active and passive management is so passionate.

So deciding which method of investing—active management or passive management (indexing)—is better depends on how clairvoyant you are. My suggestion to John and Chris is to take a sort of have-your-cake-and-eat-it-too approach: Do both. Create a concentrated, active portion of your portfolio in which you strive for overperformance, and an index part that provides broad diversification. Some would argue that this is a fence-sitting posture, neither wholly timid nor wholly bold. But I would rather be 50 percent right than 100 percent wrong.

Such fence-straddling allows you to get the market-like performance of an index fund with the possibility of receiving from the active-management portion a "positive alpha" performance (that is, one that exceeds the benchmark).

To do this you need to (1) hire an oversight manager, (2) design an asset-allocation model, and (3) instruct the manager to invest some of your stock money into a concentrated portfolio of mutual funds or separate accounts that he or she selects, and the balance into index funds or exchange-traded funds. The latter helps to broaden the risk and lower costs.

No money-management strategy is perfect 100 percent of the time. One investment strategy will outperform another sometime. But you do need to *have* a strategy. This is one that I've used in my own personal money management, and one that I think will work well for our friends John and Chris and maybe you.

It's important to remember that this is separate from fixed investments and real estate. This strategy is designed for the aggressive, long-term growth portion of your portfolio that consists exclusively of stocks and stock funds. And other than the need for some occasional rebalancing, it shouldn't be touched for several years.

With that in mind, let's see how this goes down with John and Chris.

John: We're eager to hear what you have to say about stocks, because about 40 percent of our portfolio will be invested in them.

Chris: We like stocks. As we said earlier, we've accumulated most of our money by being diligent savers and by investing in stocks.

Ray: Stocks historically have provided the best long-term rate of return, and because we've bought plenty of time with our relatively safe buckets and our real estate investments, the risk of owning stocks in the long term has been all but eliminated as long as we diversify and hold over a 15- to 20-year time horizon. And, of course, the stock portion of your Bucket No. 3 is where you expect to get your long-term growth.

John: What strategy do you recommend?

Ray: Actually, for you it's plural: strategies. Because you have both qualified (IRA) and nonqualified (taxable) accounts, I would use two entirely different strategies. According to Lipper, an investment research firm, the average fund investor gives up 2 percent to 3 percent per year in performance due to taxes. So for your personal funds I would design a core *strategic* portfolio. And because your IRA funds are already sheltered, current taxation is not an issue. Thus, I'd employ a more *tactical* strategy there.

Chris: Strategic? Tactical? Help! I don't understand.

Ray: Let's take them one at a time. A strategic asset allocation is one based on science; a tactical allocation is based a bit more on art. Strategic asset allocation is a product of the Nobel Prize–winning Modern Portfolio Theory, or MPT. What we've learned from MPT is that the variability of the returns you get on your portfolio is mostly dictated by the combination of asset classes and styles. Asset allocation—meaning how you divide your money among, say, stocks, bonds, real estate, and cash—is far more important than what stocks you choose or how good your timing is in buying them.

So the way you go about doing that is, first, hire a strategist, or oversight manager. That's an individual or firm that creates an asset allocation, and that selects several different style-specific managers or several index funds or other passive investments. That person or firm then manages the equities within that portfolio, or manages the managers who buy the equities. This firm also overlays a tax screen in order to minimize the impact of taxes. So this strategic portfolio is usually somewhat passive and fairly inexpensive to run.

Further, strategic allocation is more tax efficient because the asset allocation is fairly static, and the money managers stay very close to their investing style. They typically use passive investments such as index funds, tax-managed mutual funds, and ETFs, and hold down the turnover. Because there's less buying and selling, there are fewer short-term capital gains and transaction costs. So a strategic allocation is less expensive and more tax efficient.

Chris: What does the term *tax efficient* really mean?

Ray: Whenever multiple assets are managed by multiple managers, gains and losses occur. If someone sitting in an oversight position can see, for instance, when taxable gains are being made, he or she can sell some of the losing stocks in the portfolio to offset the gains. The result: a lower tax bill. Also, the fact that a strategic portfolio is passive means fewer moving parts and therefore, fewer costs and fewer taxable events.

John: Are there a lot of these tax-efficient managers?

Ray: A few. My job would be to find the right ones for you, then constantly monitor what they're doing relative to our expectations against their peers and against certain benchmarks.

John: Okay, so we turn over our taxable account to a strategic money-management firm. What about our IRA? Is that where the tactical strategy comes into play?

Ray: Exactly. Tactical money managers design an asset allocation based on how they see the financial world and do overweightings or underweightings accordingly. These managers are looking to take advantage of short-term pricing anomalies, sectors that seem poised to outperform, or supercharged individual stocks that show great promise. Most of these portfolios are concentrated, which means fewer stocks instead of a broader, indexed approach.

For example, a strategic model might include a 15 percent allocation to international equities invested in a broad international index fund. By contrast, a tactical manager who believes that the dollar will weaken and the overseas markets will flourish in the next year or two might overweight the international allocation to perhaps as high as 30 percent, and fund that with 30 to 50 international stocks. If he or she is right, the portfolio will likely produce an enhanced rate of return.

These tactical managers make educated allocations in an attempt to outpace the market benchmarks. Due to the sometimes high turnover, this portfolio tends to create short-term gains and losses. Short-term gains in a taxable account could really upset our game plan because they're taxed at ordinary income-tax rates. But short-term gains in an IRA have no impact. So to take advantage of a strategic, tax-efficient asset-allocation model, we'll employ a strategy of broad diversification with low turnover in your personal account. And to generate a little more potential alpha—that is, benchmark-beating performance—we would hire a manager who employs a tactical approach for your IRA. The aim is to get high alpha with low beta.

John: What does that mean?

Ray: It means going for the gusto, or alpha, while taking into account how much risk is being taken in order to get it. What I'm interested in are money managers who have delivered consistent alpha with a low-to-manageable beta. Beta compares the risk a manager takes to the overall market or benchmark. If a manager has delivered an alpha of 5 with a beta of .85, this means that he or she has delivered a performance 5 percent better than the benchmark at 85 percent of the risk.

Chris: But isn't tactical more complicated, costly, and risky?

Ray: Perhaps, but when the stock market is in a downward trend, or trading sideways, for a number of years, you'll appreciate having an actively managed, tactical portfolio. Active managers can more easily respond to changing economic environments. By using sophisticated trading techniques, they can even attempt to make money, or at least lose less, when the markets are headed south. And, of course, they do this with little regard for the tax implications. So yes, it's more costly but usually well worth the price in both performance and security.

Chris: So I guess there's no good answer to the question of which is better—tactical or strategic?

Ray: Nobody knows. There have been prolonged secular bull markets lasting decades in which a strategic approach worked great. But there also have been similar long-running bear markets in which good stock-picking has far outpaced the indexes. The problem is, we won't know if we're in a bull or bear market, a secular bull or secular bear market, or simply in an up-or-down trend until it's over. Sometimes bull-and-bear years occur inside of secular bull-or-bear markets. Trying to predict what will happen next is, at best, a guess.

In fact, just when we think we know what's going to occur, the market sometimes throws us a curve, and we strike out. That's why I recommend that you employ both methods. Sometimes I even recommend two or three different tactical managers, because they sometimes concentrate their holdings in different areas. For example, one may be excellent at picking value stocks, while another specializes in small cap. Or, one may use individual stocks, another prefers mutual funds or exchange-traded funds, and a third one uses some combination of those. Nonetheless, tactical allocation always works best when added to a core, broad-based strategic portfolio.

John: So short-term gains are okay in our IRA because there the taxes are deferred. But naturally, we want to minimize taxes on trades in our taxable account, right?

Ray: Correct. In your taxable account we'll put more passive investments and then place the more swift-moving tactical portfolio in your IRA. That way we have the best of both worlds. So I recommend that you place $150,000 from your taxable account in a strategic, tax-managed allocation and go with a tactical allocation with the $100,000 in your IRA. We'll have a chance later on to go through the prospectuses and select from a list of institutional strategists.

John: Sounds great, but couldn't we simply buy an index fund and be done with all this?

Ray: Sure. That would give you broad diversification, but you're certain to never beat the market or the benchmark. By using a strategic, tax-efficient allocation and adding tactical strategies, we're attempting to not only match a benchmark, but, it's hoped, outpace it consistently.

Chris: Would these tactical choices involve individuals stocks or funds?

Ray: Probably both. That's because most separate account managers have a high minimum account size—say, $100,000 or $250,000 to $1 million or more. With a portfolio of your size, we may be able to use one or two separate account managers . . . then fill in the gaps with mutual funds, indexes, or ETFs for the allocations that don't meet the minimum. All of this, however, is under the direction of an oversight manager responsible for managing your account.

Chris: What if we've already had some big gains in specific stocks and we don't want to sell those?

Ray: We look at the company whose stock you own and study its overall size and style. Then we build a custom asset-allocation model around that particular stock or stocks. For example, if you own a large position in a big-cap tech stock, we might consider underweighting big-cap tech in your new asset-allocation model. And as your portfolio creates some losses over time, we can begin to sell off parts of the tech stocks, washing out any gains and rebalancing the portfolio allocation.

John: So who are these money managers?

Ray: They're usually quite substantial and accomplished, perhaps overseeing billions of dollars. He or she uses numerous screens to determine which are the best and most appropriate managers and mutual funds. My job would be to hire the oversight guy or gal and then be the liaison between you and him.

John: Sounds simple enough. But also kind of expensive.

Ray: Not really, considering that the average growth-mutual-fund shareholder pays about 1.5 percent to have the fund managed. It's likely that your total costs should be in that ballpark. The key, of course, isn't how much you pay, but how much value you receive for what you pay. And these strategists have proven track records over long periods.

John: So what steps do we need to take to do this?

Ray: First, we decide on an asset-allocation model. I recommend a global model, which includes overseas stocks. That adds diversification and lowers the risk and the volatility. I also recommend that you use a little more of an aggressive strategy because you have set aside significant dollars in safe accounts and real estate, the combination of which should easily meet your income needs for the next 15 to 20 years.

Chris: We can be more aggressive because we've already taken care of Buckets 1 and 2? And because we have a real estate buffer as well?

Ray: That's right.

John: Our plan now seems to be really coming together. I like it because we'll be reducing our risk by lowering our stock allocation well below the current 70 percent. But we'll still have a well-managed Bucket No. 3, and some Bucket No. 2 investments that are tied in some way to stock-market performance.

Ray: Correct. So here's how your buckets look:

John and Chris's *Buckets of Money* Plan
(not including $50,000 emergency fund)

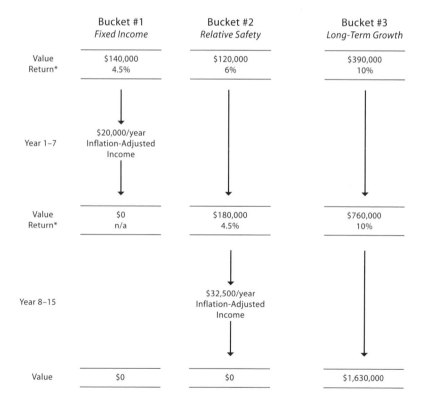

	Bucket #1 *Fixed Income*	Bucket #2 *Relative Safety*	Bucket #3 *Long-Term Growth*
Value Return*	$140,000 4.5%	$120,000 6%	$390,000 10%
Year 1–7	$20,000/year Inflation-Adjusted Income		
Value Return*	$0 n/a	$180,000 4.5%	$760,000 10%
Year 8–15		$32,500/year Inflation-Adjusted Income	
Value	$0	$0	$1,630,000

*Assumed rates of return not guaranteed.

If we place $140,000 from your IRA in the short-term income Bucket No. 1, assuming a 4.5 percent growth rate, that money should provide

$20,000 in annual inflation-indexed income for the first seven years. Then we can tap into Bucket No. 2—your mid-term, relatively safe bucket—that will be funded with $120,000 of IRA money. That should continue the inflation-indexed income stream for years 8 through 15.

That leaves Bucket No. 3, the long-term bucket, funded with $140,000 of IRA funds in REITs (both traded and nontraded), as well as the $100,000 balance of your IRA in a tactical stock portfolio and $150,000 of your personal funds in a tax-efficient strategic portfolio.

John: So let's say we spend Buckets 1 and 2 over the next 15 years. What might Bucket No. 3 be worth at the end of that time?

Ray: Assuming that real estate grows at only the dividend yield of 6 percent and stocks grow at 8 percent, in 15 years your portfolio could be $1,128,000—or even more if real estate and stocks grow at something near their historic rates.

Chris: How much is that?

Ray: Actually, over the last 23 years they've both averaged more than 10 percent.

John: So let's dream for a moment. If, indeed, real estate and stocks grew at 10 percent, what would our portfolio look like in 15 years?

Ray: Let's calculate: $1,630,000 (see chart on previous page).

Chris: That's awesome.

John: So are we done?

Ray: Almost. But remember, Chris asked about whether we actually deplete the buckets. That gets us into the issue of rebalancing. And something I suggest for sophisticated investors is value-averaging their Bucket No. 3.

John: How does that work?

Ray: Let's say you expect an annualized 8 percent rate of return in your Bucket No. 3. In a year like 2003 in which you might have earned, say, 25 percent, you actually made 17 percent more than you expected. At that point, you'd skim the extra 17 percent off the top and place it in Bucket No. 2, buying a few more years of safe income.

Chris: But what if stocks dropped?

Ray: One thing we've learned from history is that the best time to buy stocks is shortly after a bear market or a big decline. According to Jeremy Siegal, a finance professor at the Wharton School, if you'd invested at the bottom of the last six bear markets (not including 2000 to 2002), you would've averaged 8.6 percent per year after inflation. So in a case where you expect an 8 percent annual return for Bucket No. 3 and it drops 10 percent, it might be wise to take money from Bucket No. 2 and buy into Bucket No. 3. Ideally, if the portfolio dropped 10 percent and you could afford it, adding 18 percent to your Bucket No. 3 portfolio from new contributions would be the thing to do. Otherwise, taking surplus money out of Bucket No. 2 and funding the 18 percent into Bucket No. 3 would get you back on track. Then, if Bucket No. 3 rebounds, you can replenish Bucket No. 2.

John: Why 18 percent?

Ray: You'll need 10 percent to make up for the 10 percent loss, plus 8 percent to catch you up to the 8 percent expected return. This forces you to buy low and sell high. And you're assured that your portfolio's value is growing by 8 percent per year one way or the other.

John: So when you do better than 8 percent, do you sell some of the profit off the top? And when you do worse than 8 percent, do you put more money into Bucket No. 3 by either adding new money or tapping into your Bucket No. 2? So the account grows at an 8 percent rate regardless of the return.

Ray: That's right. Like dollar-cost averaging, only better.

Chris: Sounds like a lot of work.

Ray: Not really. You and I will be looking at your portfolio annually and doing some rebalancing anyway. We just need to be sure to check on the tax effects of any moves before we act.

Chris: How do you mean?

Ray: Well, whenever you move money around in your personal account, chances are you'll be creating a short- or long-term gain, or a short- or long-term loss. When rebalancing, it's usually better to take your gains by selling inside your IRA and take your losses in your personal account. That is, of course, in an ideal world.

The next best thing to do is to match up your losses and gains. This way they offset one another, and no taxes will be paid. If you can't do that, be sure to at least attempt to hold on to your winners for a minimum of one year. That minimizes the tax liability. Remember, long-term capital gains on assets held more than one year are taxed at a maximum 5 to 15 percent, depending on your taxable income. Short-term gains (held less than one year) are taxed at your higher personal income-tax rate. Also, if you're regularly adding money to your accounts—such as funding IRAs and 401(k)s—you can rebalance or value-average by adding more money to the areas that have gone down and not add to those that have gone up. That way you're not selling the winners and creating gains; you're simply adding new money to the losers, buying more shares when prices are lower.

But, as I said, you don't need to stress out over all of this. I will be working with you on an ongoing basis to help you make tax, rebalancing, and asset-allocation decisions.

John: That's great.

Ray: So, are you okay with what we've come up with for your buckets? And do you understand it all?

John: Yes, I think we're on board. I get it.

Ray: And you're going to do what each year?

Chris: Relax. And let the money compound.

Ray (laughing): True. That's for sure. But what else?

John: Call you whenever we have a question.

Ray: Good. Any other questions?

John: Well, just this: We have wills and living trusts, but we don't have any life insurance to speak of. Is that okay?

Ray: To retire in comfort, you probably don't need any significant coverage. If either of you were to die, your income would be reduced by Chris's Social Security payment of $800 per month, inflation-indexed. That's tantamount to about $150,000 of capital required to replace that. With a total of $700,000 in assets, the survivor should have no problem making it. So I wouldn't consider buying life insurance for the traditional reasons.

Chris: Is there anything else you *would* recommend?

Ray: Remember when we talked about your emergency bucket? I said that you might consider putting that money into something that would potentially protect you against the cost of a long-term illness or nursing-home stay.

John: So you think we need long-term-care insurance?

Ray: Probably not for one another. But if you want to maximize the kids' inheritance or what you could leave to charity, you might consider a single-premium life-insurance policy that would cover both of you in a long-term-care situation.

Chris: How would that work?

Ray: There are a few companies that will take a lump-sum payment—usually the money allocated for emergencies—and place it in a guaranteed-principal, single-premium life-insurance policy with a joint long-term-care rider.

Say, for instance, you deposit $50,000 into this policy with a death benefit of $130,000. If you die, your beneficiary would obviously get the $130,000 tax free. But if you need to pay for home health care or nursing-home care, the death benefit can be commuted into monthly payments to pay for that care. Once the death benefit is used up, the policy lapses. But if there's a balance upon your death, it's paid to your heirs.

John: But what if you need the cash value for an emergency?

Ray: Most emergency funds sit for a long time at low yields because the emergency never arrives. In this type of a policy, the principal is 100 percent guaranteed. So if you need the cash for emergencies, it's always there. It may not earn a lot of interest—usually a net of 1 to 2 percent—but it's guaranteed to be at least equal to your original contribution.

This isn't something I think you need to hurry up and buy, but it's something to consider if one of your primary goals is to leave as large an estate as possible to your kids and charity.

Chris: Sounds as if we should learn more about that. Anything else we should be thinking of?

Ray: Sure. Things like tax-credit investments, Roth IRA conversions, health savings accounts—dozens of ideas like that we can discuss in the future at our regular update meetings. Meanwhile, I'll give you information to read so you'll be better schooled on some of these other strategies.

John: Thanks. We didn't know that financial planning could be this interesting and informative.

Ray: Well, it can be. In fact, some of these strategies we'll look at can be pretty fascinating.

$ $ $ $

CHAPTER NINE

Sampling Other Strategies for Making Your Money Last

Stockpiling money for retirement and putting it in the right spot, as we've seen, is critical. But yet another challenge will be how you draw down that money. In other words, how do you crack that nest egg without scrambling your finances?

When you start depending on your savings for income, expect the training wheels to come off your retirement plan. This will be for *real.* Time, the rate of inflation, and expected returns will loom much larger than when you were working. When you were on the job, for example, a couple of bad years of investing could be overcome by adding to your savings or by working longer. But in retirement you'll be withdrawing money in both good years and bad. So you'll need to manage those reserves wisely by maximizing earnings and reducing taxes. And that means you'll be confronted by a bewildering number of tax angles, rule changes, longevity predictions, and inheritance dilemmas.

The basic problem? How to siphon enough consistent cash out of what are probably too many retirement plans and other sources burdened with too many rules. Take, for instance, our mind-boggling alphanumeric stew of retirement plans, each with its own regulations. There are, to name just a few, traditional IRAs (deductible and non-deductible), Roth IRAs, 401(k)s, 403(b)s, 457s, SEPs, Keoghs, Simple IRAs, and—in a recent addition—even Roth 401(k)s. And our tax system makes understanding them tougher than it ought to be. The regulations are so complex because the tax structure seeks to do so many things at once: be fair but also achieve social goals, meet political objectives, and undo previous tax-policy blunders. The trick is to know what rules pertain to your particular situation.

Indeed, pitfalls are plentiful for those who don't understand the sometimes-complicated rules of retirement accounts. Mistakes can be costly. To take just the simplest example, let's say that a 59-year-old retires and transfers a lump sum from his or her 401(k) to a bank savings account. He or she could suffer a major tax penalty and lose as much as a quarter or more of his or her life savings because of this one uninformed decision. (That transfer, unless it was made directly to an IRA in a timely fashion, would be subject to federal and state tax and a 10 percent federal penalty tax.)

So in this chapter I'm going to seek to simplify the rules and give you some further strategies to help ensure that you get the money you need to live on. We've already talked about when to take your Social Security, but here I'm going to get into how and when to tap your retirement plans and other accounts, ways you can use your home as a source of retirement dollars, how to lower the taxes due on your stock options, and when investing in low-income housing tax credits can help you taxwise even as you assist others.

The truth is, most folks aren't aware of the importance of planning for how to receive cash during their retirement. They've spent decades accumulating wealth but haven't thought much about converting those savings to retirement income. One study by ING's U.S. financial services found that almost 70 percent of 50- to 70-year-olds had no plan in place for their "retirement paycheck"—that is, how they're going to convert their savings into a lasting income stream.

Making this change is easier if you start planning for the transition well ahead of time. It's easier with some lead time, for example, to pay off credit cards, car loans, and other debts, which should be a priority before you retire. And, of course, it goes almost without saying that you shouldn't be taking on any new debt.

Withdrawing Money in Retirement

Tapping your tax-advantaged retirement accounts. Once retired, you need a strategy that includes withdrawing at least the minimally required amounts from traditional IRAs and 401(k)s. The IRS doesn't really much care how you tap into your IRA or 401(k), so you're free to take the money as a yearly lump sum or a steady amount each month. Further, the IRS doesn't care if you own just one IRA and draw down on it, or if you have several and drain a little from each of them monthly or yearly or whenever. It also doesn't care if you draw out more than it requires you to. And it doesn't care what you do with the money you withdraw from your IRA—you can spend it or reinvest it in a taxable account.

But the IRS *does* care mightily that you take out at least the minimum once you turn age 70½, whether you need the money or not. After all, the tax man has been patiently waiting for this day through probably what were decades of tax deferral.

But to put first things first, make sure that you handle your 401(k) correctly when you retire or otherwise leave the company. In general, you can do four things with those retirement savings: You can (1) cash out, (2) leave the money in the plan, (3) roll it over into an IRA, or (4) roll it over to a new employer's plan. If you cash out and you're under 59½, you'll be hit with a big federal penalty (and maybe a state penalty, too) as well as income taxes, not to mention missing out on the benefits of your money compounding tax deferred. So that's not smart.

The big benefit of rolling over the 401(k) balance into an IRA is that you'll have more investment options than in a 401(k) plan. Also, you can consolidate all your wayward retirement accounts in one place. But be careful how you do this. It's best to have the money transferred directly between financial institutions without your touching it.

You also could choose to leave your 401(k) with your old employer or roll it over into your new employer's plan. Either choice would make the most sense if you're enamored of the prescreened group of investments offered by that plan. But the selection varies from company to company, and those offered by smaller employers may be pretty skimpy. And if you leave it with your old employer, make sure that you know about any rules that may apply to the 401(k) accounts of departed workers and how they'll affect your heirs if you die. (Most companies don't offer stretch-out distributions from 401(k) plans.)

For most people, establishing a rollover to a traditional IRA is the best option. That's because your money grows faster than it would if you had cashed out the 401(k), paid the taxes, and put what was left in a taxable account. (An exception may be company stock, which I address later in this chapter, or individuals with low or even negative taxable income.) But many choose to cash out their 401(k)s to buy a new car, a new kitchen, or a Tahiti vacation. Long after the thrill of the purchase has waned, they'll be feeling the shock of the tax-and-penalty bite—and wondering how they're going to afford to retire.

You can establish an IRA rollover account at just about any financial institution. But again, I want to emphasize the importance of doing this carefully. Don't have the check sent to your home. Have it deposited directly into the IRA to minimize the costly complications, such as the mandatory withholding of 20 percent of any distribution made payable to an individual.

With either an IRA or a 401(k), you *may* start withdrawing amounts as early as age 59½ without penalty. And you *must* begin such withdrawals no later than the year after you turn 70½—otherwise, you face monetary penalties. Of course, those withdrawals will be taxed at your ordinary income-tax rates. (Roth IRAs, which I'll get into shortly, also allow you to begin withdrawing tax free at 59½, but there's no mandatory withdrawal at 70½ or any other age, provided you didn't inherit the Roth. That's one big reason why Roths are more desirable for certain individuals. Another is that withdrawals, whenever taken, are tax free.)

So how much do you need to withdraw? The required minimum distribution (RMD) at age 70½ will be the total of your account balances divided by the distribution period calculated by the IRS. In its Publication 590 (see **www.irs.gov**), the IRS sets out three different tables to be used to determine that divisor. Under the most common, the Uniform Lifetime Table, for example, a 72-year-old would divide his or her retirement account balances by 25.6, meaning that a $100,000 balance would require a withdrawal that year of $3,906.25. Failure to take out that much would result in a penalty of 50 percent of what the withdrawal should have been.

But if ever there was a trap awaiting unsuspecting seniors, it's these rules governing RMDs. Many seniors get tripped up, especially during the first couple years of having to take a distribution. In some cases they fail to take the RMD, saying that they don't need the money. (They may not, but, as I mentioned, the IRS—which has deferred taxes all those years—still wants its payback.)

In other cases, retirees use the wrong year-end account balances or the wrong life-expectancy factor from the Uniform Lifetime Table to calculate their RMD. If you mess up, you will not only pay ordinary income tax on the distribution, but you'll also get stuck with a 50 percent penalty on what you should have taken out but didn't. How do you avoid this? Check and double-check the life-expectancy factor and year-end account balance, and in most cases, you should really consult a knowledgeable financial advisor.

Adding to the necessity of working with an expert is the fact that the other tables come into play when, for example, you're married to someone more than ten years younger than yourself and you've named that spouse as a sole beneficiary. (The effect is to make the required minimum payouts smaller.) If that sounds like you, you'll definitely want to get a financial advisor to help you calculate the withdrawals.

And it really gets dicey when deciding which set of rules to follow if you inherit a retirement plan. Further, the rules vary, depending on whether the owner died before or after beginning minimum distributions and whether the beneficiary is the spouse or a non-spouse. (More on inherited IRAs later in this chapter.)

Trust me, it's complicated stuff. If your situation is even a little bit out of the ordinary—or even if it's as ordinary as white bread but you're at all financially challenged—don't try this at home. Find yourself an experienced, competent advisor (see Chapter 11 for suggestions); and come up with a withdrawal system that works for you *and* the IRS.

Drawing down your total retirement resources. Understand, of course, that every person's situation is different, and that a required minimum distribution from your tax-advantaged retirement accounts is only that, a *minimum*. You may well want or need to take out more. How much more? Well, that's debatable and something your advisor—after looking at your other retirement resources, such as personal savings, pension, and Social Security—can help you figure out.

You need at least enough money to meet your basic needs but not so much that you run out of cash in your sunset years. Your advisor will need to look at the "big picture." How much income can you expect to get from a pension, stock options, a part-time job, Social Security, personal savings, or perhaps an expected inheritance? And how much can that income be expected to grow during your retirement?

I believe that a realistic rule of thumb—confirmed by numerous academic studies—is that most people shouldn't withdraw more than 4 percent of the balance of their total retirement resources every year. (That's a *real* 4 percent, meaning that it should be increased each year by the previous year's inflation rate to help you retain the same purchasing power.) That 4-plus percent gives you the best shot at not outliving your assets.

How Much in Stocks?

But that raises a related question: How much of those retirement resources should be in stocks and real estate? (Unlike bonds, stocks and real estate may grow in value, making up some of the depletion as you withdraw money for income.) You may have heard the axiom that says your exposure to stocks should equal no more than 100 minus your age. In other words, if you're 60, you shouldn't have more than 40 percent of your resources in stocks. Indeed, that may have been a reasonable rule generations ago when life expectancies were shorter, but it's probably too conservative now.

Obviously, the greater allocation you have in stocks and real estate, the more growth potential—and also the more downside risk you'll have. Larry Swedroe, in his book *Rational Investing in Irrational Times*, says, "With at least a fifty percent allocation to equities, the historical evidence suggests that you will have less than a five percent chance of outliving your assets. . . ." If you follow my Buckets of Money strategy, you can actually design an asset allocation that matches your future need for income with a time horizon. For instance, we know that stocks are risky in the short run, but if left alone, with dividends reinvested for 15 years, you're likely to have a positive return. More aggressive investors or younger retirees may want to go with 10-year buckets, while those fainthearted about stocks may prefer a 20-year strategy.

Indeed, this is something that you need to seriously discuss with your advisor. But the truth is, a lot of people are too conservative with their money. They underestimate their life span, and they overestimate how much of their nest egg they should keep in fixed-income assets. Take this example: If you had $1 million and invested it all in bonds at

4.5 percent interest, you'd get $45,000 a year and, of course, at the end of, say, 25 years, you'd still have your million bucks.

Or, you could divide that million into two piles. One pile, let's say $731,000, you invest at 4 percent, and spend it down to zero over 25 years. That would also give you $45,000 a year every year for 25 years, the same as you would have gotten with the all-bond portfolio.

Meanwhile, what happens to the other $269,000? Well, you could have invested it in stocks and, based on historical data, you probably could have done pretty well. (Burton Malkiel, a Princeton University professor and the respected author of *A Random Walk Down Wall Street,* says that the *worst* 25-year period since 1950 for domestic stocks as measured by the S&P 500 was about a 7.94 percent rate of return.) So let's suppose you stuck that $269,000 in stocks and did only as well as the worst quarter-century since the year I was born. At the end of 25 years, you'd have $1.8 million in stocks, $800,000 more than you started with—and you would have still enjoyed your $45,000 a year. And that's calculating the worst 25-year period since 1950. If your stocks grew at, say, 9 percent, you'd end up with $2.3 million and could leave your heirs more than double what you started with. And if stocks grew at their historical 10 percent return, that $269,000 would have grown to almost $3 million—three times what you started with.

This example is akin to a highly simplified version of the whole Buckets of Money approach: Spend down part of your money to live on while putting the rest into growth investments that you won't touch for a long time. Understand, the point of the example is not that stocks will grow at some predictable rate but that there's a downside to being too conservative. Putting all your wealth into fixed income may not be the smartest thing to do.

When Will You Need the Most Income?

When figuring out how much income you're going to need in retirement, there's reason to believe that you ought to take out more income in the early years. Retirement planning traditionally has assumed that a person retains the same lifestyle throughout retirement, but some research now suggests that spending tends to decrease with age. One study in *The Journal of Financial Planning* showed that spending in practically every category—from housing to entertainment—declined with age. (The one big exception: health care.) Retirees over age 75 spent an average of 26 percent less than those in the 65- to 74-year-old age-group. What's more, the greater the difference in age, the greater the difference in spending. For instance, those over age 75 spent 46 percent less than those 55 to 64 years old, and 51 percent less than those aged 45 to 54.

So this raises the possibility that, rather than the inflated 4 percent withdrawal previously discussed, you could withdraw a higher percentage of your savings in the early years of retirement and moderate the annual inflation adjustments. But, of course, as we've seen, many variables exist, including projected life span and stock/bond mix. Also, the kind of insurance you buy to help cover rising medical costs and nursing-home care will also figure into this equation.

Your future spending pattern is something worth investing some time on with your financial advisor. On one hand, the few thousand dollars extra that you might withdraw could be what puts the quality in your "quality of life"—like that extra vacation with the grandkids or that newer-model car. On the other hand, you can't go back and unspend in your later years if you take too much out to begin with. For my part, I'd lean toward being conservative, especially at first.

Penalty-Free Ways to Crack Your Retirement Plan Early

Age 59½, whether you continue to work or not, is generally when you can start drawing down your IRA without a 10 percent federal-tax penalty. But there are ways you can get that money earlier and penalty free.

Why would you opt to shrink your retirement cache early? Only for serious reasons, I would hope. You might do so if you were grievously short of income and/or in poor health. Or perhaps you're starting a business or have another once-in-a-lifetime opportunity that demands cash. If so, here are some of the possibilities:

Withdraw Roth contributions. The Roth IRA permits penalty-free (and tax-free) withdrawals for any reason after age 59½ if you've had the account for at least five years. Even if you're younger than 59½ or have had the account for less than five years, you can withdraw your *contributions* tax free. In other words, if you've contributed $30,000 to a Roth over time and it's grown to $40,000, you can withdraw the $30,000. But if you tap into that additional $10,000 in earnings, you'll pay taxes and penalties if you do so before the five years are up and before you reach 59½. Understand, once you've taken out the money, you don't have the option of replacing it. You'll still be limited by the relatively small annual contributions, currently $4,000 a year ($1,000 more if you're 50 or older in 2006) and rising to $5,000 in 2008.

Take a 60-day "loan." Once in any 12-month period, you're allowed to withdraw funds from your IRA for up to 60 days, tax free and penalty free. But if you don't place the money back in the IRA within that time frame, it will be considered a withdrawal subject to taxes and penalties.

You can do this with multiple IRAs. So if you have more than one IRA, you may be able to buy yourself longer than 60 days by using a second IRA to pay back the first one within the 60-day period. However, this strategy is cumbersome and dangerous. (For example, we're talking about 60 calendar days, including weekends—not two months.) Miss the deadline by a day and you could incur taxable income and possible penalties.

Withdraw for special situations. The IRS allows penalty-free withdrawals of up to $10,000 from a traditional IRA for a first-time home purchase. (In a seasoned Roth IRA, the $10,000 of earnings plus post-tax contributions can be withdrawn tax free.) Similarly, you can make withdrawals for qualified education expenses, such as post-secondary education, tuition, books, supplies, and—if the student is enrolled at least half-time—room and board. In addition, you may also make withdrawals if you're disabled, have unreimbursed medical expenses that exceed 7.5 percent of your adjusted gross income, or are unemployed for more than 12 weeks and need money for health insurance.

However, I emphasize that if you take advantage of any of those provisions, you're stealing from your future. No matter how noble the reason, taking money out early can easily become a bad habit.

Use these options only as a last resort, asking yourself, "Will I still have enough to support my actual retirement?"

My advice? Explore other options, including a standard bank loan or a home-equity loan. If you must withdraw funds early from an IRA, avoid tax consequences by drawing down your original contributions (not earnings) from your Roth IRA first.

What stops—or maybe *should* stop—most people from withdrawing IRA funds early is that 10 percent early-withdrawal penalty on top of the ordinary income taxes due. But apart from any of the above provisions, here's another way you can overcome that hurdle and systematically draw down your IRA:

72(t) election. This is a way to annuitize your IRA, meaning you can take regular payments before you turn 59½ and still avoid paying the 10 percent penalty. This can be done at any age by agreeing to take a "series of substantially equal periodic payments" (monthly, quarterly, or annually) that continue for at least five years or until you're age 59½, whichever period is longer.

For example, if the IRS longevity tables show that you have a likelihood of living another, say, 25 years, then you can withdraw 1/25 of the balance in your account in the first year; then, 1/24 of the new balance in the second year, and so on. Or, you can simply take out a fixed amount each month based on your life expectancy and the interest rate the government makes you use for the calculation.

Sounds inviting? Maybe, maybe not. Don't do this without a lot of thought, because you can only change your mind and recalculate your payments lower once. After that, they can't be stopped (until after the longer of five years or age 59½) or modified without penalty even if you win the Publishers Clearing House sweepstakes. You can, though, annuitize one IRA under 72(t) and leave the others alone.

Further, the IRS actually allows three methods of calculation, and it's easy to make mistakes with these payments by taking out too little or too much—and that could cost you thousands of dollars in retroactive penalties and interest. So once more you're going to want to work closely with a lawyer, CPA, or competent financial advisor if you want to set up a 72(t).

And understand that a 72(t) doesn't let you off the hook taxwise.

You'll still owe income taxes on whatever you take from the IRA. (Though again, of course, the Roth IRA is an exception.) The remainder of your IRA will continue to grow tax deferred. And when the payout period is over, you can modify the schedule, take a lump-sum payment, or stop taking distributions altogether until age 70½.

How to Get the Most from an Inherited IRA

Another complication with retirement accounts is that IRAs often outlive their owners. And therein lies another problem. Don't assume that any of the rules governing the IRAs you own will apply to any that you inherit.

Well-meaning benefactors and recipients—sometimes even abetted by well-meaning advisors—frequently run afoul of the complicated IRS guidelines. The result: the gutting of what could have been a growing asset that would have nurtured your family for years.

The confusion starts with the fact that Uncle Sam only allows widows and widowers to roll an inherited IRA into their own accounts. For everyone else, the money is taxable the minute it's removed from the deceased's IRA. So if you inherit an IRA from your spouse, you can roll it over, you can make contributions to it, you can designate your own beneficiaries—and usually you won't owe any tax on it until you start receiving distributions.

But what happens if you're *not* a spouse of the deceased but you roll over an inherited IRA into your own IRA? The IRS considers the rollover both a withdrawal of assets from the deceased's IRA and an excessive contribution to your own IRA. You end up with a big tax bill, huge penalties, and a much smaller inheritance.

You also can't withdraw the assets from an inherited IRA and deposit them into a new IRA. And you can't consolidate IRAs you inherit from different benefactors into one account.

So what should you do if you expect to inherit an IRA? For starters, talk to your mom or dad or whoever might be bequeathing it. They may be among the lucky ones who can live comfortably off other sources of income and, thus, intend to pass along some or all of their IRA assets. Make sure their beneficiary forms are up-to-date. If they fail to fill out the form or simply leave the IRA to their estate, the account would have to be liquidated upon their death. That would scuttle the heirs' chance to stretch out distributions across their life expectancies and reap more tax-deferred growth. Also, try to find out if the parents understand the issues involved in passing along an IRA. If not, try to convince them of the advantages of hiring an estate-planning attorney, CFP®, or CPA to double-check their arrangements.

But if they've already died and willed the IRA to you, consider retitling or disclaiming the account.

Retitling. This means changing the name on the original account and, specifically, including the name of the person who died and noting that it's "for the benefit" of you. For example, if the original owner was John Brown and the beneficiary was his son James, the new title might read, "John Brown, IRA (deceased March 1, 2006) F/B/O James Brown, beneficiary."

And while keeping the account in the original owner's name, make sure you change the Social Security number on the account to that of the beneficiary.

If you correctly retitle an inherited IRA as a beneficiary IRA, you can stretch out the withdrawals across much of your lifetime rather than taking a lump sum (provided you take the first stretch-out payment by December 31 of the year after the date of death.) That, of course, gives you a chance to postpone most of the tax bite and extend the time that tax-deferred earnings can accrue.

Disclaiming. Another possibility—if you inherit an IRA but don't need the money—is to disclaim it, meaning to waive the rights to the IRA in favor of the contingent beneficiary. Why would you want to do that? Well, an affluent widow, for instance, might prefer that the IRA be inherited by her son and/or daughter who could enjoy the tax benefits for a much longer time.

But again, it's important to emphasize that this retitling and disclaiming is very tricky. Anyone contemplating such a move should be advised by an experienced estate-planning attorney. Too often, even bankers, brokers, and others who work in the financial industry have only superficial knowledge of these IRS rules. There's no substitute for competent guidance. You will not only have to deal with retitling or disclaiming, but the whole question of when and how distributions from the inherited IRA need to begin.

Another tricky point: If you inherit an IRA along with other siblings or heirs, you can split up the account and allow each heir to spread withdrawals across his or her own life expectancy. Otherwise, you get stuck using the life expectancy of the oldest heir, meaning larger distributions and a bigger tax bill.

So, as you can see, mishandling an inherited IRA can cost you plenty of time, money, and stomach lining. Please talk to a professional and avoid costly mistakes. In fact, you may want to get a second, or even a third, opinion on how to proceed.

Don't be eager to cash it out all at once. If you don't need the money immediately, you may be able to keep the IRA alive for decades. Remember, the IRAs you inherit do have one important thing in common with the ones you personally own: You can stretch out the withdrawals across your lifetime rather than taking them as a lump sum. That gives you a chance to postpone a lot of the tax hit and lengthens the time that tax-free earnings can accrue—and that potentially translates into additional thousands of dollars.

When you do withdraw money from an inherited IRA, whether it's the minimum required or more, you'll pay income taxes on the cash. The only exception is a Roth IRA. Anyone lucky enough to inherit a Roth won't need to pay taxes on the required minimum withdrawals.

Would You Benefit from a Roth Conversion?

The attraction of an IRA, of course, is that as long as the money stays inside one, you won't owe any taxes. The feds can't claim a piece of it unless you withdraw some. In fact, with the Roth IRA, you never owe any income taxes. And, as I said, with a Roth you don't need to withdraw (and pay taxes on) some minimum amount when you turn 70½.

So why not convert your regular IRA into a Roth? Wouldn't that be an obviously wise move? It could be *if* you can stand the initial shock. Because when you convert your traditional IRA to a Roth, you'll owe ordinary income taxes on the amount that you convert the next time you file your annual federal income-tax return. If you transfer $100,000, say, and you're in the 28 percent tax bracket, you'll owe $28,000.

Why? Because that's going to be the last chance the IRS will have to get its mitts on the money. Money inside a Roth can grow for a lifetime without ever being subjected to income taxes again. And beneficiaries can continue to defer tax free, subject to a RMD of usually just 3 or 4 percent for the first several years, depending on their age.

The affluent are spared the problem of figuring this out. If your modified adjusted gross income (MAGI) is more than $100,000 during the year of an intended conversion, you can't qualify. For a married person, that means *joint* MAGI. (Beginning in 2010, any taxpayer can do a Roth conversion.) Also, you can't do a conversion if you're married but filing separately or if you inherit a regular IRA from someone other than your spouse.

When Does Conversion Make Sense?

Whether converting makes sense for you depends on a lot of factors. If you're in, let's say, your 40s or younger, there's more logic in converting than if you're older. After all, you probably don't have much in your IRA yet, so the tax pain should be minimal and you have a number of years to compound your Roth tax free.

Another good conversion candidate would be someone who was, say, a high-income earner during his or her career but who's now living frugally on Social Security and investment income, and has a large, yet-untapped IRA. That person is a good bet for conversion because that IRA is going to be kicking out RMDs at age 70½. And when it does, the retiree could shoot back up into the top tax brackets. So he or she should consider using up the lower income-tax bracket levels now by converting some of that traditional IRA to a Roth each year.

For example, a married couple can have more than $319,000 of taxable income before they hit the top bracket of 35 percent. So if their annual income was $80,000 and they had pensions, IRAs, and 401(k)s in the millions, they could convert more than $220,000 of their IRA to a Roth each year before hitting the top bracket. The payoffs would be numerous.

For one thing, their future required distributions from the traditional IRA would be smaller because that IRA will be smaller. Second, the Roth will give them a tax-free fund to draw from in case of emergency needs later in life. And, third, their heirs will be happy because for them a Roth's tax-free distributions will be simpler to deal with. However, doing a sizable conversion would create a wicked tax bill, and that added cost must be figured into the economics of doing so.

Most of the time, Roth IRA conversions are done to use up the lower income-tax brackets while you're alive so your children, who may be in a higher bracket when they inherit your Roth, won't be forced into higher brackets. Roth conversions are also advisable when you're expecting to pay tax on your Social Security benefits. Because Roths are not part of the MAGI calculation, you might be able to supplement your Social Security payments with tax-free Roth distributions.

If you expect to leave your IRA to your heirs, a conversion might also make sense, because converting a regular IRA to a Roth shrinks your taxable estate. Thus, the savings to heirs can be sizable.

But for most folks, their tax bracket goes down, not up, when they retire, so they probably shouldn't convert. Nor should they convert if they don't have the cash to pay the taxes. It's probably not worth doing if you have to steal from your IRA to pay the tax bill. Yet another reason not to convert would be that you fear the tax rules will be changed again with some new or better IRA that would make the Roth less desirable or even eliminate it, however unlikely that may be.

Is it possible to convert, then change your mind? Yes, you can reconvert a Roth to a traditional IRA, although that isn't common. Most people who make the initial conversion—once they get over the shock of that initial tax hit—are pleased.

When you convert a traditional IRA to a Roth, some of the assets typically go up in value after the conversion, while others go down. You can reconvert the Roth back to a traditional IRA and even later re-reconvert to a Roth at a lower tax cost. But ordinarily you can't "cherry-pick" (as it's called) losses without factoring in the gains as well. (When you convert to a Roth, the amount of the IRA transferred must be included in your gross income. But you can reduce your tax bill if you recharacterize a Roth IRA that has declined in value.)

One way around that, though, is to create several Roths and specifically identify assets to be transferred to the newly established Roth IRAs. You might group, for example, a particular fund, a particular stock, or a particular bunch of stocks within a market sector. That way you could recharacterize the Roth IRAs that have declined in value back into a traditional IRA and keep in the Roth those that have risen in value.

But, of course, that's a super-tricky maneuver. And what's important in any conversion or reconversion is to understand all the tax consequences before you proceed. Again, talk to a professional.

The New Roth 401(k)

The Roth 401(k), just introduced in 2006, can add another arrow to your retirement-savings quiver. This is a new kind of retirement account that's especially promising for young workers and for highly paid employees. Combining features of Roth IRAs and 401(k) plans, the Roth 401(k) allows workers to set aside money from their paychecks that's already been taxed. The money then grows tax free, and all withdrawals after age 59½ are tax free.

Workers with access to both types of accounts can continue to contribute solely to a standard 401(k), divert their contributions to the Roth 401(k), or split their contributions between the two, but they can't switch money from one plan to the other after it goes in.

In a regular 401(k) plan, contributions are made with before-tax dollars. The money isn't taxed while it remains in the account, but each dollar taken out is taxed as ordinary income. So it provides a tax break on the front end. The Roth 401(k) won't initially reduce an employee's tax bill, but it will give him or her a break on the back end. Which plan will be more attractive depends on how long the money stays in the account, how much it earns, and your tax brackets when you put the money in and when you take it out.

What's clear is that the Roth 401(k) will be a much quicker route for saving than a Roth IRA, with its more restrictive contribution limits and income restrictions. (The most you can currently put in a Roth IRA is $4,000, or $5,000 if you're age 50 or over. By contrast, the comparable amounts would be $15,000/$20,000 for either a 401(k) or a Roth 401(k). The Roth 401(k) also has no income limitations.)

Is the benefit of tax-free withdrawals down the road worth the up-front cost? To figure that out, workers will need to predict their personal tax situation in retirement. As a general rule, the Roth 401(k) is a good solution for those who expect to be in a higher tax bracket in retirement. But employees also must try to forecast what the national tax picture will look like when they're ready to draw down their nest egg. If tax rates rise to pay off the growing budget deficit, paying taxes now, as in a Roth 401(k), probably would be a good deal. On the other hand, if the tax system is reformed in favor of a lower flat tax or some kind of national sales tax, those who've invested in the Roth 401(k) might lose in a big way.

The new Roth 401(k) appears to be a boon for two groups: high-income workers and young people in low tax brackets. That's because the higher-paid employees may be excluded from having a Roth IRA because of its income limitations. (Single filers with adjusted gross incomes of $110,000 or joint filers earning $160,000 or more are barred from contributing to Roth IRAs.) So, previously, highly paid workers didn't have access to a retirement savings account that offers tax-free withdrawals in retirement. But anyone can invest in a Roth 401(k) so long as their employer provides that option.

Another advantage for highly paid workers is that a Roth 401(k)'s withdrawals can help them manage their tax situation in retirement. If they already have sizable savings in traditional 401(k)s, these new plans will let them pull a portion of their retirement income from a Roth 401(k), thereby lowering their overall tax burden. But highly compensated employees need to weigh the costs of the post-tax contributions today while they're in a high tax bracket versus the benefits of tax-free withdrawals when they retire.

The Roth 401(k)'s tax-free withdrawals are also likely to appeal to younger workers who expect their income to climb and carry them into a higher tax bracket later. That's because they're paying taxes on their contributions today at lower rates, but later will be able to withdraw the money without paying any taxes. Still, because those contributions are after-tax, a worker with a Roth 401(k) will have lower take-home pay. And, of course, many younger people have a hard time finding spare cash to contribute to a standard 401(k), let alone a Roth.

Workers contributing to a Roth 401(k) typically have access to the same mutual funds and other investment options that their firms offer in a regular 401(k). And as with a Roth IRA, a Roth 401(k) account must be open at least five years for a tax-free withdrawal, and the account holder must be at least age 59½.

Educational and nonprofit employers that offer 403(b) plans will also be able to add Roth 401(k) accounts. However, the Roth option will not be permitted in 457 plans, offered by government employers.

Early indications are that employers are acting cautiously, with many not yet adopting the Roth 401(k). Some may be reluctant to add the option because it could confuse their retirement offerings and because the Roth 401(k), like most provisions of the 2001 tax act, is set to expire after 2010. (Unless Congress extends the Roth 401(k), the money already invested will be allowed to remain after 2010, but no new money could be added.)

You'll likely be hearing much more about this new program, but you might ask your employer about it. Don't assume that your firm will automatically make the arrangements.

Using Your Home Equity to Best Advantage

Pondering a big equity in your home is like looking through the window at a Häagen-Dazs. You spy this splendid ice cream sundae and start asking: *How could I get that right now _and_ not wreck my diet?*

That "sundae" is probably one of your largest assets, especially if you've been in your home a while. Many Americans, especially those living on either coast or in the Sunbelt, have an enormous buildup of equity in their homes. In fact, that equity is likely one of their largest assets, especially if the mortgage has been paid down over the years or even paid off. That home equity can be a valuable source of extra income during retirement *if* you can figure out a way to mine the value that's locked in that property.

That's what people do, for instance, when they take out a home-equity loan or a home-equity line of credit. But, of course, that means taking on more debt, which is not what you want to do as a retiree. So let's look at some of the other options.

Trading down. If your home is larger than you need, trading down to a smaller place or moving to a less expensive region may be a good way to increase your retirement income. (The tax laws encourage this: You can generally exclude up to $250,000 of the profit—$500,000 if you're married—on the sale of your principal residence from capital-gains tax.) The difference between what you sell your old house for and what you pay for the new one can give a sharp boost to your retirement nest egg. Of course, you need to factor closing costs and moving expenses into that equation as well.

A smaller home—or one in a less expensive area—usually means lower real estate taxes and smaller bills for heating, cooling, insurance, and maintenance. If your move is from a single-family house to a condominium, your costs will be reduced even more because outside painting, roof repair, landscaping, and similar costs will be covered by your condo fees.

But consider the drawbacks, too: likely less space and perhaps a less attractive home. Besides, you may not want to be uprooted from your home and from the friends and associates you're used to dealing with. While you may be sitting on a huge chunk of cash, you may not want to sell the house and move because you like it and the neighborhood—after all, that's why you've stayed there so long. So, increasingly, people are coming up with other creative ways to deal with this problem.

Pay off your mortgage. You'd probably like to own your family home free and clear. That's the goal of the mortgage-burdened everywhere. Not having to send in that check every month is bound to give anyone a warm and fuzzy feeling. And think what you could do with all those extra bucks. Plus, paying off your mortgage—or even paying a bit more each month than is required—will reduce the interest you pay by thousands of dollars.

Few investments—maybe *none*—give you this kind of risk-free return. Spending, say, $10,000 to pay down a 7 percent mortgage will give you a return of $700 a year—the same guaranteed yield as a 7 percent Treasury bond, if there currently were such a thing. (Taxes complicate this a bit. Prepaying means there's less interest to deduct, and that will lower your yield if you actually file a Schedule A.)

Great! So why not do it? Well, lots of people do, but is it the best solution for *everyone?* No, for several possible reasons, such as the fact that you may have more pressing needs for that extra cash. For example, you shouldn't even *think* about prepaying your mortgage if you have credit-card debt. Interest rates on your plastic are at least twice that of your mortgage, and the interest on credit-card debt is not tax deductible. So any extra cash should go toward getting out from under that debt first.

Further, before you try to pay off your mortgage, you need to make sure you've got an emergency fund. That means stashing enough cash—say, in a money-market or bond fund—to cover your expenses for several months in case you lose your job, are injured, or suffer some other unexpected setback.

What's more, owning your home debt free won't be much of help if you can't afford to put food on the table after you retire. So before committing a large sum toward your mortgage, make sure you've taken full advantage of tax-favored retirement plans, such as 401(k)s or IRAs; and ensure that you have enough life insurance to cover the mortgage, living expenses, and education costs. Even if you don't have others depending on you, disability insurance or long-term care insurance are good ideas, too.

Also, can you earn a higher return elsewhere? If your mortgage rate is 6 percent and you can make 8 percent in a different investment, you'd come out ahead, dollar for dollar, with the other investment. (But be careful! How predictable *is* that 8 percent return?)

Be mindful also that if you pay down or pay off your mortgage, you'll reduce or eliminate your mortgage-interest deduction. Depending what else is going on in your financial life, this could end up increasing your taxes.

Finally, note that some lenders penalize you if your prepayment exceeds a certain amount (say, 20 percent a year) or if it occurs within a certain period (such as in the first five years of the loan). Be sure to check your mortgage contract.

Okay, let's say you've got those bases covered: Your other cash needs are taken care of, you won't be hurt taxwise, be assessed a penalty, or be forsaking significantly higher returns elsewhere. Then shouldn't you press ahead with plans to pay off the mortgage? Maybe.

Paying off a mortgage early is especially attractive for some home owners who have small loans and, thus, pay an amount of interest that doesn't exceed the standard IRS deduction for nonitemizing taxpayers. Paying extra or paying off early also allows some borrowers to avoid paying private mortgage insurance. And if you're about to send a kid to college, taking money out of your savings and using it to prepay your mortgage may reduce the assets that are counted against you when applying for college financial aid.

So, good reasons exist to pay off or pay down your mortgage. *But what if you could have the mortgage covered and still get that important tax deduction?* That would be the best of both worlds, wouldn't it? Consider this strategy:

Pay your mortgage from a Roth. If you're able to save enough to send in extra mortgage payments, maybe you could instead put some or all of that money to work in a smarter way—say, into a Roth IRA. If you were able to wisely invest that Roth money, you might get a better return than you would from prepaying a mortgage of 6 or 7 percent. Remember, mortgage interest is tax deductible, and a Roth accumulates its earnings tax free.

So let's say you're in a combined 33 percent tax bracket. A deductible 6 percent mortgage would only cost you 4 percent. So anything you earned in your Roth IRA above 4 percent would be gravy.

Further, when you decide you're ready to be mortgage free and if you're over age 59½, you can withdraw money from the Roth to either pay off the mortgage balance in full or simply withdraw enough money to cover the mortgage payments. The latter tactic would allow you to keep your mortgage-interest deduction *and* use the Roth money tax free, thus building your wealth more quickly.

Even if you're younger than 59½, withdrawals from a Roth IRA are treated first as a return on your principal contributions, then interest. So as long as you're 59½ by the time you start tapping into the interest accumulated in the Roth, you'll be okay.

Yes, you'd need to start on this plan early enough to build up a sufficient balance in your Roth. (Remember, the current maximum yearly contribution is $4,000, or $5,000 if you're age 50 or more.) And you'd still need to write that check each month to the bank or savings and loan.

But if you knew the tax-free source from which the money was coming—*and* you kept what's likely your biggest tax deduction—wouldn't it be worth it? Think about it.

Reamortize the loan. Another tactic for those who are retired, or are about to retire, is to refinance—not necessarily to lock in lower rates, but to reamortize the loan. Let's say there are ten years left on your loan. You might be able to refi and get a 30-year loan, which would cut your payments greatly, keeping much more cash in your pocket.

What do you care if you die with a loan outstanding? Maybe you'd be leaving your children a $750,000 home with a $100,000 mortgage instead of a house that's paid off. But meanwhile, you'd be freeing up cash flow for your standard of living. (Keep in mind that interest on refinancing or home-equity loans is deductible only on principal amounts of $100,000 beyond your acquisition debt—that is, the amount of the loan before you refinanced.)

Take advantage of an interest-only mortgage. Interest-only mortgages, in which you pay no principal for a period of years, are growing in popularity. Eventually, though, the initial low-payment period (often ten years) ends, and monthly payments soar because borrowers must pay the principal in a compressed time frame and possibly at higher interest rates than when the loan originated.

These are potentially riskier than conventional mortgages, and I usually recommend them only for sophisticated borrowers who understand the pitfalls, but they can work well for those who are disciplined in their investing, who don't overspend, and who expect their incomes to rise sharply in the future. For instance, you could take out an interest-only mortgage and dedicate the savings to a Roth IRA. When the low-payment period ends, you could pay the principal and interest with tax-free money from the Roth while still retaining your mortgage-interest deduction.

Take out a reverse mortgage. Reverse mortgages used to be thought of as largely a last resort for impoverished seniors who had no other income, but this kind of mortgage has now become widely popular with seniors because it allows them to turn their home equity into tax-free cash. With a reverse mortgage, you can increase your income and continue to live in your present home for life.

Historically, high home values and low interest rates have combined to give the arrangement added allure. In one recent year, the volume of such loans soared 112 percent, according to the National Reverse Mortgage Lenders Association.

It's called a *reverse* mortgage because the principal balance gets larger, not smaller, over time, and because the bank pays you; you don't pay the bank. Only home owners age 62 or older can take out a reverse mortgage. Generally, the older the applicant, the higher the value of the house, and the lower the interest rate, the bigger reverse mortgage a home owner can qualify for. (Many seniors don't qualify for home-equity loans or home-equity lines of credit because of low income. And in any case, such loans require a monthly repayment, so they don't solve cash-flow problems.)

So the interest on a reverse mortgage just accrues, and the loan doesn't need to be repaid until the borrower dies or moves out of the home. In the 1970s and '80s, some questionable reverse-mortgage programs resulted in owners being put out of their houses when the size of the debt exceeded the value of the property. But government safeguards now ensure home owners will never owe more than the home's value. That's because if the value of the house falls below the loan amount, the lender absorbs the difference.

The money can be used for any purpose, and the proceeds can come in the form of a monthly check, a lump sum, or a line of credit, or some combination of these. The payout doesn't affect your Social Security payments. And you don't need to repay the loan as long as you live in the home. (The loan is usually repaid from the proceeds from the sale of the house after you move or die.)

The size of the loan depends in part on the specific reverse-mortgage program you select. Most home owners qualify for the biggest cash advances under the U.S. government's home-equity conversion mortgage (HECM) program, which is backed by the Federal Housing Administration (see **www.hud.gov**). Generally, figure on getting no more than about 30 to 50 percent of the equity in your house because lenders don't want to be left holding the bag if house values plummet. But if the market value of your home is well above the average house price in your area, you might be able to get a larger loan from a private lender.

Ideally, you want the biggest loan at the lowest cost. But the two don't always go hand in hand, and their complex features can sometimes make them difficult to evaluate. For help in figuring out the best terms, talk to your financial advisor. You may also want to contact the AARP's Reverse Mortgage Education Project (**www.aarp. org/money/revmort**).

Reverse mortgages can be an expensive way to generate income compared to, say, trading down to a smaller home. Loan fees and closing costs are higher than for traditional mortgages, often running into the five figures. However, these may be wrapped into the loan amount, meaning that there's little up-front cost. Because the loan is payable at death, heirs may feel shortchanged, although they can take out a conventional mortgage to pay off the reverse mortgage.

Reverse mortgages make the most sense if you're looking for an ongoing source of income through retirement or you need a large lump sum. It doesn't make much sense if you might move in a few years or just need cash for some relatively small bills. That's because the stiff up-front expenses—such as origination fees, closing costs, and mortgage insurance—can drive the effective short-term loan rate skyward.

Also, note that a reverse mortgage doesn't reduce your housing costs unless it's used to pay off your existing mortgage. Because you stay in your home, you still face real estate taxes, insurance, repairs, and other costs associated with the property.

While the payouts are tax free, the accrued loan interest isn't deductible until or if the borrower starts paying off the loan. Each payment that you receive from the lender reduces your home equity—and increases the amount of principal and interest that you owe on the mortgage. This means that the owner will net less when the home is eventually sold, unless the value of the home appreciates more rapidly than the rise in the reverse-mortgage balance.

On the other hand, if you face a serious retirement-income shortage, this reduction in equity—really a lessening of your heirs' potential inheritance—may be better than lowering your standard of living. So for an increasing number of retirees, adding to their cash flow trumps the downsides of reverse mortgages. It can be especially helpful in the early years of retirement when you can travel and get out more. And as noted, if you have a balance on your existing mortgage and need more cash flow, a reverse mortgage can allow you to pay off your home loan and give you cash-flow relief in a hurry.

However, here's a word of caution: Be disciplined about how you use any retirement windfall, whether it's from a reverse mortgage or from some other equity-tapping techniques. The Securities and Exchange Commission has come out strongly against individuals borrowing against their homes to buy investments such as stocks, and the commission is especially critical of borrowing to buy variable annuities.

I often hear from people wanting to use their home equity to buy more real estate. While that can sometimes produce phenomenal results, it's also very risky. An individual really has to have staying power—a good job and quite a bit of cash in the bank—to do that successfully. Because while leverage (borrowing) can make you money, leverage can also take you down. Before taking money out of the home to invest, be sure to do the math. If the deal doesn't pencil out, back off.

Get an unofficial reverse mortgage. If you're put off by the fees involved and/or the administrative hassle of applying for a reverse mortgage, here's another idea: Work out a deal with your kids. Tell them the house will eventually be theirs but meanwhile, you need more cash flow to live a comfortable retirement lifestyle. Perhaps they could take over some or all of the mortgage payments and provide you with the additional income you need. They could even charge you an interest rate below that of a traditional reverse mortgage. So, your kids would be creating a low-cost reverse mortgage for you.

A trust deed can protect the repayment of the loan plus interest before the balance is distributed to the heirs. The kids will be paid back after you die when they sell the house. My strong suggestion would be to get any such agreement in writing. Reach a clear understanding of who gets what and when.

Another suggestion: Take your time and think carefully through any plan to tap into your home equity. After all, it has taken many years to build up that value. Whether you're trading down to a smaller, less expensive home; paying off or paying down the current loan;

reamortizing; or taking out an official or unofficial reverse mortgage, don't act in haste. Remember, it doesn't hurt to have equity in your home. So take the time to unlock that value in the smartest way.

Getting the Most Out of Your Company Stock

Another way to bolster your income in retirement is to use the NUA—net unrealized appreciation—strategy. That's a way to pay less in taxes if you hold company stock in your retirement plan.

Ordinarily, when you begin taking distributions from a retirement plan, you pay ordinary income tax on the current market value of those assets, plus tax on any cash they've kicked out. But by using the NUA strategy, you can defer paying tax on the appreciation in your company stock and, when sold, only pay the long-term capital-gains tax rate (currently a 15 percent maximum tax on the gain) rather than your ordinary income-tax rate, which could be as high as 35 percent.

In essence, those who retire or leave a company *and* who own company stock in a retirement plan have two choices: (1) They can roll the stock over into an IRA and eventually pay taxes at ordinary-income rates after selling the stock and withdrawing those funds; or (2) they can ask for a lump-sum distribution of the company stock into a taxable brokerage account, pay a tax on the cost basis of the stock, and then pay the lower long-term capital-gains rate when they ultimately sell the stock.

For those who have large amounts of appreciated company stock, it's usually better to go the latter route. For example, let's say you own 5,000 shares of company stock with a market value of $500,000, or $100 a share. You paid $60 a share, for a cost basis of $300,000, so your NUA is $200,000 ($500,000 - $300,000).

If you elect to roll the company stock to an IRA and eventually take a $500,000 distribution, you'd owe (assuming a 35 percent federal tax rate) $175,000 in taxes. But if you instead adopt a NUA strategy and take a lump-sum distribution of the employer stock to a separate account, you'll owe $105,000 in ordinary tax on the $300,000 (35 percent x $300,000), and the $200,000 of appreciation wouldn't be taxed until the securities were sold . . . and even then would only be taxed at the long-term capital-gains rate of 15 percent. Any additional appreciation from the original distribution date also would only be taxed at the long-term capital gains rate, provided it's held for 12 months after the date of distribution.

So you'd end up paying the $105,000 tax on the original distribution plus $30,000 (15 percent x $200,000) as you withdrew the money. That makes a total tax of $135,000 on the original amount of stock instead of $175,000 if you'd paid 35 percent on the entire amount.

Of course, the higher your income-tax bracket and/or the more your stock has appreciated, the greater the benefit from this technique. For highly appreciated stock, the cost basis could be quite low, leaving you with a substantial gain that's taxed at 15 percent instead of ordinary income-tax rates.

There are some rules to consider: For one thing, you must take a lump-sum distribution of *all* assets in the plan to qualify. If you also have mutual funds in the retirement plan, you may have them (or the proceeds after they're sold) distributed into a traditional IRA to maintain their tax-deferred growth. Also, keep in mind that to preserve your retirement savings, it's probably best to pay the taxes due on the cost basis from another source of money.

The NUA strategy is less beneficial if your tax rate is likely to decline in retirement. State income taxes should also be considered. Also note that the stock price could decline or tax rates could change, defeating the tax-saving benefits of the strategy.

The NUA strategy can aid your beneficiaries if you hold the stock in a taxable account and it appreciates before your death. When they sell the inherited stock, they will owe long-term capital-gains tax on the unrealized appreciation. However, any additional appreciation between the date of distribution and the date of your death is never taxed. Instead, that amount is treated as a step-up in cost basis for your beneficiaries.

Tax-Credit Investing

Here's another strategy I've used several times to help retirees and preretirees solve two problems at once:

Problem No. 1: Because millions of renter households spend more than half of their incomes for housing, there's a great need for privately built low-income housing that rents at below-market rates.

Problem No. 2: Many older investors have large IRAs, pension plans, or annuities that may or must be withdrawn and are taxed at hefty ordinary-income rates.

The solution: Consider investing in low-income housing tax credits. This promotes affordable housing for the poor and allows investors to effectively convert their taxable retirement money into a tax-free Roth IRA.

As with any strategy, risks exist, and due diligence is always a must. But for the right investor, low-income housing tax credits can be a win-win.

Here's the background: Low-income housing tax credits were created about 20 years ago by Congress. One way to qualify for the tax credit is by directly building, buying, or renovating apartments to rent to low-income people. But more commonly, investors pool their money in a limited partnership and receive tax credits that lower their federal income taxes each year for the next 10 to 12 years.

A key point is that a *tax credit* is a lot more beneficial than a *tax deduction.* (Credits cut your tax bill outright. Deductions merely lower your taxable income.)

Calculating the maximum tax credit you can take each year is pretty complicated and depends on your tax bracket, so you'll want to work with a financial planner or tax specialist who knows his or her way around this kind of tax shelter.

But let's say you invest $60,000. You may get credits of $5,000 to $6,000 a year for ten years (although it may take a year or two before full access to the credits is available). That's almost like getting a tax-free check for $6,000 a year over the next decade.

Meanwhile, let's say you've got a substantial traditional IRA from a 401(k) rollover or one that you've built up over the years. Using this $6,000 a year in tax credits, you can take approximately $25,000 out of your IRA each year for the next ten years and use the tax credit to offset the tax, so it's like a tax-free distribution from your IRA.

You then convert that $25,000 into a Roth and let it grow. After ten years, you will have stashed away $250,000. Plus, of course, it will likely have increased in value. For instance, if you invested that new Roth money in a real estate investment trust paying 6 percent, at the end of the ten years your $250,000 may have grown to perhaps $350,000. That $350,000 would have been funded tax free and can be withdrawn and used tax free when, and for whatever purpose, you wish. Or, because there are no distribution requirements on a Roth, you can decide to let it sit and appreciate for your heirs.

That first $60,000 that you invested in low-income housing, then, would have given you the power to create this "super Roth" without penalty and without paying tax on the conversion. What's more, you could get a further payback from the low-income property you invested in. Under the law, the partnership you invested in must hold the low-income units for 15 years before selling them.

If, unlikely as it seems, the partnership sold the property after 15 years and got nothing—in effect, bulldozed it—you would have still have gotten your tax credits, which would probably amount to about a 4 to 5 percent tax-free rate of return. If the sale merely returns what the partnership put into actual bricks and mortar, you'd get perhaps $50,000 of your original $60,000 back, the rest going toward fees and sales charges. That would increase your return to maybe 6 or 7 percent after taxes. And if the property had appreciated at 2 to 3 percent, you might get a return of 8 to 10 percent or more after taxes.

So in the worst-case scenario, you would have performed a useful social service while making about the same as you'd likely get from a tax-free municipal bond. But in the best case, you could receive about double what a tax-free muni pays. But, more important, by using the tax credit in concert with a Roth conversion, you could build up a tax-free nest egg—as much as $350,000 in our example.

If that Roth were invested in our hypothetical REIT with a 6 percent yield, it could produce a tax-free income of $21,000 a year. And that's income that wouldn't increase your modified adjusted gross income (MAGI), meaning that it wouldn't make more of your Social Security taxable. In fact, the $21,000 wouldn't show up anywhere.

As I said, though, with any investment there are risks. That's why individuals must meet minimums for income and net worth. Even so, this is an illiquid, long-term investment, with any capital-gains payoff being more than a decade away and not guaranteed. You shouldn't count on any cash flow because rents may barely cover debt and operating expenses.

Further, you need to be careful with whom you choose to partner. The firm you choose should have a track record for bringing properties to market and being able to comply with the complicated federal rules so that the property remains qualified as a low-income rental. But for the right person, tax credits can be potentially a lucrative and socially beneficial strategy, especially when coupled with a Roth conversion. (Tax credits do not reduce the Alternative Minimum Tax (AMT), so if you're close to being hit with the AMT, you should be especially careful to get competent tax advice before proceeding.)

Maximizing the Benefits of Home Ownership and Rental Property

Serial primary-home ownership. Of course, one of the best investments anyone can make is to buy their own home. That's because you have to live somewhere, and when you sell, there's an exemption of up to $500,000 ($250,000 if you're single) of capital gains tax free. What's more, you can sell a principal residence every two years, provided you occupy it for 24 months out of the preceding 60 months and wait at least two years between sales.

That creates an interesting strategy for folks who own rental homes. Let's say you own your home as well as two rentals with lots of appreciation. You could sell your primary home and pocket up to $500,000 in capital gains tax free. Then you'd move into one of the rentals and make that your principal residence for two years before selling it. Finally, you'd move into the second rental, live in it for a couple years, and then sell it.

Thus, over a four- to five-year period, you could liquidate all three properties and maybe walk away with several hundred thousand dollars (or more) tax free, with the exception of recapturing a bit of depreciation on the rentals. (Only depreciation after May 7, 1997, must be recaptured.)

1031 exchange. Some people (my wife is one) don't want to move into their rental property just to get out of paying some tax. For them, another strategy is to use built-up equity in the rentals to improve their income and long-term growth by doing what's called a 1031, or "Starker," exchange.

What you do is list the property and add some language to the sales contract that informs all parties that you intend to do a tax-deferred exchange. Upon the sale, 100 percent of your proceeds go directly to an "accommodator," which is usually a title company. From the date of sale, you have 45 calendar days to identify three or so potential properties that you what to exchange into. And you have 180 days to close escrow on at least one or more of those properties. The exchange must be for investment purposes (not vacation), and the ultimate exchange investment must be for an equal or greater value than the net sales price and carry an equal or greater debt.

If you follow all the rules, you may be able to create more real estate value as well as more income. For those needing some of the equity out of their real estate, either for an infusion of cash or to give Donald Trump a run for his money, they can borrow against the property without tax consequence after the exchange occurs.

If you do change your mind and decide that you want to move into an exchanged property and make it your principal residence, a few rules apply. First, it must be a bona fide exchange—you must intend at the time of the exchange for this property to be for investment purposes and not used as a principal residence. Thus, it probably needs to be rented out for at least two or three years. Then, if you decide to kick the tenants out and move your family in, you can't sell it as a principal residence and qualify for the $250,000 to $500,000 exclusion unless you've lived in it at least two years, and at least five years have passed since the exchange took place. Again, if you sell it as a principal residence, you'll still recapture the depreciation taken after May 7, 1997.

This technique is especially valuable if you're a few years from retirement and plan on moving to your retirement dream home. You could, in effect, do a 1031 exchange from your rental into a property in an area where you'd like to retire. Then three or so years later, establish that property as your retirement home, or after living in it for two years, sell it tax free and buy the home of your choosing.

Tenant-in-common (TIC) exchange. The hassle of managing the property is one of the big downsides of investing in real estate. Unfortunately, many smaller investors may not be able to afford the kind of quality property management that's available on larger deals. That's where this strategy may be valuable.

A group of smaller investors sell their property and buy a fractional share of a building or other real estate. Usually, a big REIT or major real estate firm is involved as the property manager and organizer of the deal. Sometimes the REIT itself will actually own a tenant-in-common interest in the building or buy up any unsold units inside the REIT so the deal can close on or before the deadline. I prefer that the organizers have some "skin in the game."

TICs have been around for years, but their popularity has soared since 2002 when the IRS said they would be allowed for 1031 exchanges. TICs are thought to be especially attractive to baby boomers who invested in real estate years ago but now, as they enter retirement, are looking to shed the hassles of management, such as dealing with tenants and keeping current on maintenance.

While TICs are a way to potentially convert low-cash-flow, high-maintenance real estate into a low-hassle cash generator, they're not without risk. As with all real estate, doing due diligence is important. The popularity of TICs may be bidding up prices on marginal deals, meaning the property may fail to meet projected returns. In addition, investors need to make sure they understand the up-front loads and ongoing fees, as well as whether they can get out before a property is sold. But if you select the right company and the right real estate deal, a TIC may be an excellent way to generate hassle-free cash flow at retirement.

Buying real estate with your IRA. Promoters often hold seminars on how you can buy property—such as condos, single-family rentals, and apartments—using money within your IRA. True, this can be done. But there are lots of good reasons not to do so.

First, ask yourself: "Should I even consider this?" Real estate has some significant advantages if personally owned that are lost when the property is put within an IRA. For example:

— *Appreciation.* When appreciated real estate is sold, you get long-term capital-gains tax treatment that maxes out at 15 percent (if held more than a year). That contrasts with tax as high as 35 percent on ordinary income distributed out of an IRA.

— *Depreciation.* Personally owned property can be depreciated on your tax return. This potentially lowers your income tax now or later. But inside an IRA, depreciation provides no benefit.

— *Step-up in basis.* Personally owned real estate receives a step-up in tax basis at death. Thus, all capital gains and unrecaptured depreciation are wiped out, and the beneficiary inherits the property tax free. Real estate owned inside an IRA is taxed to the beneficiary at ordinary income-tax rates.

— *Better financing.* A property-owning IRA must qualify for any loan without the help of the individual IRA holder. Because traditional lenders are reluctant to make loans to an IRA, those who do tend to be hard-money private lenders charging exorbitant rates. This makes the real estate economics of the deal less attractive when it's owned in an IRA.

— *Double taxation.* If your IRA secures financing, any future gain relative to that financing may be construed as unrelated-business taxable income to the IRA. This means that your IRA must actually pay tax, then you pay tax again when you withdraw the funds. The tax rates for unrelated-business taxable income in an IRA are very high on fairly small sums, again potentially hurting the economics of the deal.

So what's the answer? Well, there is a way to use your IRA to help buy personally held real estate. For example, I heard recently from a 50-year-old woman who, after going to one of those seminars, wanted to use $200,000 of her $500,000 IRA as a down payment on $1 million worth of real estate. I discouraged her for the reasons I just cited and gave her a better idea instead.

Because her home had appreciated greatly in the last few years, I recommended that she get a $200,000 interest-only, home-equity loan for about 6.5 percent for ten years. By then the newly acquired property is likely to have been sold and the loan repaid.

As a result, she now has easy access to the down payment for the new property and owes about $13,000 per year in interest. So I proposed that she take her $500,000 IRA and split it into two IRAs of about $250,000 each. We place the first $250,000 IRA under a 72(t) election and begin receiving payments of about $1,250 per month, enough to cover the interest cost on the home-equity loan. While this $1,250 is taxable income (although penalty free), most, if not all, of the interest she pays on the home-equity loan will be tax deductible. (Interest on $100,000 can be deducted on Schedule A, and the balance deductible on Schedule E; see your tax advisor.)

The bottom line is that she was able to buy the real estate personally, retaining all of the tax and estate benefits. Her out-of-pocket costs were near zero. And she still was able to use her IRA to make the transaction work without incurring the disadvantages of actually having the property within her IRA. This strategy can not only be used to buy investment property, but also vacation property (Schedule E deduction not available) or other personal-use property not available to be purchased within an IRA.

Choosing the best legal structure for your rental properties. Forming a limited liability company (LLC) isn't a strategy that will make you money—but it might help you avoid losing a lot of it in a lawsuit. An LLC is a hybrid combining some of the best features of a corporation and a partnership.

Like a corporation, it exists as a separate entity and is the entity of choice when holding investment real estate. Lawyers often advise clients to form multiple LLCs when they have multiple properties, placing a single asset within each LLC. Assets within the LLC aren't protected from lawsuits from, say, tenants and creditors, but the members of the LLC can't be held *personally* liable for claims against them resulting from a lawsuit for something that happened at that property, unless that lawsuit was the result of the LLC owner(s)' negligence. Thus, it's recommended that LLC owners subcontract as much as possible and not perform services (such as electrical construction and the like) that could cause them any personal liability.

Other advantages of LLCs include flexibility in how the profits are distributed; no meetings or minutes are required; and all losses, profits, and expenses "flow through" to the individual members, avoiding the double taxation of paying corporate and individual tax.

All 50 states allow for the formation of LLCs. You need to file articles of organization and an operating agreement, which is akin to corporate bylaws or partnership agreements.

However, state statutes vary, so it's advisable to seek legal counsel to determine the best choice for your situation.

Investigating Other Investment Strategies

Principal-protected variable annuity. Although I touched on this briefly when talking with our hypothetical couple John and Chris, I want to revisit this strategy because it can be a good one for certain individuals. I should say that normally I don't favor variable annuities— the fees are high and the gain produces ordinary (not tax-advantaged) income for the investor or the heirs. But for individuals who loathe the risk of the stock market or are concerned about outliving their assets, these annuities can have merit.

A variable annuity is an insurance contract that allows investors to participate in the stock market through separate accounts similar to mutual funds. If the account value declines and the investor dies, the insurance inside the annuity makes the investor's heirs whole. So there's no way to lose at death.

Insurance firms have gotten increasingly creative in adding other benefits. For instance, some new and improved variable annuities have a 5 or 6 percent guaranteed-lifetime-withdrawal benefit as well as principal protection. Fainthearted investors can pay extra and invest their variable annuity's subaccounts' cash value in a stock allocation, knowing that if their portfolio hits the skids after several years, they can walk away with their original principal. Or, in some cases they get a guarantee of a high-watermark sum in which a percentage of the highest value is paid at the end of the contract period regardless of future declines. The total cost for variable annuities is usually about 1.5 percent more than traditional mutual funds. Thus, they shouldn't be considered by younger investors but instead by those in their 50s and beyond who want and need the assurance they will not lose money in the market. (All annuities carry a pre-age 59½ penalty on any with-drawal of savings.)

I particularly like a principal-protected variable annuity as a bond alternative, not necessarily as an alternative to investing in stocks. For example, combining a fixed annuity in which interest rates are adjusted annually with a principal-protected variable annuity may work better than bonds in a Bucket No. 2. If interest rates go up, the fixed annuity's rate likely will follow suit, while bonds will decrease in value. If rates go down, unless it's an extreme recession, stocks usually go up and pro-duce better returns than fixed annuities, CDs, or even bonds. So using principal-protected variable annuities along with other fixed investments may bolster Bucket No. 2 returns without assuming stock-market risk.

Equity-indexed annuity. This is another strategy that John and Chris discussed but may be worth reiterating because it can help the bond investor who's looking for more potential return while still getting downside protection. An insurance company will usually guarantee a floor return of, say, 3 percent, while giving the investor the ability to earn an interest rate tied to the performance of a stock index, such as the S&P 500. It differs from a variable annuity because there are no ongoing fees for money management, although there's usually a cap on how much you can earn. Also, dividends are excluded from the return calculation.

If the stock market does very well, the variable annuity will look better. If the stock market does average, the equity-indexed annuity and the variable annuity will likely look average. And if the stock market craters, the equity-indexed annuity will still offer a guaranteed return of, say, 3 percent versus a simple principal protection in a variable annuity. Combining equity-indexed annuities and variable annuities, along with bonds, can sometimes produce a very competitive fixed-income portfolio for your Bucket No. 2.

Prepaid variable forward contract. This is a sophisticated tool that can work well for an investor with a lot of money tied up in just one or two stocks and who's worried about capital-gains taxes or the stock plummeting before he or she can sell. It's akin to an options "collar" in which an investor both buys put options and sells calls to protect a stock position. It requires doing a lot of homework.

Take Gil and his wife, who sit on $9 million in one firm's stock with a cost basis of nearly zero. If they sell, they'll pay $1,350,000 in federal capital-gains tax and about $810,000 in state income tax. They're contemplating a move to Nevada (a no-income-tax state), where they can buy a fine house for cash with just the savings from the state tax alone. But with a kid who's a senior in high school, they can't move for a year. They want to diversify but can't stomach the more than $2 million in taxes they'll pay if they sell the stock now. Plus, they think the stock may go even higher. What can they do?

They explain their dilemma to a competent financial advisor who hooks them up with a couple of major investment houses that put together a contract that places a floor on the underlying stock. Thus, they don't need to worry about the stock plunging in a bear market, and they can participate to the upside of the stock if it rises. The contract can be written so that it matures in a year or two after they move to Nevada. Sound perfect?

Well, consider the costs involved. To finance this would probably cost 10 to 15 percent. Here's how it would work: The couple would get a tax-free, advance payment of about $7.5 million now. They'd repay that advance with the stock when the contract matures. Meanwhile, they'd get to redeploy the $7.5 million, deferring the taxes for a couple of years, avoid paying the state income tax, and still be able to participate in at least some of the upside.

Again, though, understand that such an arrangement involves extremely sophisticated derivatives. Setting this up would require the most knowledgeable of professional advisors.

$ $ $

For now, that should give you plenty of strategies to work on with your financial advisor, and you'll learn how to best find him or her later in this book. In the next chapter, I'm going to tell you how to get some of the fundamentals covered—such as long-term care, estate planning, and life insurance—and I'll also detail several insurance strategies that could serve you well.

$ $ $ $ $

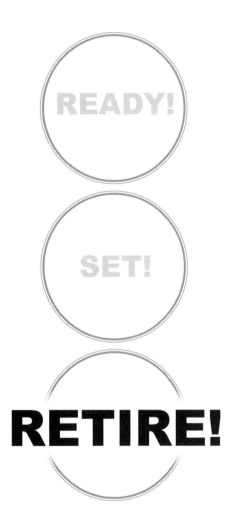

PART III

READY!

SET!

RETIRE!

CHAPTER TEN

Getting Your Ducks in a Row

Setting up a Buckets of Money plan and following some of the strategies outlined in the previous chapters can deliver big benefits for your financial future. You might compare those strategies to a fleet running back who darts and twists and leaps for big bursts of yardage on the football field. His talent electrifies the crowd and puts points on the board. But what makes his success possible? Good fundamentals, such as blocking and tackling, by his teammates.

In this chapter we'll look at the financial equivalent of blocking and tackling—putting in place the needed legal structures and the right risk protection to build a solid foundation under your retirement finances. Doing so may not directly or immediately fatten your bank account, but it will help get your financial life in order—and keep it there—so that your other strategies can work their magic. Specifically, we'll look at the role of estate planning, and the related issue of trusts, as well as insurance and charitable giving.

Estate Planning

Making an estate plan is a process laden with emotion. After all, it's about life and death, about personal values as well as financial value. But too often that emotion gets in the way and ends up complicating—or even defeating—efforts to reach one's estate-planning goals. At a time when the giver's or receiver's judgment may be clouded by grief, he or she may be forced to wrestle with a great many financial issues that neither has thought much about. A wrong move on the part of either can end up costing time or money or both.

To avoid such headaches and heartaches, it's necessary to try to think clearly and not just lead with your gut. That's why working with an objective third party often is a good idea because he or she—an attorney or financial planner, for example—can pose the tough questions that you may be loath to ask.

You may have elderly parents or other relatives who wish to leave you something. And if you're nearing retirement, you've probably given at least a little thought to your own estate. Of course, "estate" sounds so pretentious, like something only somebody like Bill Gates might have. But, in truth, everybody has one, even if it's just an under-nourished bank account and a ratty, old car. Your estate is just what you own minus what you owe. And the purpose of estate planning is to answer the questions: Who gets what? And under what conditions?

Estate planning can help ensure that your money and other assets go to the people you want—not those determined by state law. Further, it allows you to divide your assets in such a way as to manage the money efficiently, create the fewest possible legal hassles for your survivors, and possibly minimize the tax bite.

To do this, you first want to figure out what your assets are and how much you want to pass on to heirs. Then come up with a plan that takes into account probate (the legal process that distributes your estate) and estate taxes (transfer taxes that can take a big chunk out of your estate if it's large enough).

Currently, the amount excluded from the federal estate tax is $2 million. That's set to rise to $3.5 million in 2009, then the tax is scheduled to disappear entirely in 2010—but only for that year. Go figure! Unless Congress acts before then, the tax will be resurrected in 2011, reverting to a tax-free limit of only $1 million. (There's some talk of raising the basic exclusion to $5 million or even higher, thus eliminating the tax for all but a few multimillionaires and billionaires. But for now Congress seems deadlocked.) Meanwhile, the top rate at which estates are taxed by the feds will gradually fall to 45 percent in 2007 and then disappear in 2010. But—you guessed it—the rate is set to spring back to life in 2011 at 55 percent.

As if that's not confusing enough, many revenue-starved states have moved to protect their own death-tax revenue, creating a crazy-quilt pattern of rules around the country. Residents must file with both the federal and their state government when they pay estate taxes. But on their federal taxes, they're given credit for the amount they pay the state.

So, as I say, you're probably going to need the help of professionals, such as an estate-planning lawyer and a financial planner. But meanwhile, here are some ideas about how to receive—or give—an inheritance.

Receiving an Inheritance

First, figure out if the estate is likely to be taxable. If a person dies in the years 2006 to 2008 and leaves more than $2 million to anyone other than his or her spouse, the estate will be subject to taxes. But, as noted above, that's a moving target and may be changed by Congress, so it's important to stay abreast of changes in the estate tax.

Talk to affected parties. Make sure the benefactors have a will and that they've filled out the beneficiary designations on their retirement accounts and life insurance. Ideally, they should avoid owning too many illiquid assets, like real estate and rare coins. Also, you might encourage them to simplify their finances by paying off big debts. And they should make their intentions really clear to all their heirs. A family legal fight to determine what they *really* meant is a sure way to drive up the cost and drag out the process.

In fact, this is probably the most important chat you'll ever have with your parents. And it's a tough one because most parents don't want to talk about what happens in their latter years. They may fear loss of independence, loss of privacy, and even loss of dignity when they can no longer make their own decisions. Besides, they—and *you*—may be uncomfortable with this radical role reversal: the "kid" looking after the parent.

But uncomfortable or not, you've got to have this talk, because if they don't plan well, your parents' sunset years and their eventual demise could create unintended consequences. You and your siblings might be picking up the pieces for a long time.

Take, for instance, the basics: a will and durable powers of attorney. If your parents haven't drawn these up, it's not hard to imagine a situation in which they might become incapacitated by, say, a stroke (four million Americans live with the effects of stroke, one of the leading causes of disability), and no one—not even you—can pay their bills or make key health-care decisions for them. Even if they escape being incapacitated, wouldn't it be better to talk about such subjects *now* when your folks are relatively healthy and lucid?

But how? The key to a successful dialogue is showing your parents that you're not interested in their assets but in seeing that they're cared for and their wishes are fulfilled.

You don't want to be threatening, and you don't want to appear grasping, especially when you inquire about their investments and insurance. So try to be casual and unemotional. Perhaps the icebreaker is something along the lines of "I'm worried that if something happens to you, I won't know what to do," or "With the cost of health care being what it is, I want to help you make sure you're not wiped out by a major illness."

It's important to have your own financial house in order first and be a good example. Then perhaps you can use that as a wedge to discuss similar issues with your parents. "You know, I was talking to an attorney the other day about revising my will,"—and show it to them—"and that got me to thinking: Do you have a recent will? Where do you keep it?"

Make sure they have a will; a durable power of attorney for financial matters (appointing someone to handle their money if they can't); a durable power of attorney for health care (empowering someone to make medical decisions if they're unable); instructions on funeral and burial wishes; and if appropriate, a "living will" that directs doctors not to take extraordinary measures to prolong their lives. You don't want to be scrambling to get these documents when your parents are ill or not at the top their game mentally.

In addition, among the important questions you should ask:

- *Have they planned for long-term care?* More about this later in this chapter.

- *What are their wishes should they become extremely ill?* This is where a health-care power of attorney comes in. When your parents can't make their own decisions about health care, you may have to step in. Have they given you that author- ity? Have they been very clear about their wishes?

• *Do they have an up-to-date estate plan?* Are they aware of recent changes in the law that may affect their wills, trusts, and other estate-related documents?

• *Do they have sufficient insurance?* Medicare alone is at best an iffy partner to rely on for your parents' health-care needs. And lack of good health-care coverage can gouge a big hole in your parents' financial safety net (and your inheritance). And while your parents may no longer need life insurance to provide financial security for their children, it's often the best and most cost-effective source of cash for estate taxes. Again, more on this later in this chapter.

• *Have they budgeted enough so they won't outlive their income?* You want your parents to have enough money to cover their costs and enjoy their retirement years, but that requires planning and must take into account the possibility of seri- ous illness.

In short, you really need to know everything: not only what plans they've made, but also where the crucial documents—wills, trusts, bank accounts, and investment records—are kept and whom they use as advisors, such as attorneys, accountants, and financial planners. Remember, unless they're doing something terribly self-destructive with their money, you want to honor their choices. But you don't want to encourage procrastination or denial. (And, incidentally, the above questions also are very good ones to ask about your own preparations.)

Once your parents have passed on, the process of getting the assets is probably going to take longer than you think. Typically, no distributions are made until after estate taxes are paid, which is usu- ally within nine months after the date of death. So don't buy a yacht or make any major lifestyle change until you receive your share of the estate and pay all taxes and fees that may be due. For estates above the exclusionary limit, federal estate taxes now run in the neighborhood of 45 percent, and as I mentioned, several states also levy inheritance taxes. In addition, the lawyers, executor, and perhaps an accountant must be paid. And don't forget the ordinary bills and debts of the estate. If you inherit a piece of property, for example, the estate is obligated to pay the accrued mortgage and taxes. Or if it can't, the asset may need to be sold to pay the debt, or you could pay it out of your own pocket.

Folks fret a lot about estate taxes. But in many cases, legal costs will take a bigger bite out of the assets. Some states allow lawyers to charge a percentage of an estate's value while others permit them to bill by the hour. However the fees are calculated, they usually relate only to assets that pass through probate court and are governed by the will.

So to keep a lid on legal costs, benefactors can ensure some assets pass directly to the beneficiaries and bypass probate. Examples include retirement accounts, life-insurance proceeds, and property that is owned jointly with right of survivorship.

Assets held in a living trust (which differs from a living will) also go directly to the designated heirs, avoiding probate. Such a trust can be especially useful if the decedent owned real property in more than one state. Property placed in a trust avoids the need to go through probate in each of the states involved.

Understand, too, that retirement-plan owners can face double taxation. If you inherit an IRA, 401(k), or a tax-deferred annuity, you face this dilemma: Such assets are included in the value of the estate (and could make it subject to estate tax), but you will also generally pay income tax when these assets are distributed.

As discussed in the previous chapter, a way to minimize taxes on the proceeds of an IRA is to set up an Inherited IRA and stretch out the period over which payouts are made. The beneficiary still must pay taxes on the required minimum distribution, but because the withdrawals are taken over a longer period, the annual distribution—and the taxes owed—will be less. Meanwhile, the remainder of the Inherited IRA can continue to grow tax-deferred.

Planning Your Own Legacy

You probably have a will. Maybe even a living trust. But there's probably more you can do to plan your estate so it makes a personal statement as well as assists your heirs. For starters, one of the smartest, quickest things you can do to make the most of your legacy is to be diligent about specifying your beneficiaries.

Stay current with your beneficiaries. In the old days, this was pretty simple. The term *beneficiary* largely was used in relation to insurance and meant "spouse and kids." But both families and finances have become more complex. The phenomenon of "blended" families—spouses with children from previous marriages—heightens the need for estate planning. In addition, we now have many different kinds of investments, such as retirement accounts, college savings plans, and insurance policies that require updated beneficiary designations.

Some people think that they can sidestep the naming of specific beneficiaries by naming their estate as their beneficiary. Bad idea! That subjects the money to probate, tying up the funds and keeping them out of the hands of your heirs for what could be a long time.

On the other hand, by selecting the right beneficiary or combination of beneficiaries, you may be able to greatly extend the potential value of your assets, expedite distributions, reduce the tax bite, and encourage peace in the family.

Some specific issues with beneficiaries:

- *Retirement plans.* With the 401(k) plans, the primary beneficiary must be your spouse unless he or she agrees to waive his or her rights. Yet that doesn't mean the spouse is always the best choice. In fact, if you name your children or even grandchildren as beneficiaries of IRAs and other retirement accounts, you may be able to spread out the distribution of these assets for years beyond your death. That's a plus, because the longer the assets remain invested in tax-deferred accounts, the more they will have the potential to grow.

- *College savings plans (Section 529s).* While there can be only one beneficiary named, that beneficiary can be changed. For example, if a student doesn't use all the money for college, you can name another, although the new one is supposed to be a sibling, cousin, or other relative of the initial beneficiary. Maybe unused assets can even be used by the student's children after the asset has grown tax-deferred for several decades.

- *Insurance policies.* If you've been divorced and don't update your beneficiary, it's quite possible for an ex-spouse to collect your life-insurance proceeds instead of your current spouse. Even if marital assets are divided under a divorce decree, you need to change the beneficiary.

- *Joint accounts.* Legally known as "Joint Tenancy with Rights of Survivorship" or "Tenants by the Entirety," these accounts pass to the joint owner when the other one dies. A common example would be joint savings or checking accounts. (When there are multiple "tenants," keep in mind that the last one living inherits everything.)

- *Contingent beneficiaries.* Be sure to name these. That is a safeguard in case your primary beneficiary dies before you do, or if you and your primary beneficiary die simultaneously, say, in an auto or plane crash.

Remember, insurance policies, IRAs, and other retirement accounts all require that you name beneficiaries. When you die, that asset is immediately owned by the beneficiary. What your will says won't take precedent over whom you've named as beneficiaries.

If you haven't reviewed your beneficiary designations lately, contact your plan administrators, insurance companies, trust companies, and mutual funds and ask them to tell you whom you have currently listed. Or ask your financial advisor, who routinely handles such paperwork. You won't be imposing, and you may well be able to correct an oversight that will prevent problems later on.

Are you sure you really want to "leave everything" to your spouse? This is a noble idea and sounds "right," but can backfire. The marital deduction allows you to pass on an unlimited amount to your spouse. But in 2007 you can also leave as much as $2 million to someone other than your spouse estate-tax free. So by leaving everything to your spouse, you're wasting that other $2 million exemption and potentially subjecting your estate to unnecessary taxes.

For instance, let's say you and your spouse each have $2 million in assets. When one of you dies, the other inherits the $2 million without estate taxes. But when the second spouse dies and the combined $4 million estate passes to the children, that $2 million could be hit with a tax bill of several hundred thousand dollars. So the impulse to leave everything to the spouse could end up increasing the family's ultimate tax bill. (Again, Congress is perennially tinkering with these rules. So be sure to check with an attorney about the latest law.)

One way around this is to set up a bypass trust funded with, in this case, $2 million in assets. The children, as beneficiaries of the trust, would have access to those assets upon the surviving parent's death. The trust also can be set up so the surviving spouse receives income from it while he or she is still alive. More on trusts later in this chapter.

Choose an executor carefully. You want to pick someone whom you trust to carry out your estate plan. But again, sentiment can lead you to choose the wrong person.

For instance, your business partner may be a terrific guy who really cares for your family. But he's also probably the obvious buyer for your business. So if you pick him as executor, he's going to have a natural conflict of interest: The less he pays for the business, the more he hurts your heirs. That's a tough position to put him in. Either he or your heirs are likely to feel cheated.

Or you may be inclined to pick as executor either your oldest child or maybe the relative who's the closest, emotionally and/or geographically, to you. But does that person have the time, the interest, and the ability to carry out these serious duties? Also, do you want one family member having to negotiate with another for money after you're gone? That's a quick way to spur family unrest at a time when you won't be there to intervene.

Be cautious about giving money to minors. Naming children and grandchildren as beneficiaries is another noble impulse. But if they're still minors, you'll also need to name a guardian. If you don't and if you don't create a trust to manage those assets, these underage beneficiaries generally won't have access to the assets until the court has appointed a guardian or trustee for them.

Even if your kids aren't minors, you may want to think long and hard about the impact of giving them too much money with too few restrictions. A lot of wills and life-insurance policies provide sums for children who, even though legal adults, don't have the emotional or financial maturity to manage large sums all at once.

Keep assets as liquid as possible. If you bequeath to your family your antique coin collection or a wall full of Impressionist masters, your heirs may wish you hadn't. Not only are such items tough to divide among heirs, they're also considered part of the estate, which means that executors must have them valued and possibly pay estate taxes on them.

If estate taxes are due and there isn't enough liquidity in the estate to pay them, beneficiaries may either pay the taxes from their own savings or sell the assets—often at fire-sale prices—to raise money for the taxes.

Life insurance can help here. Although the death benefit of a policy is included in the taxable estate if the decedent owned the policy, the proceeds (minus the estate tax, if any) pass directly to the beneficiaries without having to go through probate.

A properly executed irrevocable life insurance trust can also shelter life-insurance proceeds from estate taxes. When the insured dies, proceeds aren't included in the estate because he or she didn't "own" the policy—the trust did. (This must be done correctly, so make sure you see an estate-planning lawyer.)

Set up a living trust. This is a popular way of seeing that other assets, such as your home, bank accounts, and brokerage accounts, are kept out of probate. A big advantage is that although you've placed assets in a trust, you can name yourself as trustee and keep control over them until you die.

Among a living trust's many advantages are that it's nearly impossible to challenge, and it's valid throughout the United States—unlike wills, which are challenged all the time. Further, most people opt for a *revocable* living trust, meaning they can change or cancel the trust arrangement at any point during their lifetime. However, even if you have a living trust, you probably should still have a will.

A couple of important points: First, a trust is really just a container, an envelope of sorts. It has no intrinsic value and no worth until and unless you retitle assets into the trust. Otherwise, all that legal effort is fruitless. Second, it avoids probate but not taxes. Your heirs will get their legacy sooner than they otherwise would, but they still may need to pay taxes on it if the estate exceeds the tax-free limits.

Often included in a living trust is a *living will.* It has nothing to do with a regular will, which divides property. Instead, a living will declares your preference for medical treatment if you become seriously ill. And it, in turn, is often accompanied by a *durable power of attorney for health care* and a *durable power of attorney for financial matters.* These can avoid prolonged, costly court proceedings if you become incapacitated.

Consider multiple trusts. A comprehensive estate plan may include several trusts set up for a number of different purposes, such as to protect against creditors, court judgments, and ex-spouses; provide for heirs who aren't capable of managing money themselves; stretch out money for more than a generation; benefit favorite causes; or ensure privacy.

We've already looked briefly at a bypass trust as a way to provide for your spouse after your death. But others would include:

- *Generation-skipping trusts.* These allow income from your trust to be used by your children, although some or all of the principal passes to your grandchildren.

- *QTIP (qualified terminable interest property) trusts.* Such trusts ensure that your surviving spouse gets income but that the assets eventually go to your children, not to a new spouse of your former husband or wife. This allows a person who has been divorced or widowed to provide the new spouse with lifetime income but eventually pass assets to the biological children from the earlier marriage.

- *Charitable remainder trusts.* These trusts permit you to contribute assets to a charity and get a tax deduction as well as an annuity from the income. A person establishes the irrevocable trust with, say, their stocks, bonds, or real estate and then names a favorite charity as beneficiary. It's a win-win because the donor gets an immediate income-tax deduction for a percentage of the gift, and then can opt to take income from the trust as long as the benefactor or his/her spouse lives or for a specified period of time. When the time period expires or the second spouse dies, the charity gets the assets.

Let's look at how this might work: Joe has a piece of raw land he paid $50,000 for 25 years ago. The property around it has been improved, so Joe's parcel is now valued at $500,000. If he sells it, he'll pay capital-gains taxes, and in a high-tax state, those taxes could exceed $100,000. The $400,000 he'd have left after the sale could be invested at, say, 6 percent, to net him about $24,000 in annual income.

By contrast, he could transfer the $500,000 property to the charitable remainder trust, a tax-exempt entity that could sell the property tax free and reinvest the proceeds. If the $500,000 earned 6 percent, the trust could distribute at least $30,000 a year in income to Joe for the rest of his life and his wife's life. Further, because after Joe and his spouse pass on the charity gets whatever is left in the trust, Joe also gets a current income-tax deduction. He can't deduct the entire $500,000. But depending on his age, his wife's age, and the amount of the distribution, he will probably get a write-off of $100,000 to $150,000.

What's not to like about a deal like that? Joe gets a current tax deduction, zero capital-gains taxes, and more income. The only worry might be that the charity, not Joe's heirs, would eventually wind up with whatever is left in the trust. But there's a way around that, too. If Joe also wants to leave money to his heirs, he can take his tax savings and maybe a few extra dollars for premiums and buy a life-insurance policy that will pay $500,000 when the second spouse dies. That way Joe and his wife receive more income while they're alive and get a decent tax write-off. And after they die, the charity gets what's left in the trust, and under the second-to-die life-insurance policy, the kids get $500,000.

CRTs aren't for everyone. But for those who want to give to charity after they die, this is a way to do just that but also benefit yourself while you're still alive.

- *Charitable lead trust.* This is the opposite of a charitable remainder trust. In this case, the charity receives the income from the trust assets, and the donor takes an immediate deduction for the assumed value of the donation over the entire period. At the donor's death or expiration of the trust, the principal reverts to the donor or his or her heirs.

Other kinds of trusts can help with additional estate-planning issues. For example, if minor children are involved, a trust can manage the assets and control the timing of their distribution. Or if you have minor children from a previous marriage under the care of an ex-spouse, you can use a trust to help ensure that your bequests to them are used as you desire.

Learn about disclaimer wills or disclaimer trusts. This type of will or trust arrangement is gaining popularity as the future of the federal estate tax becomes murkier. The rationale is to give surviving spouses discretion over how much they choose to inherit so they can adjust that amount as estate-tax rules change. What makes a disclaimer will/trust different from traditional ones is that the survivor, usually a spouse, has nine months to disclaim (give up) all or part of the inheritance to the contingent beneficiary.

Thus, the spouse can adjust the amount he or she will receive as estate-tax rules change but still keep enough money to live on. The amount disclaimed typically goes into a bypass trust set up for the children and is also estate-tax exempt.

A major advantage of a disclaimer will/trust is that it helps married couples solve a snag with the very popular bypass trusts (also known as credit-shelter trusts). With a bypass trust, typically whatever is the current maximum exemption goes into the trust. Then the spouse gets income from the trust but not access to the principal, which eventually goes to the kids.

With the exemption rising, though, more spouses are getting little or nothing. An entire $3.5 million estate, for example, would go into the bypass trust in 2009.

Instead of rewriting the will/trust every year to reflect the new exemption levels or writing in it some sort of limit on how much children will receiver under a bypass trust, many are now opting for disclaimer language to give the surviving spouse the discretion to decide how much, if anything, he or she needs.

Practice gifting. Another way of avoiding taxes—or shifting taxes to someone in a lower tax bracket—is giving away some of your assets while you're still alive. Most gifts are by older people to their children and grandchildren with an eye on helping them buy a house or get an education. Each year you can give up to $12,000 ($24,000 from a married couple) to each family member or heir without incurring gift or estate taxes. (By contrast, if the money stays in your estate, the tax at death could be as much as 45 percent.) If you have the cash flow and plan far enough ahead, you can avoid much in estate taxes through this gifting strategy.

Those with appreciated assets can take advantage of the $12,000 annual gift-tax exclusion by gifting the property (in $12,000 increments) to someone in a much lower tax bracket. When the recipient sells the stock or real estate, he or she will pay the much lower capital-gains tax.

Individuals also can give $1 million to a beneficiary without having to actually write a check for gift taxes. Under current law they would be using up half of their $2 million estate-tax exemption after they die, but giving $1 million away today saves about 50 percent tax on the future appreciation if the estate is large enough to be hit with federal estate tax. Many large estates use the $1 million gift exemption to buy a life-insurance policy.

If a person has a $12 million estate and expects a $4 million exemption, he or she could use the $1 million gift exemption today by giving it to the kids or to a trust for the kids. The kids could take the $1 million and buy a $3 million or $4 million life-insurance policy to pay the federal estate tax and keep the assets in the estate. This is an especially good idea when the kids want to keep the family business or the family real estate and there's not enough liquid cash to cover the estate taxes due within nine months after the date of death. This strategy also can be combined with the formation of a family limited partnership to further reduce the taxable estate by making it less liquid and less marketable.

So, as you can see, there are lots of possibilities when it comes to creating a plan for your estate. What's more, such plans require periodic review and revision if they're to stay current and viable, especially if your marital status changes, you change your state of residence, or your health or income changes.

One last bit of advice when it comes to your estate: Don't fail to level with your adult kids the way your parents probably didn't level with you. The truth is, poor parent-child communication can cause big money problems. Just telling the kids that "everything is taken care of" isn't enough. After all, they may be forced to make vital health-care choices without understanding what kind of insurance you have, take care of your house and car without knowing the details, and pay bills without even being sure of where you keep the checkbook. What's more, if they're likely to inherit some money—or *not* inherit any—that is information that would be very helpful for them for planning purposes.

Why is it so hard for the generations to talk? Discussing death and disability isn't a million laughs, and such a discussion reminds us of an unwanted change in the relationship. The parents feel old, and signing a power of attorney feels like losing control. Plus, many adult children don't feel competent themselves when it comes to money.

Nonetheless, such talks are absolutely necessary. Most people, if they get up the nerve at all, wait until their parents are old and frail. But the best time to have a financial dialogue is when parents are, say, in their 50s or at the latest in their 60s. And if they're older, the best time to talk is *now*.

You should make sure that your kids know:

- Where you store your financial records, including tax returns, pension information, and investment data

- What kind of medical insurance you have

- Who your doctors are and what kind of medications you take

- The status of your estate planning, including wills and trusts

- Who the executor of your will is

- How you would expect to handle the costs of an extended illness

- Where your emergency paperwork is kept, including powers of attorney, will, living wills, trusts, and so on

- Your monthly income and expenses

- How you plan to divide your assets

- The names, addresses, and phone numbers of all your advisors, including estate lawyer, accountant, investment advisors, trust officers, insurance agent, banker, and the like

Charitable Giving

Do you have a hankering to be a philanthropist? You can deal with that urge and at the same time actually derive income from your gift. In fact, in some cases, you can even grow your estate as you help your favorite charity.

If you have virtually unlimited wealth, like, say, a Gates or a Rockefeller, you can create a large private foundation that will carry on good works in perpetuity and perhaps make your name a household word. But what if you have more dreams than riches? What if being a philanthropist seems too lofty but you'd still like to do some good?

Moreover, what if you'd like to both do good—*and* do well—by saving on your taxes? All that is possible. And increasingly, those who are making such choices are not the super-rich, but affluent middle-class folks with a passion for helping others as well as themselves.

After a rough few years, charitable giving is enjoying a resurgence because of the stock-market bounce. Donating appreciated stocks is one of the most popular forms of giving because you can immediately deduct the stocks' market value from your taxes and eliminate capital-gains liability. But there are a number of ways to structure such giving, each with advantages and disadvantages. What's the right choice for philanthropic purposes may not be the best answer in terms of tax strategy.

Let's take a look at the most common vehicles:

Giving gifts directly. You can, of course, just write a check to your favorite charity and take a tax deduction for that amount (subject to the limitation of 50 percent of your AGI). But if you sold, say, appreciated stock to raise the money, you'll owe taxes on the capital gain. For example, if you sold for $50,000 stocks you bought for $10,000, you'd owe tax on the $40,000 profit. So a better plan might be to give the stock directly to the charity. That way you avoid capital-gains taxes, and you can claim a tax deduction based on their $50,000 current value (subject to the limitation of 30 percent of your AGI) rather than their original cost ($10,000).

But there are a couple of downsides. For one thing, smaller organizations may not be set up to accept noncash donations. Second, you will want to see your money put to good use, not eaten up in administrative costs. So, especially if you're talking about multiple recipients, your giving ought to be preceded by considerable due diligence.

For most people, the giving—not the detective work—is the fun part, and so the investigating may lessen the zest of giving. But the rough rule of thumb is that at least 60 percent of a charity's dollars should go to fulfill its mission or program, and 40 percent or less to administrative costs. But that number can vary widely based on the overhead associated with the type of work being done. Several Websites have sprung up to help you assess the effectiveness of various charities. Prominent among them are **www.Guidestar.org** and www.CharityNavigator.org. They offer free access to large amounts of information that charities are required to file each year with the IRS and give guidelines for evaluating those to whom you might make a donation.

Starting a private foundation. For more sophisticated giving, the classic choice involves two popular donor tools: private foundations and donor-advised funds. The two differ greatly in organization, degree of control, and tax impact.

For starters, to launch a private foundation you must form a separate legal entity, apply for tax-exempt status from the IRS, and follow the complex tax-code provisions that regulate these entities. To justify the expense of setting up and running a private foundation, most planned-giving advisors recommend an initial endowment of $1 million to $5 million.

But if you're willing to deal with the paperwork, a private foundation can allow you enormous freedom in your giving. You retain near-total control over your grants and can involve future generations in philanthropy. You can donate to the foundation almost any kind of asset, including tangible personal property. Those assets are controlled by a board—usually you and those you pick—that disburses the funds. You can appoint relatives to the board, give them responsibility, and—subject to certain limitations—even pay them a salary. You can hire an investment manager. And, most important, you can gift as much as you want and to whomever you want. You have complete control over grant making.

The disadvantages? The tax advantages aren't quite as good as with a donor-advised fund. Generally, deductions for cash gifts are limited to 30 percent of adjusted gross income (AGI) and 20 percent of AGI for appreciated property, compared to 50 and 30 percent, respectively, for a donor-advised fund.

The other negative: a lack of privacy. A public record must be filed with the IRS each year showing the foundation's assets, contributors, and grants. To the giver who seeks anonymity, or to the donor who prefers that Recipient A not know what Recipient B gets, this can be a sizable downside.

Using a donor-advised fund. This is an individual account within a public charity. For those of more limited means, a donor-advised fund (DAF) can be attractive because initial donation size, expenses, and red tape are minuscule compared to private foundations. In fact, it's said that setting up a private foundation is a lot like opening a bank, while creating a DAF is more like opening a bank account.

Typically, a DAF can be set up with an initial contribution of as little as $10,000, payable in cash or marketable securities. The process is as simple as creating a brokerage account: Fill out the paperwork, contribute the assets, and take an immediate tax deduction for their full market value. Donated securities are usually liquidated immediately and credited to your account. The brokerage or community foundation provides a range of funds with different risk levels and asset-allocation models.

Once the fund is set up and invested, you can direct it to make grants (minimum $250) to the charity of your choice at any time. Or, instead of writing out a check right away, you can postpone that decision while you build up the account and/or ponder your prospective recipients. Your money is invested until you're ready to disburse it. When you decide to make a gift to charity, you simply contact the fund, which will double-check the beneficiary's tax-exempt status and then send the donation.

You can open a DAF at major brokerages like Fidelity, Schwab, Vanguard, Oppenheimer, and T. Rowe Price as well as at your local community foundations. The charitable fund takes a small percentage of assets under management as a fee for its services.

One of the big changes in the giving business has been a migration toward DAFs. However, you don't have nearly the control you would under a private foundation. Your DAF contribution is irrevocable, and control actually lies with the fund's trustees. You're not likely to have much say about investment choices, and even your choice of charities is technically viewed as a nonbinding recommendation.

Other downsides? Most DAFs take just cash and marketable stock. Also, a DAF generally can't recommend grants to individuals, create scholarships, or support charities organized under the laws of other countries.

However, DAFs can be useful estate-planning tools, allowing individuals to move money out of their estates and set the stage for children and grandchildren to develop their own charitable impulses. Grandparents, for example, may open a DAF for their grandchildren and build a charitable account to which they can donate. (Contributions to a DAF don't trigger gift taxes.) Sometimes heirs set up memorial accounts. That way, friends and family members can contribute in memory of the deceased. The family then makes donations to the deceased's favorite charities.

Donors to DAFs can name successors to take over their grant making after they die. And if there aren't subsequent generations who will want to be involved, the donor can name the public charity itself as the beneficiary. Even large donors who might have the wherewithal to set up a private foundation sometimes use a DAF for privacy reasons. Simplifying the donation process also leaves the donors free to concentrate on the causes they hold dear.

When considering a DAF, take care to avoid making grants that regulators might view as lining your own pockets. Gifts to the fund shouldn't be used to benefit you, your family, or related parties. If you stick with a DAF from a community foundation or a known investment company, you're unlikely to run afoul of the IRS or other regulators.

Other suggested actions before committing to a DAF include:

- Nail down the nature of the assets it will accept, such as appreciated securities, life-insurance policies, or artwork.

- Determine any restrictions on your grants. May donations be made outside your city, state, or country? Is there a minimum grant amount?

- Look carefully at fees.

- Determine what services the DAF offers. Does it give you the option of anonymity or publicity? Does it offer grant-making support? Does it allow you to talk to the charity you're supporting? Does it provide staff services?

- Find out whether the fund stops when you or your spouse die.

Setting up a charitable gift annuity. When you sign up for a gift annuity, you hand over a sum of money to a nonprofit. In return, you get an immediate, partial tax deduction and a fixed amount of income every year for the rest of your life. You don't get as much as if you'd purchased an immediate fixed annuity from an insurance company, but with the insurance company, you wouldn't get the tax break. And of course, if you die prematurely, the windfall goes to the charity instead of to the insurance company.

However, you must be careful about the financial health of the charity. That's because most nonprofits don't take donors' money and use it to buy an immediate annuity from an insurance company. Instead, they hang on to the money and make the annuity payments themselves. And in recent years, there have been a couple of notable defaults on gift annuities.

Exercise some due diligence. Go to the Website of the American Council on Gift Annuities (**www.acga-web.org**) and read about gift-annuity regulations in your state. Ask the nonprofit if it keeps a separate reserve fund to backstop its annuities and find out who administers the gift-annuity program and how the money is invested. Some states, such as California, New York, and New Jersey, strictly regulate these operations, but many others do not. This has led to abuses.

While most annuities offered by charitable organizations are legitimate, the North American Securities Administrators Association, which represents state regulators, has warned investors to be cautious of little-known organizations or those that provide only sketchy information. In one Arizona case, for instance, 430 investors lost an average of $133,000 when a promoter used investors' money to buy himself property, pay child support, book charter flights, and subsidize his gambling habit.

Establishing a trust. Among the most popular forms for giving are two we've already discussed briefly in the preceding section, the charitable remainder trust (CRT) and, its opposite, a charitable lead trust (CLT).

You'll recall that a CRT permits you to contribute assets to a charity and get a tax deduction as well as an annuity from the income. It's an especially good idea to fund a CRT with appreciated securities. That doubles the tax benefit because you avoid paying tax on the unrealized gain, yet you get a tax deduction based on the current value of the future gift.

So CRTs are popular because you can actually reduce your income taxes, avoid capital-gains taxes, maintain or even increase your income for life—*and* donate large sums to charity. Also, the trust assets are not included in your estate, and thus are exempt from estate taxes.

In addition, there are ways you can create a CRT and still provide for your children. As previously mentioned, this involves having another trust, or having your heirs buy an insurance policy equal to the size of your gift and name the kids as beneficiaries. Because they'll receive their inheritance from insurance, not from your estate, the children get the cash free of taxes and probate.

A CLT is kind of a CRT in reverse: The charity receives the income from the trust assets. In return, you take an immediate deduction for the assumed value of the donation over the entire period. At your death or the expiration of the trust, the principal goes to you or your heirs. CLTs are especially popular among people (like athletes or entertainers) who earn a greater portion of their income in their early years rather than at the end of their lives.

These trusts also work best in a low-interest-rate environment. That's because then the rate used by the IRS to value the gift results in a higher deduction for you and less of a tax liability for your heirs. And if the trust investments perform better than the IRS assumptions, you—or your heirs—could end up with a larger principal amount than you began with.

Whatever philanthropic vehicle you use, it's important to develop your giving plan. My advice: First, find your passion. Figure out what's really important to you and how can you help others make their lives better. For maximum impact, it's probably a good idea to focus your gifts, not scatter them.

Second—you're heard me say this before, but it's true—you're probably going to need help. The tax rules can be complicated, and in all but the simplest of donations, you're going to want the assistance of, say, a financial planner, an accountant, the planned-giving officer at a well-run charity, and/or an attorney, especially if you're setting up a trust. But by thinking through the choices I've described, I hope that you can begin to maximize your tax savings and achieve your personal goals, including minimizing potential estate taxes. And most important, experience the joy of giving.

Insurance

As someone either retired or close enough to retirement age to be reading this book, you have, I hope, your basic life-insurance needs covered. Or at least your assets well exceed your liabilities and your family's need for income. Because I've already briefly mentioned the difference between term insurance and permanent, or cash-value, insurance, I won't go into that again. But I do want to go over the importance of disability and long-term-care insurance as well as to outline three insurance strategies that can be particularly helpful for certain individuals.

I should mention the need to do what's called a "capital-needs analysis"—that is, what do you have and what will your family need if you should die prematurely? It's important to cover all the needs—food, clothing, shelter, and education—that are likely to arise. One rule of thumb is that life insurance should cover at least five to seven times the policyholder's annual earnings. That may sound like a lot, but note that college costs, for example, can be expected to continue to grow rapidly.

On the other hand, perhaps your children are grown or nearly so. So you and your spouse may think you have enough assets to see you through your sunset years. But what if a catastrophe occurred? What if one of you had a stroke? Or got cancer? Or suffered a heart attack? Or contracted Alzheimer's disease? Even a broken hip or a bout of pneumonia can devour decades of savings in a matter of months if you need home health care or must be admitted to a long-term care facility.

Today's extended life spans have upped the odds of something like this happening. So unless you're very wealthy, protecting against such a catastrophe should be a priority. (In fact, even wealthy folks often buy long-term-care insurance because they'd rather spend a little bit of money on a policy now than expend their assets later on the care itself and thus, shortchange their heirs.)

As you approach your retirement years, ask yourself: *What are my biggest potential financial losses?* Well, your house could burn down, your job could disappear, or through injury or illness, you could become unable to take care of yourself.

You probably already have fire insurance, and you might be able to replace your job, but what if you lost your ability to produce an income? Or, if you're already retired, what if you were forced to enter a nursing home? Either would qualify as a major financial reversal, the kind that insurance is best designed for. So you should also consider:

Disability insurance. If you become sick or injured and can't work, that's when big trouble begins. You could lose your home, your ability to put your kids through school, and your shot at building a retirement nest egg. After all, medical advances can keep you alive in cases where you would have died a generation ago—but that doesn't mean that you won't be devastated by the costs and by the loss of income.

Disability insurance *is* expensive, but guess why: Because there's a good chance you're going to need to file a claim. In fact, insurers figure that you're five times more likely to be disabled than to die during your working life. Of course, if you weren't likely to need it, the policy would be cheap, but is that a reason not to have it? I don't think so.

Be very careful when buying disability insurance. Do a lot of research and compare and contrast policies on such points as the definition of disability; the waiting period (known as the "elimination" period)—that is, how long after being disabled before you get the benefits; monthly income; cost-of-living adjustments; what kind or amount of work you may continue to do, if able; and the "integration," or how the policy meshes with other benefits or income you receive.

Long-term-care insurance. While disability insurance is important for those still working, the big issue for retirees becomes long-term-care insurance. LTCI is a question you could someday face for yourself, or maybe even sooner for your parents. LTCI is a good way of avoiding a terrible cash drain in your retirement years.

Arguably, the cost of long-term care is the biggest threat to America's retirement assets, more so than the problems with Social Security, the prospect of another bear market, the falling dollar, energy prices, or even the federal budget deficit. Those are all macro problems that presumably great minds are grappling with. But I'm talking about a crisis that you and I can do something about if only we were paying attention.

Here are the facts:

- The national average cost of a semiprivate room in a nursing home is more than $74,000 annually. Home health care is expensive, too, with a national average cost of more than $20,000 annually.

- One out of every two persons over age 85 will require such care.

- And contrary to popular belief, private health insurance usually doesn't pay for it, nor does the government (unless you're impoverished).

By 2030—when today's 50-year-old is about age 75—the estimated cost of a year in a nursing home will be more than $190,000. Because the average nursing-home stay lasts 2.4 years, that's $456,000 that somebody's got to pay. Where does that leave the average Joe or Jane who's managed to squirrel away a few bucks for their sunset years? In a tight spot.

In fact, with many families having trouble saving *anything*, it's hard to see how they could even begin to scrape together that kind of cash. Result: big problem. So unless you're very wealthy, LTCI should be a priority. Yet most people are pretty ignorant when it comes to LTCI. Many people mistakenly assume that Medicare will foot these bills. But Medicare doesn't pay for a long stay in a nursing home, and neither do the supplemental, private health-care policies, known as Medi-gap. And Medicaid, the state-run welfare program, pays only if you're impoverished, or nearly so.

It's middle-class people who face the biggest risk. After all, the very rich can afford a nursing home or nursing care, and the poor in many cases are backstopped by the government.

LTCI, a disability plan that's been around since the mid-1980s, pays the expenses of folks confined to a nursing home or needing other forms of long-term care, such as assisted living, adult day care, or care in their own home.

The cost of LTCI relates directly to your age. In fact, a policy purchased at age 65 is three times more expensive than a policy purchased at age 45. Any policy you buy should contain benefits that will pay for care wherever you'll likely need it: at home, in adult day care, assisted living, or a nursing home. It should also provide inflation protection.

Once you buy a policy, the premiums you pay usually remain the same for life, so there's an advantage in buying it early and getting a cheaper premium—but perhaps not too early because you'll be insuring yourself against a very unlikely event. (The average age of a person admitted to a nursing home is 83.) So late middle age is probably the optimal time to buy. But, remember, this is insurance you must qualify for. So if you wait to buy it until you actually need it, you will probably be out of luck.

Figuring out if, when, and how much LTCI to get can be a mind-numbing experience. Many complicated factors vie for your attention, such as length of coverage, amount to be paid out each day or month, how long you'd need to wait to collect after you're judged eligible, and whether you want to account for inflation.

And don't forget to check the financial stability of the insurer, too. Even the best or most expensive policy will do you little good if the company isn't around 20 or 30 or 40 years from now when you need to collect.

Consumer Reports looked at the range of LTCI firms and options and concluded, "Long-term-care insurance may be a lousy deal, but right now it's just about the only deal." It recommends buying at around age 65, from a financially strong insurer, a policy that covers care in nursing homes, assisted-living facilities, and at home. The policy should provide a daily benefit that increases along with the price of care. The magazine further suggests that a four-year period of care should be sufficient, and it favors a 30-day "elimination" period.

But don't do what a magazine says to do. Rather, evaluate your family history and make a decision that best suits your needs. Your state insurance department sets the standards for LTCI. You might want to check with that agency or with an advisor who specializes in LTCI before you buy.

So, LTCI is worth thinking about, especially when you're young enough to afford it and your health is good enough to qualify for it. For sure, not thinking about it won't make the problem go away. But it will make it more costly.

Unless you're insured, ending up in a nursing home can destroy the assets that took a lifetime to build. But more than just covering nursing-home care, these policies can also cover costs such as home health care and adult day care, and thus allow a policyholder to remain longer in his or her home.

Three Other Insurance Strategies

Three other insurance strategies may be worth mentioning. One most often appeals to the cash-strapped, while the other two can benefit high-net-worth individuals.

Selling your policy. When a cash-poor senior needs to get money out of his or her life insurance policy, one option is sell that policy to an investor. But while it may provide some initial cash flow, this is not usually a good idea. A recent study by researchers at Deloitte Consulting and the University of Connecticut looked at the issues involved in what are called "life settlements." In such settlements, the insured typically sells the policy to a third party, often an institutional investor, which takes over the premiums and reaps the payment when the seller dies.

The study, funded by insurers, focused on people over 65 with policies of at least $250,000 and who have some health problems but have a life expectancy of 2 to 15 years. (Similar are "viatical settlements" in which the insured is terminally ill, usually with less than two years to live.) Researchers looked at the value of selling the policy compared with keeping it until death, or surrendering it for its cash value. After looking at more than 500 life-settlement contracts filed in New York

State from 2000 to 2003, the study found that the investors paid an average of about 20 percent of the face value of the policy. By contrast, the "intrinsic economic value of the policy" (the estimated future pay-out minus future premium costs) was 64 percent of the policy's face amount.

Thus, using a life settlement to get rid of a high-yielding, tax-free asset is an expensive way to get cash, the authors said. That's especially true when compared to other options the senior might have. For instance, he or she could raise money by selling other assets, taking out a reverse mortgage, or borrowing against the life-insurance policy. The policyholder who needs to free up cash might also ask his or her children or other beneficiaries to assume the premium payments. After all, they're going to get the ultimate benefits.

It's rare that an individual is forced by necessity into such an arrangement. Nonetheless, it's likely that you'll be pitched this concept sometime. So be aware and informed.

Irrevocable life-insurance trust. Wealthy individuals who wish to pass their assets to their children often face a tax dilemma: While they can bequeath $2 million to their heirs without paying federal estate tax, any amount above that could trigger a tax of almost 50 percent on the excess.

For instance, I recently came across a 62-year-old man who was married (for the second time) and who had sold his company for more than $20 million. Let's call him Mr. Rich. His net worth is $25 million, and he'd like to leave that amount to his two kids from his first marriage. However, he realizes that even if Congress kicked up the estate-tax exemption to $5 million, there would be a $10 million tax bill due 90 days after his death. Such a person is the classic candidate for an irrevocable life-insurance trust funded with a $10 million guaranteed-death-benefit universal life policy.

Here's how it would work: First, the trust is set up by an estate-planning lawyer, and an independent trustee is named to transact its business. Step 2 is for Mr. Rich and his wife to each make a one-time gift of $1 million to the trust as well as joint annual gifts of $12,000 to each of the two kids, or $48,000 per year. (They'll need to file gift-tax Form 709 in Year 1.)

The third step is when the trustee sends notices to all the trust beneficiaries—in this case, Mr. Rich's two kids—and informs them that they have a 30-day right of withdrawal. This makes it a legitimate gift of a present interest. After the 30 days is up, the trustee purchases a $10 million life-insurance policy on Mr. Rich. Once the policy is issued, it's funded with the one-time $2 million gift and the $48,000 gifts annual thereafter.

When Mr. Rich eventually dies, $10 million will be paid tax free to the trustee for the benefit of Mr. Rich's two children. That will be enough money to cover the estate taxes on the $25 million estate (assuming a $5 million future exemption instead of the current $2 million). So how good of a deal is that?

Well, let's say Mr. Rich dies without the trust and the life insurance, and he leaves a $25 million estate and Congress raises the exemption to $5 million. The tax due would be about $10 million. Assuming that the estate was liquid enough to raise $10 million in cash within nine months after the date of death, the kids would get the $15 million left over. But with the trust, the children would get the whole $25 million because the $10 million insurance death benefit would be available to pay the estate tax.

What if Mr. Rich, instead of buying the life insurance, just gave the kids the money anyway and they invested it in, say, 4.5 percent tax-free bonds? At what point does the life insurance make no sense? Let's take a look:

	Munl-Bonds @ 4.5%	Death Benefit	Difference in Favor of Insurance Trust
Year			
5	$2,776,775	$10,000,000	$7,233,225
10	$3,722,315	$10,000,000	$6,277,685
15	$4,913,095	$10,000,000	$5,086,905
20	$6,397,020	$10,000,000	$3,602,980
25	$8,246,260	$10,000,000	$1,753,740
30	$10,550,750	$10,000,000	- $550,750

So if Mr. Rich died anytime before age 90 to 91, the life-insurance trust works out better than a tax-free bond portfolio. Because average life expectancy for a 62-year-old is about 20 years, this seems to be a reasonably good investment.

Of course, these numbers are all hypothetical and strictly for illustrative purposes. Individuals in such a situation should always seek professional assistance and get proposals from several insurance companies in writing before acting.

Variable universal life (VUL). This strategy is complicated. In fact, it's so complex that most financial pundits dismiss VUL as something less than desirable. But for certain individuals with high incomes, significant cash flows, and a mind-set for long-term investing, VUL may prove to be very valuable. For such people, the usual reason for owning life insurance—to provide income replacement upon death—probably isn't as big a priority as accumulating tax-favored retirement income. So for them, VUL could be just what they're looking for.

Under this strategy, their money grows tax free, and they can choose to invest among a large selection of mutual-fund-like sub-accounts. Later, they can make tax-free withdrawals of their cost basis and borrow their gain tax free. And when they die, the death benefit pays off all of the loans, and the rest is paid to their heirs income tax free. In fact, I'd say that no other investment vehicle offers the potential—all in one package—for tax-deferred growth, tax-free transfers among portfolios, tax-advantaged access to cash accumulation, and a generally income-tax-free capital transfer at death.

If you either can't qualify for Roth IRAs because your income is too high, or if you're already funding your Roth, SEP, Keogh, 401(k), or other retirement plans to the max, VUL might be for you. You would need to fund the policy liberally, especially in its early years so there's adequate value accumulated later when you want to access funds. But once you've built up accumulated value, you could take money out tax free by loans or withdrawals to supplement your retirement income.

In fact, a well-funded VUL policy—compared to investing the same amount in mutual funds over a long period of time—would likely produce a similar income stream, but that income would be tax free. In addition, you'd be insured every year for the rest of your life, and your family would get the tax-free death benefit upon your death. Understand, though, this is neither a short-term investment nor a simple one. Many of the tax advantages can disappear if IRS restrictions are exceeded.

If you're in a moderately high tax bracket and have surplus cash to invest beyond what Roth IRAs and other retirement plans allow, socking away excess money in this way will allow you to:

- Earn tax-deferred returns from a portfolio of subaccounts (like mutual funds) that you choose

- Get tax-free income to enjoy while you're still around

- Provide your family with a sizable death benefit that guarantees continuing income or acts as a hedge against future inflation

Those in the higher tax brackets with surplus cash flow may want to consider investing in such a VUL policy because the tax laws allow insurance to accomplish things you can't do with ordinary mutual funds or stock accounts: grow assets on a tax-deferred basis; make withdrawals of your principal on a first-in, first-out (FIFO) basis; borrow tax free from your earnings; and pay nominal, if any, net interest.

Again, though, let me emphasize this strategy's complexity and the need for getting expert help. Before taking action, one must consider all of the charges and underwriting costs, insurability, and the long-term nature of the contract. Consult a tax professional and insurance agent before acting.

$$$$$

CHAPTER ELEVEN

Assembling a Team

ndecision, it's sometimes said, is a key to flexibility. But, I would add, procrastination is the archfoe of personal finance. And at some point you're going to need to dig in and get some of these important money decisions made.

A decision you don't think through is still a decision—and probably a poor one, so it's smart to get some help in plotting out the best strategies for you. But because finding that assistance can be a bit of a chore, many people never seek help. And that's sad.

So in this chapter I'm going to try to nudge you in the right direction and give you some suggestions. After all, it doesn't take much more energy to plan than it does to just wish—and planning is *much* more likely to produce results.

I hope that the last few chapters showed you that, yes, while you theoretically can do this stuff yourself, you'll need to deal with a lot of moving parts. And the truth is, a good financial planner can aid you in setting priorities and developing specific strategies. The whole process lends itself to a team approach. For starters, only you can examine your dreams and set your goals. Like John and Chris, our hypothetical couple, you need to do some thinking about your comfort level with risk, about how much you need to live on, what you want to leave to your heirs, and how much of a cash cushion you'll need to sleep well at night.

Get your priorities straight. It doesn't make any sense to spend hundreds of hours poring over stock-market strategies if you still have big credit-card bills bogging you down. For sure, paying off your expensive debts is one of the best, safest investments you can make in your future.

Do you absolutely need a financial advisor? No. You don't absolutely need a car either. But you probably have one and can't imagine how you would get around without it. If you're tempted to be your own financial planner, ask yourself five questions:

1. Do I have the interest in doing this myself?
2. Do I have expertise in planning, asset allocation, and investment-product nuances?
3. Do I have the temperament?
4. Do I have the time now?
5. Do I expect to have the time to keep up later?

If the answer to any of those is no, you need some help. Probably, if you're intent on doing a good job with your portfolio, you're going to need to pick an able financial advisor or a team of advisors. Because, yes, you've got to do the right thing. But you've also got to do the thing right.

When you're near retirement is when, more than at any other time, you need such an advisor. One reason is that the sheer variety of assets held by most middle-aged investors—IRAs, 401(k)s, stocks, bonds, options, real estate, insurance policies, annuities, taxable and retirement accounts—make it difficult to know when and why to tap particular investments for retirement income. Second, many older investors make decisions by looking at the leaves instead of the forest or the trees . . . or, maybe even looking at the veins on the leaves on the trees. They obsess about buying this stock or selling that one or about dropping a certain mutual fund for another, but they fail to think about the tax consequences of their decisions, or about how they're overloaded with one asset class and anemic in another. A good planner takes these jigsaw-puzzle-like pieces and assembles them into a big picture.

Specifically, how can a financial advisor help you? Let me count the ways:

Reviews your financial situation and draws up a plan. He or she puts your plan and the recommendations in writing so there's absolutely nothing left for interpretation now or later. Next, the advisor selects the right kind of investments, insurance, estate planning, tax planning, trusts, budgeting, and other ingredients to reach those goals and fulfill the plan's objectives. Then you can sleep well knowing that you've got a plan tailored for you and a portfolio that's fully diversified and minimally volatile.

Manages your money if you have a good deal socked away but don't have the time or interest to stay on top of the details. An advisor can pick—and/or work with—strategists and money managers. It's these money managers who will do the hands-on choosing of your specific Bucket No. 3 stock investments. Your advisor will hold these managers to their style discipline, know how to judge their performance, and terminate those who consistently underperform relative to their benchmarks. The latter isn't fun, but it's sometimes necessary.

Tax-manages your portfolio. The planner helps you keep your taxes as low as possible by using tax-efficient funds and tax-efficient managers. He or she also may employ HIFO (highest-in, first-out) tax treatment, tax-loss harvesting, and use other tax-efficient screens.

Keeps up-to-date with changes in the financial world. That might mean changes in interest rates, changes in kinds of available investment vehicles, tax-law changes, or personnel changes in the money-manager ranks. It also means staying abreast of many new retirement vehicles offered by banks, brokerages, and insurance companies. Some of those products may make a lot of sense, some may not, and most will be very complex.

Rebalances your investments. The planner assists you in sticking to your asset-allocation model.

Handles a raft of other financial jobs or refers you to someone who can. These could include creating an estate plan; writing or reviewing your will; developing a plan for paying for your children's educations; helping you navigate a financial transition, such as divorce or the death of a spouse; or assisting you in choosing a long-term-care policy.

Not surprisingly, you may need to spend a few bucks to get this kind of help, but if you hire a really sharp advisor, his or her advice and contacts should pay for itself—and *a lot more.*

How Do You Find Such a Wizard?

Well, first make sure you know what you're looking for. If you don't want a full-blown financial plan and really just want someone to give you investment advice, then almost any qualified planner or broker can do that. And in some states, almost anyone can advertise him- or herself as being a financial planner. So you won't have any trouble finding one if you're just aiming for, say, a stock- or mutual-fund picker.

Locating a qualified one, someone who digs deeper than just stock picking, will be a chore, but probably well worth it. Several hundred thousand practitioners are angling for your business, and they're not as uniformly trained as professionals in some other fields. In other words, you have stockbrokers, insurance agents, tax preparers, accountants, money managers, and lawyers all calling themselves some kind of financial consultant. You can narrow the task by limiting yourself to looking for certain designations, which I'll soon explain.

For starters, though, just as you would if you were hiring a plumber or a brain surgeon, be sure to ask around. Query friends or co-workers whose judgment you respect and whose financial situation and risk sensitivity are somewhat akin to yours.

Many advisors give free seminars. This can be a way to not only learn more about investing, but also to check out the planners themselves. These seminars are often advertised in the newspaper or on radio/TV or through flyers that come in the mail or are hung on your doorknob. Of course, you could always resort to the Yellow Pages, and the Internet provides another way to connect with the right planner.

Among the best places to start are referrals from your attorney, banker, or accountant. You might also check the Websites for the big financial-planning organizations. Each offers useful information and usually referrals. Among the major sites are:

- **The National Association of Personal Financial Advisors** makes referrals to its fee-only planners at **www.napfa.org**, or 800-366-2732.

- **The Financial Planning Association,** whose membership includes but is not limited to Certified Financial Planners, at **www.fpanet.org** or 800-322-4237.

- **Certified Financial Planners Board of Standards** is an independent regulatory organization at **www.CFP.net** or 888-237-6275. It can tell you if someone is entitled to claim the CFP certification and about any disciplinary actions.

What Do All Those Letters Mean?

Investment advisors have developed a baffling array of titles and certifications. Currently, there's no uniform accreditation to become a financial advisor. In fact, one recent study revealed that there are more than 80 certifications or degrees aimed at the financial-planning profession.

But if—as I strongly urge—you want a full-blown financial review and a real plan, you probably want to look for a CFP, a ChFC, a CLU, a CPA, a PFS, or some similar designation. Or at the very least, look for someone working hand in hand with such a skilled, credentialed advisor. (Call me biased, but I think the CFP designation is the gold standard, although ChFC, CFA, CPA, and CLU are also particularly well regarded.)

However, what the abbreviations stand for is not as important as what they signify in a broader sense—that this person took the time and made the effort to study the field, subscribe to its code of ethics, and take continuing-education courses. And more important than any initials after someone's name is what kind of trust and rapport you have with the planner . . . how knowledgeable he or she is . . . how interested he or she is in your situation . . . and how well you like and understand the plan he or she comes up with. Still, knowing a little about this alphabet soup may help you make a better choice.

It used to be that a banker loaned cash, an insurance agent sold insurance, and a stockbroker peddled stocks and bonds. But over the years lots of new products got introduced, and new types of sales-people sprouted up to sell both the old and new investment vehicles. Thus, the distinctions among those salespeople blurred, so that bankers now also sell stocks, stockbrokers now lend money, and insurance agents now can get you into all manner of investments.

Thus, the task becomes not only *what* to buy, but *from whom* to buy it. That's one of the big reasons for the popularity of financial planners. At their best, they help you cut through the clutter and make the best financial choices. But just because he or she is a financial planner—even a credentialed financial planner—doesn't guarantee a successful relationship.

The Securities and Exchange Commission recently enacted a new rule designed to make it easier for consumers to know what they're getting when they hire a financial professional. It mandates that stock-brokers who hold themselves out as financial planners must be clear about the role they're playing. So if they're providing advisory services, they're bound to act in the customer's best interest, as are traditional financial planners. And if they're acting as a broker, which is to say as a salesperson, that must be clear, too. This is a small but important step.

The keys to finding the right financial advisor include locating some-one (1) whom you're comfortable with, (2) who's willing to explain your options, (3) who charges a reasonable fee/commission, and (4) who has enough experience to add value to your overall plan.

That's not as simple as it sounds. For starters, there are those alpha-betical designations. And then there's the question of how planners are paid. Let's take those issues one by one:

Alphabetical designations. Some of the initials you see after a plan-ner's name exist because of federal licensing requirements, while others represent ways in which the industry seeks to market its services. For example, planners who sell securities must hold a federal securities license. Most are also members of the National Association of Securities Dealers (NASD), a quasi-governmental agency that regulates the industry.

Any person who provides financial planning also must be a registered investment advisor. That means that he or she is registered with the SEC and/or the state. He did so by filing a form, paying a fee, and showing that he understands SEC rules. While you should never work with anyone who's not registered (because it's a federal crime to be an unregistered planner), neither should you take the designation oh-so-seriously, because what it really means is that the registrant knows SEC procedures, not necessarily the finer points of financial planning.

The other designations are issued by the various financial industry associations, not by the government. Applicants must complete course work and continuing education, and meet other prerequisites to be awarded these designations, which include:

- **CFP®:** This well-known set of initials stands for Certified Financial Planner and is earned by those who take a two-year course, pass a rigorous two-day examination, and meet continuing-education requirements.

- **ChFC:** Chartered Financial Consultant is an advanced designation usually given to insurance agents or financial planners who undergo a two-year program and complete exams and continuing education. Many ChFCs are also CLUs, or Chartered Life Underwriters, which involves a similar course of study and continuing education.

- **CFS:** A Certified Fund Specialist has taken a course and exam centering on the selection and monitoring of mutual funds.

- **CPA:** A Certified Public Accountant has passed a rigorous exam to certify his or her knowledge of accounting, auditing, and tax issues. A growing number of CPAs, who traditionally have been thought of as just tax preparers, are getting into the personal-finance field, where they can also earn a PFS (Personal Finance Specialist) designation.

- **CMFC:** Like CFS, this designation reflects the advisor's expertise in the mutual-fund industry, but this one stands for Chartered Mutual Fund Counselor.

- **CRPC:** A Chartered Retirement Planning Counselor specializes in retirement planning issues.

- **RFC:** Registered Financial Consultants must meet education and licensing requirements and take a minimum of 40 hours of professional education each year. That's roughly two to four times as much as the other designations require.

Certainly, the designations with the longest history and requiring the most rigorous testing and continuing education are the CFP, ChFC, CLU, and CPA. If your planner doesn't have any of those designations, then he or she at least ought to be working in tandem with somebody who does.

How they're paid. A great deal is written and discussed in the media about how financial planners are paid: commission only, fee only, or some combination. I'm not so sure that it matters all that much. But just so you'll be fully informed, let me explain the pros and cons of each.

First, understand the difference between a financial planner and, say, a captive stockbroker or insurance agent. While many captive agents and brokers are becoming more independent in their advice, usually they'll talk to you about their proprietary products and will give you lots of advice about which of their products might be best. Some proprietary products are just fine; others may not be so fine.

Independent planners, on the other hand, usually don't have proprietary products per se. What they do is take a comprehensive look at your situation, offer advice to help meet your goals, and then fill your needs with various nonproprietary products. But, as you'll see, most planners work for banks, brokerages, or insurance firms, or work as independent advisors. And they all pretty much sell the same types of products as insurance agents or stockbrokers.

Product sales aren't necessarily bad. After all, someone has to get you to act, but it's important for you to understand the compensation arrangement.

Commission-only planners. These planners almost always work for a bank, brokerage, or insurance company. But like planners elsewhere, they'll ask about your income and expenses, your goals, your comfort level with risk, and so on, before suggesting appropriate investments. They would argue that instead of paying two fees—one to hire a planner and one to a broker to buy the investments—you can do one-stop shopping: Just hire the commission-only planner, and only pay when he makes a transaction for you.

Others contend that the commission-only planner is naturally biased toward his firm's products and thus has a built-in conflict of interest. Some folks say that they'd never work with someone who's paid on commission because that planner may recommend products that are best for his or her financial future, not necessarily yours. And that's possible.

However, that same person may buy a plane ticket from a travel agent, vitamins directly from a doctor or from a multilevel marketer, or a vacation from an online source—all of whom might be paid a commission for the transaction. The important thing is to do business with honest, knowledgeable people. If they're paid by commission, don't be afraid to ask the tough questions—but don't automatically rule that person out either. If their products are good and the costs reasonable, then their commission arrangement may be quite acceptable.

Just be careful. Stay on your toes because, while rare, some commissioned brokers are just there for the commission.

Fee-only planners. These planners usually get a fee to make the same kind of analysis of your situation and to give you recommendations. Much like an attorney, they usually charge for their service by the hour or by an up-front planning fee. Because they don't have specific investments to sell, you may need to go to someone else to actually purchase the product or products recommended. However, "fee only" is sometimes disguised as a rolling, annual commission and may, in fact, turn out to be more expensive than if you paid a load in the first place.

Advocates of fee-only planning say that it's free of conflict of interest, but critics argue that you may still need to pay a commission or sales charge to a broker to implement the plan. The fact that you're paying twice, they say, doesn't necessarily make the advice any better or the process cheaper or more pleasurable.

Theoretically, the fee-only advisor is free to make the best invest-ment recommendations rather than steer you toward investments that trigger commissions. The financial press clearly favors fee-only advisors even though the vast majority of planners probably depend at least partly on commissions. That's because a fee-only planner not only helps you draw up a plan, but may also manage your portfolio. If the planner does oversee your assets, he typically charges a fee that decreases as your assets grow.

For example, he might charge 1 percent for assets under $1 million and .8 percent above that figure. This means that they're not entirely free of conflicts. What do you think he would advise if you had a choice, say, of rolling your 401(k) into an IRA under his supervision or keeping it at your old employer?

Again, many fee-only planners do an excellent job. However, due to their no-commission mantra, they sometimes ignore some excellent products simply because those products are priced with a built-in com-mission. Some fee-only planners, for instance, might pass up a fixed annuity paying an interest rate of 5 percent with a 4 percent broker commission priced into the product in favor of, say, a 5 percent bond fund that charged a 1 percent ongoing fee. But all things being equal, 5 percent is better for you than a net of 4 percent. Thus, investors are usually best served when the planner, whether fee-only or otherwise, leaves all of the investment options open.

Fee-offset planner. These are advisors who charge a fee, and if you choose to do business with them, "rebate," or offset, the fee against their commission. This avoids double-dipping, but in some respect cheapens the plan itself and may skew it toward the products that the advisor wants to sell.

Me? I don't think that the whole debate amounts to much. In fact, it's simplistic to say that a fee-only advisor is necessarily better than someone who charges a commission. So many aspects of financial planning—such as integrity and knowledge—loom larger in impor-tance. The truth is, you're going to pay either way, and in some cases you may end up paying more to a fee-only advisor in the long run and less in the short run.

So the bottom line is this: If you hire the right advisor, it shouldn't matter how he or she is paid. If he does a good job, he'll be worth the fee and/or commission. If he doesn't do a good job, then whatever way you paid him will be misspent.

But you don't want to overpay. For example, paying a 1 to 2 percent annual advisory fee for a portfolio that's 50 percent stocks and 50 percent bonds is outrageously high. If you pay a one-time commission to set up a bond portfolio, then pay an asset-based fee on just the managed portion of your portfolio, you'll have wisely cut your fees in half. So be smart about what you're paying for. But as to the form of payment, who cares?

What's more important is that the planner discloses fully his financial arrangement. The planner should explain to prospective clients *how* he's paid, *how often* he's paid, *how much* he's paid, and *by whom*. You should insist on full disclosure when working with any financial advisor. If he refuses to talk, you should walk.

What to Expect Once You've Found a Planner

Much like a good doctor, a planner will give you a top-to-bottom financial checkup. He or she will want to know your retirement goals, cash-flow requirements, estate-planning needs, and much more. He won't even touch investment issues until he has a good grasp of your overall fiscal health. Good planners will draw out needed information from you by asking questions. Their aim will be to figure out your objectives. They may also request copies of wills, trusts, partnership or prenuptial agreements, insurance, employee-benefit manuals, investment information, and perhaps even ask you to draw up a budget and balance sheet listing everything you own and everything you owe.

But *you* ought to be asking questions, too. Unless the advisor comes highly recommended by several people you trust, such as your lawyer or CPA, or you know this advisor by long-standing reputation, you should interview at least three planners who seem appropriate and interview them as if they were applying for a job. Ask about their experience and credentials. You might try these ten questions:

1. How long have they been in the business and in your community? Planners who have roots in the community may be more cautious than Johnny-come-latelys. Even more important is how long they've been planners.

You want someone who's been around long enough to have suffered through a bear market. Prior to the bear market of 2000 to 2002, a lot of younger planners hadn't experienced such a downturn. As a result, you could run into, say, a talented, aggressive, young planner who forgot about safe money, forgot about value, threw caution to the wind, and really overexposed his clients to risk. Many folks right now are paying the price for that and may need to delay retirement because their planner, having never experienced that sinking feeling of losing a lot of his clients' money, was too aggressive. Make sure that your advisor has enough experience to deal with your situation and understands the degree to which you need safety as well as growth.

That doesn't mean younger advisors should be avoided. To the contrary, I've found many to be exceptionally bright and very tech-savvy. But be sure they're partnered with someone who also has the street smarts and the experience to empathize with your situation.

2. What will they do for you? Design a plan? Implement it? Or both?

3. What's their investment philosophy, and what investing style do they favor? This is important. You don't want to be force-fed financial choices. Be clear what your goals are and how you'll be most comfortable getting there. You want to be sure that your planner understands modern portfolio theory—that is, asset allocation—and isn't just trying to time the market, use gimmicks, try out risky strategies, or bet your money on his ability to pick "winner" stocks.

4. What kind of investments do they specialize in? Be wary if they talk *just* about insurance . . . or limited partnerships . . . or mutual funds . . . or any one investment vehicle to the exclusion of most others. In short, you want those who are planning driven, not product driven.

5. Who's their typical client, and what's the typical size of a client's account? Once you know that, then you can judge: Are you a good match with how much the average client has invested? Are you comfortable with roughly the same amount of risk? You also might ask to talk with some clients whose situations are similar to yours, especially those who have been through down as well as up years with this planner.

What you'll want to find out from those clients is not so much the state of their investments but the state of their relationship with the planner. Has he or she kept them informed? Has he done what he promised? Has he exceeded expectations in some ways? How? Disappointed in others? How?

6. How will this relationship work? Who will make the decisions—you or the planner? Will you retain control of your assets? What kind of paperwork will this person send you? Will you have to sign a contract? If so, how can you opt out if the relationship sours? How often will you meet face-to-face?

7. How are these advisors paid? If by fee, what do the fees include? If by commission, how much will that likely be? Are these figures negotiable? Ask for a full, clear explanation because, as we've seen, some planners claiming to be "fee only" actually receive commissions as well.

8. Have complaints been filed against them? Ask the planner directly. But also, especially if you have any doubts, check the National Association of Securities Dealers at **www.nasd.com** (if this person has a securities license), the state insurance commission (if he/she has an insurance license), and the SEC at **www.sec.gov** (to see if he/she is a registered investment advisor).

One phone call or Web search may save you from sending money to a con artist, an incompetent professional, or a disreputable firm. Before you invest or pay for any investment advice, always make sure that your broker or investment advisor is licensed. Also check to see if his/her firm has had run-ins with regulators or with other investors.

The Central Registration Depository (CRD) is a computerized database that contains information about most brokers, their representatives, and the firms they work for. You can either ask your state securities regulator or the NASD to provide you with information from the CRD. (You'll find contact information for your state securities regulator at **www.nasaa.org.**)

To find out about investment advisors and whether they're properly registered, read their registration form, called Form ADV. It comes in two parts. Part 1 has information about the advisor's business and whether it's had problems with regulators or clients. Part 1 includes the advisor's disciplinary record, lawsuits and arbitrations, how he or she has paid, and potential conflicts of interest. Part 2 outlines the advisor's services, fees, and strategies.

You can get copies of Form ADV from these advisors (although they're legally obligated to give you only Part 2), your state securities regulator, or the SEC. Because some investment advisors are also brokers, you may want to check both the CRD and Form ADV.

9. What kind of assumptions are they going to use in your plan?
For example, will they use life expectancy as defined in some computer program—say, 85 years old—or will they use a more conservative approach and take you out to 100 years old or beyond? If they stipulate 85 and you live to age 100, those last 15 years could be rough!

And what kind of market-return assumptions? If they project more than a 10 percent annual return for stocks (net, after fees), that's way too aggressive. (I prefer 8 percent.) Similarly, what kind of withdrawal scenario do they foresee? I've seen planners advise clients to take 8 percent a year out of 100 percent equity portfolios. That's crazy! One good downturn and that portfolio is going to do a vanishing act. (I prefer 4 percent to 5 percent.)

10. Will they give you some preliminary recommendations?
The best test for determining whether an advisor is right for you is to ask this person at the end of the first meeting to map out a tentative strategy or a list of potential recommendations. You're not asking for the planner to give the plan away for free. Instead, you're seeking for an initial impression of what might be worth exploring.

For example, by the end of a 30- or 40-minute session, planners should be able to say what direction they're heading in with regard to your estate plan—such as a simple will, bypass trust, charitable trust, life insurance (term or permanent), long-term care coverage—as well as asset allocation, tax strategies, and the like. If the planner can diagnose your situation on the spot and make preliminary recommendations without sending your data off to some home-office computer to crunch the numbers (a task you could probably do yourself for much less money), then I'd say that this individual has a definite leg up.

Other Things to Check Out

By using your eyes and ears when you visit a prospective planner, you can also connect some of the other dots. For example:

- *How big and connected is the office and how is it run?* Is the planner part of an organization of some heft and reputation? Or is it a rinky-dink outfit that, should there be trouble, won't be of much help? Does the office appear to be either too luxurious or too spare? If the staff and office is really big, that may look good, but it may also drive up costs. If the office and staff are really small, you could have trouble getting your calls returned.

- *Does this person explain things well?* Can he/she make it simple enough for you to understand? Or is this individual hiding beneath too many technical terms and a blizzard of statistics?

- *Does this advisor talk about you first?* He/she should find out about you before moving on to products that he/she believes would be good for you. A product-first approach suggests a planner who's perhaps more interested in peddling something than in coming up with a plan that matches your goals.

- *Is he/she into fad investing?* If this person is big on such things as, say, market timing or technical analysis, you should turn and run. And if he/she claims some proprietary method of picking stocks or otherwise uses a lot of razzle-dazzle, this person is probably not for you.

- *Can you work comfortably with this person?* Is this someone you would feel okay sharing highly confidential information with? Is this individual's personality a reasonable fit with yours? But on the other hand, think twice about hiring someone in your social circle like, say, somebody from your church or softball team. If you later needed to "fire" them, could you comfortably do so?

- *Can you talk to references?* Speak to at least three who have been clients for a while, but don't expect them to give out confidential information about their money.

Once you've found the financial planner for you, take good advantage of that opportunity. Be proactive, not passive. Seek to be a full partner in the discussions. Those projections of expenses you did earlier will come in handy here.

Planner vs. Money Manager

How do they differ? In short, a financial planner is a big-picture person who helps you with your strategy and who, among other things, can put you in touch with a money manager. A money manager actively oversees your investments on a day-to-day basis.

Sometimes a planner is also a money manager, but if I were you, I'd steer clear of those. Either job is a demanding one, and the odds are not good that someone can simultaneously do both well. Further, money managers tend to become experts in their own investing style—say, small caps, growth, or value stocks—and by definition, you as a diversified investor will want your portfolio to span multiple styles, not be concentrated on one. The way to get that diversification is to have a financial planner who will help you draw up a plan, set up your asset-allocation model, rebalance your portfolio, help you manage risk, and make sure you have enough liquidity. Then that planner can hire a strategist to oversee your complete asset allocation or hire style-specific managers to invest your money in accordance with your plan. Those money managers choose and buy the actual securities.

How does the planner find these money managers? He or she may hire them directly or may work through a money-manager selection firm, or both. Typically, it doesn't cost any more to go through a selection firm because its trading costs are kept low by the sheer volume of its business.

Once hired, the money managers must be monitored by the planner to see if they meet their benchmarks. Money managers who consistently underperform sometimes need to be replaced. And if they overperform, they may be taking too much risk. Your advisor can be a major help here, making sure you don't ax underperformers too soon or rely too much on the overperformers.

The planner also wants to make sure there isn't a lot of overlap with other managers or overlap with other investments you have on your own or with other investment houses. It's important that the planner know everything about your financial situation even if he or she isn't managing everything.

A Word about Wraps

A "wrap" in financial terms isn't a coat or a pricey sandwich or what movie directors say when they're done filming. Instead, it's an account that combines private management and trade execution.

Available at most brokerage and planning firms, the wrap account usually requires a $100,000 minimum investment. Thus, in order to achieve diversification in seven or eight different asset classes, you'd need at least $700,000 or $800,000. That may make wrap accounts not feasible for many retirees. There are some asset-allocation wrap accounts for smaller sums, but you'll want to check on the fees before acting. If you can find the right wrap or asset-management account that is fully diversified and you meet the minimum investment level (usually $250,000), you may be set for your Bucket No. 3.

But more important than what the account is called is what it costs. Some wrap accounts often include extra costs. Whether yours is a wrap or asset-management account, you'll want to hold the total expense to under 2 percent annually of the amount invested—that's management fees, trading costs—everything.

One problem I have with most fully allocated wraps or asset-management accounts is that the wrap fee is charged on the entire allocation. To me this defies logic, particularly if your strategy includes investments that don't require management. For instance, when using conservative investments such as CDs, annuities, and individual bonds in Buckets Nos. 1 and 2, why would you pay an extra 1 to 2 percent for a broker to "manage" accounts that require little or no management? By splitting your funds into various buckets and paying a wrap fee strictly on the stock portion of Bucket No. 3 and on the more aggressive forms of fixed income that may require ongoing management, you may be able to reduce your advisory fees by as much as 50 percent or more.

And Then a Final Word about Integrity

Most financial professionals are highly ethical and responsible. But, of course, they're not immune to the personal frailties that plague other professions. Knowledge is your best safeguard against deception and incompetence.

It will be up to you to evaluate the planner's performance and assess his or her advice. You've got to remain alert. It's not enough to say, in effect, "Here's my money. Take good care of it for me." Remember, as long as the cost is reasonable and accountable, it's not how you compensate your advisor that's most important, but rather how comfortable you are and whether you're meeting your goals within a stated risk tolerance.

Of course, you shouldn't ever sign a blank document or allow the planner to break the law by signing your name to anything. Don't give him/her authority to make transactions without your knowledge or consent. Don't agree to list this advisor as joint owner or beneficiary on any of your accounts, and don't ever name him/her as a trustee. Also, you shouldn't pay more than 50 percent in advance for planning work or pay for more than one-quarter of asset-management fees in advance.

Look out, especially, for any financial professional who promises "a sure thing" or the need to "act quickly before it's too late." There are *no* sure things, and acting quickly without thinking causes many a financial debacle. And if you become dissatisfied, don't hesitate to call this person's supervisor and, if necessary, change advisors.

Who Else Will You Need?

A CFP, for example, can help you with many of your financial needs, but you may find that you also need a tax attorney, a CPA, or some other kind of expert. And if you don't have an estate plan, you need the help of an estate-planning attorney. How would you find these?

Estate-planning attorneys. Many attorneys are capable of drawing up a will, but only relatively few are steeped in knowledge of estates and trusts. As I explained earlier, trusts can run the gamut, from living trusts—used by millions of ordinary Americans to avoid the hassle and expense of probate court—to complex instruments designed for the ultra-wealthy. Financial sophistication, though, more than wealth mandates the use of trusts that can provide options for preserving wealth and seeing that future generations are wise stewards. When setting up any trust, it's important to work with a financial advisor and an attorney who can help you meet all legal requirements.

One good source of such expertise is the American College of Trust and Estate Counsel, a nonprofit group whose members who have made "substantial contributions" to the field and have practiced estate law for at least a decade. See **www.actec.org** for details on how to locate a member near you.

Also, check your state bar to see if it issues estate-planning certification. Even if it doesn't, the state and/or local bars may be able to provide names. Yet other sources would include **www.findlaw.com**, an attorney-referral service (click on "Estate Planning"); local bank trust officers because they're likely to know the best estate attorneys; and the

AARP Legal Services Network at **www.aarp.org/lsn**. The latter provides access to 1,000 attorneys experienced in their area of the law, in good standing with bar groups, and offering a discount for AARP members.

CPAs and enrolled agents. As you've already learned, the tax accounting on some of these investment strategies is complex. So you might also want to establish a working relationship with a tax specialist, such as a Certified Public Accountant or an enrolled agent.

Many CPAs, as I mentioned earlier, are branching out and trying to become dispensers of financial advice and products. Some people bemoan this trend, saying CPAs enjoy a fine reputation and shouldn't risk soiling it by hawking stocks, insurance, or annuities. But I say: Look at the person, not the initials, and have an honest discussion about how he or she will be paid and how this individual will deal with the inherent conflict of interest in being your tax-compliance officer and investment advisor. Also notice whether the accountant has taken the effort to earn a Personal Finance Specialist (PFS) designation through the American Institute of Certified Public Accountants (AICPA).

For help in locating a CPA to meet your needs, contact AICPA at **www.aicpa.org**.

Enrolled agents, a category dating back to the post–Civil War period, are licensed by the federal government. In fact, many are former IRS agents who also are required to meet stiff continuing-education courses to stay abreast of tax law. (Only enrolled agents or CPAs are authorized to appear in place of a taxpayer during an IRS audit.) They're the only tax professionals tested by the IRS on their knowledge of tax law.

To find an enrolled agent near you, use the search mechanism on the Website of the National Association of Enrolled Agents at **www.naea.org**.

Try to avoid the one-stop shop. That's where the attorney, CPA, and investment advisor are all under one roof with no checks and balances. Instead, get an independent attorney working on your estate planning, an independent CPA or enrolled agent doing your tax work, and an unrelated investment advisor. That way you receive independent advice rather than turn your financial life over to a group of advisors who may not have your best interests at heart.

In today's complex investment world, even expert investors find it difficult to create and implement a well-structured investment plan on their own. So, again, I strongly urge you to work with investment professionals who understand your needs and can help you develop prudent strategies that will both protect and grow your wealth.

$$$$$

Don't Forget to Enjoy Life

Many people err in not paying enough attention to their finances. But you also can pay *too* much attention. You can easily confuse being well off with well-being. You can live to earn money rather than earn money to live. And that brings us to an issue that's increasingly relevant for a great many Americans: *What is our pursuit of wealth bringing us?*

More debt, yes. More possessions, sure. More contentment? I don't think so. And a lot of research backs me up on that. Now, understand, I'm in the wealth-building business. I fervently believe that when it comes to wealth, more is better . . . *but up to what point?*

A *TIME* magazine poll found that happiness tended to increase as income rose to $50,000 a year. (The median annual U.S. household income is about $44,000.) But after that first $50,000, more income did not have a dramatic effect. Even the most prosperous among us, the *Forbes* 100 wealthiest Americans—as surveyed by University of Illinois psychologist Edward Diener—are just slightly happier than average. And the sadness and misfortune that has dogged many lottery winners is well known.

Yet, with the super-rich—as glorified by the media—setting the pace, many Americans have come to believe in life, liberty, and the purchase of happiness. They don't just need a TV; they want a gigantic plasma-screen model as part of a home-theater system. They don't need a car; they want the epitome of European craftsmanship. They don't need a house; they want a 6,000-square-foot, five-bedroom mansion with computerized window shades and a three-car garage.

Some have dubbed this an epidemic of "affluenza"—not a typical virus but instead a highly contagious disease of overconsumption. Symptoms include compulsive shopping, high debt, overwork, inability to delay gratification, a sense of entitlement, and stress. Affluenza sufferers often find themselves so consumed by jobs they don't like—in order to have money to buy products they really don't need—that they end up with little time left for family, friends, or community. Or as Will Rogers put it many years ago, "Too many people spend money they haven't earned, to buy things they don't want, to impress people they don't like."

No wonder the national savings rate now hovers around 0 percent, dramatically below the long-term average of 7.7 percent. No wonder America's consumer debt has topped $2 trillion, doubling in less than ten years. No wonder personal bankruptcies have reached an all-time high.

Hope College psychologist David G. Myers, calls ours "the doubly affluent society": twice as rich as we were in 1957, but no happier. We find ourselves, he says, with "big houses and broken homes, high incomes and low morale . . . making a living but too often failing at making a life." Our "soaring wealth and shrinking spirit," he says, amount to an American paradox.

That seems to be because of what sociologists call "reference anxiety." Folks tend to ask themselves, "Is my (car, house, boat) nicer than my neighbor's?" instead of, "Is it adequate for my needs?" Buy that new car, house, or boat or pull down that bigger salary at work—and what happens? Your spirits are boosted briefly, but then you find yourself again facing a gnawing sense of dissatisfaction. This notion—that we rapidly adapt to improvements in our lives yet end up feeling little or no better off—is called the "hedonic treadmill." And it's a tough one to jump off.

So *what* would make us happier for longer?

University of Southern California economist Richard Easterlin surveyed 1,500 people over nearly three decades to see what put a spring in their step and a smile on their faces. His findings: Good health and time with family are the building blocks of happiness. Wealth, on the other hand, doesn't necessarily lead to contentment because people with more money just want more things.

According to the University of Chicago's National Opinion Research Center, the underpinnings of happiness are:

- Five or more close friends (excluding family members). People with such friends are 50 percent more likely to describe themselves as "very happy" than those with fewer.

- A loving partner. Forty percent of married American adults report themselves "very happy" versus 26 percent of those who aren't married.

- Good health.

- A connection with others, such as a community or religious group.

My conclusion? It's not—as the snarky license-plate frames or T-shirts proclaim—that "He Who Dies with the Most Toys Wins." Actually, the winner may be the one who has *some* toys but, more important, has the time—and friends—to enjoy them. In the end, happiness is about wanting what you already have. If you're never rich in anything but friends, family, and worthwhile things to do, you're still pretty rich.

Our culture has come to accept great wealth as a personal value. But, in my view, life is so short, and there is no safety in numbers or anything else. So my advice would be: *Don't let your wealth, or your pursuit of wealth, blind you or shield you from life.*

Sure, save. Invest. Use your head to make your money go as far as you can. Employ as many of the strategies in this book as you can. But don't let money, or lack of it, keep you from jumping on life's carousel. In short, living well doesn't always depend on having more money. Needs and expenses have an amazing ability to keep pace with income. So you can decide to *make more* . . . or you can decide to *need less.*

Retirement Is . . .

What do you want to do with your life once you stop working full-time? Finding that answer will require setting some priorities. What comes first? Second? Third? Is it peace of mind? A nice house? More free time? Getting those kids into Ivy League schools? Whatever you decide, try to see your money as a tool of liberation, not a financial ball and chain. My suggestions:

- **Value your time.** Retirement should be a happy time, provided your health is good. No longer ruled by the clock, many retirees say having more control over their time is one of the best things about their new life.

- **Plan ahead.** If you're compelled by health or office pressures to retire prematurely, there may not be a whole lot of planning you can do. But if you're given some time to think, focus not only on how you'll pay for retirement but what your retirement will look like? What will those priorities be? Travel? Hobbies? Volunteering?

- **Invest in friendship.** Regularly seeing good friends probably will do more for you than having the latest in German automotive engineering parked outside your door.

- **Become involved in something bigger than yourself.** "You give but little when you give of your possessions," wrote Kahlil Gibran. "It is when you give of yourself that you truly give." And he was right. So even if it's just something as prosaic as digging around in a community garden or being a docent at the museum or handing out flyers for a favorite cause, you'll be part of a team. There's merit in that, regardless of the outcome.

It's been said that real prosperity is living easily and happily in the real world, whether you have money or not. And I couldn't agree more that life isn't about just being shrewd in wealth accumulation. The joy you get in retirement won't directly correlate with how much money you have. It'll correlate with how *involved* you are . . . with family, friends, country, and planet . . . involved in trying to make this a better world, involved with physical activity and mental stimulation, involved with romantic love, involved with grandchildren and stamp collecting and model airplanes and begonias . . . and whatever else that interests you.

Interest of the compound variety is important to your financial well-being. But it's interest in people and the world around you that will really bring you happiness.

When we put money in its appropriate place, we find the rest of life emerges. We operate in trust, not greed. We think about giving before we think about getting. Balance, then, is key . . . putting money in service to ourselves instead of being in service to it.

"In the quiet hours when we are alone and there is nobody to tell us what fine fellows we are," wrote author and playwright A. A. Milne, "we come sometimes upon a moment in which we wonder, not how much money we are earning, nor how famous we have become, but what good we are doing." Consider that yet another strategy. And an important one.

$ $ $ $ $

Glossary

72(t) election: A strategy permitting fixed amounts to be withdrawn at regular intervals from retirement accounts before the age of 59½ without penalty.

401(k): A retirement plan sponsored by private employers in which employees can contribute pre-tax dollars, and the money grows tax deferred until it is withdrawn.

403(b): An employer-sponsored retirement plan for employees of tax-exempt organizations, such as schools, charities, and hospitals. Workers can contribute pre-tax dollars, and the money grows tax deferred until it's withdrawn.

457: A retirement plan for government employees that is similar to a 403(b).

529 plans: State-sponsored college-savings plans that allow investors to shelter from taxes the money they save for their children's education.

1031 exchange: Also known as a "Starker exchange," this is a tax-deferred property exchange in which the owner uses built-up equity in rental property in an attempt to improve income and long-term growth.

A

Active management: An investing strategy that seeks returns in excess of a specified benchmark.

Alpha: A measure of extraordinary return for the taking of additional risk. A positive alpha signifies the amount of extra return awarded to the investor for taking added risk rather than accepting the market return.

Annuity: An insurance product usually purchased to provide monthly payments during retirement.

Asset allocation: How a portfolio is divided among differing kinds of assets, such as stocks, bonds, and cash.

Asset class: A group of assets—such as cash, real estate, or equities—with similar risk and reward characteristics.

B

Bear market/bear/bearish: A prolonged decline in the stock market. A person who expects that prices will move lower is called a bear, and an event is considered bearish when it's expected to move prices lower.

Benchmark: An appropriate standard against which actively managed funds can be judged. For example, the performance of small-cap managers should be compared to a small-cap index such as the Russell 2000.

Beta: A measure of the volatility, or systematic risk, of a security or a portfolio in comparison to the market as a whole. A beta less than 1 means that the security will be less volatile than the market. A beta greater than 1 indicates that the security will be more volatile than the market.

Blue-chip stock: The stock of a well-known corporation with a long record of growth.

Bond: An instrument of debt issued by corporations and governments. The issuer commits to making regular interest payments to the lenders (bondholders) and ultimately repays the original investment in a specified number of years. If a firm is liquidated, bondholders are given a higher priority than stockholders and thus have a better chance of getting some of their money back.

Bond ladder: A strategy in which a portfolio is structured so as to have roughly equal amounts invested in various maturities. Thus, interest payments come due sequentially.

Broker: A person who charges a fee or commission for trading stocks, bonds, and other securities.

Bull market/bull/bullish: A market in which prices of securities are generally rising. A person who expects that prices will move higher is called a bull, and an event is considered bullish when it's expected to move prices higher.

Buy and hold: A long-term strategy to purchase stocks or mutual funds and generally keep them despite the ups and downs of the stock market.

Bypass trust: A trust arrangement in which children, as beneficiaries, would have access to the trust's assets upon the surviving parent's death. The trust also can be set up so the surviving spouse receives income from it while he or she is alive.

C

Capital appreciation: The increase in the market value of an asset since it was purchased.

Capital gain: The net profit made when assets such as stocks, bonds, and real estate are sold for more than the original purchase price.

Capital-gains distribution: A payment by a mutual fund to its shareholders for the profits made on the sale of stocks or bonds in the fund's portfolio. Shareholders are liable for taxes on these gains even though the investor didn't sell their mutual-fund shares.

Capital-gains taxes: The taxes on net profits from the sale of securities or real estate.

Capitalization: The market value of a company as determined by multiplying the number of outstanding shares times the price per share of its stock. Companies often are categorized as small cap (small capitalization), large cap, etc.

Certificate of deposit (CD): An interest-bearing deposit at a bank that locks up an investor's money for a certain period of time.

Certified Financial Planner® (CFP): A financial advisor who has passed a rigorous exam to certify his or her wide knowledge on a range of personal-finance issues.

Certified Public Accountant (CPA): A person who has passed a rigorous exam to certify his or her knowledge of accounting, auditing, and tax issues.

Charitable lead trust: A trust designed to reduce beneficiaries' income by first donating a portion of the trust's income to charities and then, after a specified period of time, transferring the remainder of the trust to the beneficiaries.

Charitable remainder trust: A tax-exempt revocable trust designed to reduce the taxable income of individuals by first dispersing income to the beneficiaries of the trust for a specified period of time and then donating the remainder of the trust to the designated charity.

Commission: The fee paid to a broker for completing a trade.

Common stock: A class of securities representing ownership in a company. A holder of one or more shares is a part owner of the firm and thus is entitled to vote on company directors and receive dividends.

Compounding: Growth that results from reinvested income as well as from the gains on the original investment.

Consumer Price Index (CPI): A measure that examines the weighted average of prices of a basket of consumer goods and services, such as transportation, food, and medical care. Changes in CPI are used to assess price changes associated with the cost of living.

Corporate bond: A taxable bond issued by a corporation.

Cost basis: The original cost of an investment that's used to calculate the capital gain when the investment is sold.

D

Deferred annuity: A type of annuity contract that delays payments of income until the investor elects to receive them. Thus, it has two main phases: the savings phase in which you invest money into the account, and the income phase in which the plan is converted into an annuity and payments are received. This annuity can be either variable or fixed.

Defined-benefit plan: A pension plan that guarantees a certain benefit based on a formula that includes salary history and years of service.

Defined-contribution plan: An employer-sponsored retirement plan that depends on employee contributions and often some employer contributions as well. The benefits, not guaranteed, depend on the success of the underlying investments.

Diversification: Holding different types of investments to reduce risk.

Dividend: A company's distribution of earnings to investors who own stock or who own shares in a mutual fund holding the stock of that firm.

Dividend yield: A ratio indicating how much a company pays out in dividends each year relative to its share price. It's calculated by dividing the annual dividends per share by the price per share.

Dollar-cost averaging: Investing a set amount of money periodically, usually monthly or quarterly. The investor thus attempts to reduce the risk that might be involved in investing a large sum all at once.

Donor-advised fund: A private fund administered by a third party and created to manage charitable donations on behalf of an organization, family, or individual.

Dow Jones Industrial Average (DJIA): The nation's most closely watched stock-market index, it consists of a weighted average of the stock of 30 major corporations.

E

Emerging-market fund: A mutual fund that invests in stocks of firms located in less-developed countries.

Equity-indexed annuities: An annuity in which an insurance company will usually guarantee a floor return while giving the investor the ability to earn an interest rate tied to the performance of a stock index, such as the S&P 500. It differs from a variable annuity because there are no ongoing fees for money management, although there's usually a cap on how much you can earn.

Estate plan: An estate is what you own minus what you owe at the time of your death. The purpose of estate planning is to answer the questions: *Who gets what? And under what conditions?*

Estate tax: A federal tax levied on some large estates when the owner dies.

Exchange-traded fund (ETF): A basket of securities designed to track an index while still trading as a stock.

Expense ratio: A charge that investors pay annually to a mutual fund. It's expressed as a percentage of the total investment and may include management, administrative, and marketing fees.

F

Federal Deposit Insurance Corporation (FDIC): A federal agency that guarantees that a customer's money (up to a certain limit) will be protected if the bank fails.

Federal Reserve: The central bank that sets U.S. monetary policy. The "Fed," along with its Federal Open Market Committee, oversees the money supply, interest rates, and credit.

Fee-based planner: A financial advisor who is paid through a combination of fees and commissions.

Fee-only planner: A financial advisor who is not paid by commission. Some are paid by the hour or by the project, while others charge a percentage of assets.

Financial advisor: A generic term used by many money consultants, such as financial planners, brokers, and insurance agents.

Fixed annuity or Guaranteed Investment Contract (GIC): A contractual arrangement in which an investor, in return for a lump sum, receives a set sum of money at regular intervals for a specific period of time or for life.

Front-end load: An up-front sales commission paid when shares of certain mutual funds are purchased.

Fundamental analysis: A method of evaluating a security by attempting to measure its intrinsic value by examining related economic, financial, and other qualitative and quantitative factors.

I

I-Bond: A government bond that provides both a fixed rate of return as well as an inflation-protection component.

Immediate annuity or Immediate Annuity Contract (IAC): A contractual arrangement with an insurance company in which an investor, in return for a lump sum, receives a set sum of money at regular intervals for a specific period of time or for life.

Index: A composite of securities that measures price changes in a specific group.

Index fund: A mutual fund that seeks to match the returns of a stock or bond benchmark by holding the same stocks or bonds that comprise the index.

Individual Retirement Account (IRA): A savings vehicle in which investors are allowed to deposit money to grow tax deferred until taken out in retirement. (*See also* **Roth IRA.**)

Inflation: A time of generally rising consumer prices, generally expressed as a percentage of increase above the previous year's prices.

J

Junk bond: High-yield corporate bonds that are rated below investment grade. While the riskiest of all bonds, these are also potentially the highest yielding.

K

Keogh Plan: A retirement plan established by a self-employed individual for him/herself and his/her employees.

L

Large-cap stock: Stocks of the largest corporations, whose capitalization (share price times number of shares outstanding) exceeds $10 billion.

Leading indicators: Major market signs that suggest the economic state for the coming months. Indicators include consumer expectations, changes in the money supply, and price fluctuations.

Leverage: The use of debt to increase the amount of assets that can be acquired.

Limited liability company (LLC): A corporate structure whereby the shareholders of the company have a limited liability for the company's actions. Basically, a hybrid between a partnership and a corporation.

Liquidity: The ability to quickly sell to produce cash.

Load: A mutual-fund sales charge used to pay a stockbroker or financial advisor's commission.

Long-term-care insurance: A policy that pays for nursing-home and/or home-care expenses when the policyholder can no longer take care of himself or herself.

Living trust: Assets held in a living trust go directly to the designated heirs, avoiding probate.

Living will: A legal document that sets out the medical care an individual wants or does not want in the event that he or she becomes incapable of communicating his or her wishes.

M

Market capitalization: The market price per share of a firm's stock times the number of shares outstanding.

Market timing: A strategy used by investors who seek to anticipate trends—that is, buying before a predicted upswing and selling when they expect a downturn.

Momentum-driven strategy: A strategy in which the trader will often take a long or short position in the stock with the hope that its momentum will continue in either an upward or downward direction.

Money manager: A professional who oversees clients' investments on a day-to-day basis.

Money-market fund: A type of mutual fund that invests in short-term securities and usually keeps the per share value at $1.

Mortgage-backed securities: Financial instruments representing an interest in assets that are mortgage related.

Municipal bonds: Obligations issued by state and local governments. Interest paid is free from federal income tax and in some cases free of state and local taxes as well.

Mutual fund: A pool of money from many shareholders that is invested in stocks or bonds and thus allows investors to own a small piece of many securities by holding shares of the fund.

N

NASD: The National Association of Securities Dealers. A quasi-governmental agency that regulates the industry.

NASDAQ: The National Association of Securities Dealers Automated Quotation system, a computerized marketplace that handles trades for thousands of stocks, including that of many technology companies.

NASDAQ 100: An index of the biggest and most popularly traded companies on the NASDAQ.

Net asset value (NAV): The value of a single share of a mutual fund's investments.

Net income: A firm's profits after taxes, depreciation, interest, and other expenses.

Net unrealized appreciation (NUA): This is the difference in value between the average cost basis of shares and the current market value of the shares held in a tax-deferred account.

No-load fund: A mutual fund that does not impose a sales charge.

P

Passive management: An investing strategy that mirrors a market index and does not attempt to beat the market.

Pension plan: A fund established by a company for paying retirement benefits to former employees.

Portfolio: All securities held by an investor.

Preferred stock: A hybrid equity that functions a lot like a bond, paying income and giving investors a higher priority than common stockholders if the firm is liquidated.

Q

QTIP Trust: A trust that enables the grantor to provide for a surviving spouse and also to maintain control of how the trust's assets are distributed once the surviving spouse has also died. Income, and sometimes principal, generated from the trust is given to the surviving spouse to ensure that he or she is taken care of for the rest of his or her life.

R

Rally: A rise in stock or bond prices following a downward movement.

Real estate investment trusts (REITs): Publicly owned companies that acquire, own, and manage income-producing real estate. *Traded* REITs are bought and sold like stocks, while *nontraded* REITs are less liquid but may produce a more stable share price and a potentially higher dividend.

Rebalancing: Restoring a portfolio to its original asset allocation.

Recession: A downturn in economic activity, generally defined as two consecutive quarters of decline in a nation's gross domestic product.

Required minimum distribution (RMD): The amount of money that federal law requires to be withdrawn from a tax-deferred retirement account after the investor reaches age 70½.

Reverse mortgage: A special type of loan used to convert a home's equity into cash. The money obtained through a reverse mortgage is usually used to provide seniors with financial security in their retirement years.

Roth 401(k): Combining features of Roth IRAs and 401(k) plans, this retirement-savings plan allows workers to set aside money from their paychecks that's already been taxed. The money then grows tax free, and all withdrawals after age 59½ are tax free.

Roth IRA: A savings vehicle in which investors are allowed to deposit money to grow tax deferred and to withdraw it tax free in retirement.

S

Sales load: A sales charge levied by some mutual funds.

Secular: An adjective used to describe a long-term time frame, usually at least ten years, as in "a secular bear market" or "a secular bull market."

Securities: Common stocks, preferred stocks, corporate bonds, and government bonds.

Securities and Exchange Commission (SEC): A federal agency, created in 1934, that regulates the securities industry.

Share price: The price of a single share of stock.

Short-term capital-gains tax: The tax on the profit from an investment that is sold after being held for one year or less.

Simple interest: Interest calculated on the original amount of money invested.

Simplified Employee Pensions-Individual Retirement Account (SEP-IRA): A retirement plan that allows the self-employed to save tax deferred.

Small-cap stock: Stocks of the relatively small corporations, whose capitalization (share price times number of shares outstanding) is $2 billion or less.

Standard & Poor's 500 (S&P 500): An index of the stocks of 500 large U.S. corporations.

Stock: A share of ownership in a corporation. Owning a share entitles one to be involved in a firm's growth or decline, receive dividends, choose directors, and to participate in other corporate actions.

T

Tactical manager: A professional who makes educated allocations in an attempt to outpace the market benchmarks.

Tax-credit investing: A strategy that involves investing in low-income housing tax credits. This promotes affordable housing for the poor and allows investors to effectively convert their taxable retirement money into a tax-free Roth IRA.

Tax deferred: Earnings remain untaxed until withdrawn.

Tax-free bonds, or municipal bonds: Bonds whose interest is paid free from federal income tax and in some cases free of state and local taxes as well.

Tax-managed or tax-efficient mutual funds: Funds that seek to minimize the yearly tax burden of their investors.

Technical analysis: A method of evaluating securities by analyzing statistics generated by market activity, such as past prices and volume.

Term life insurance: Insurance that provides no investment value but yields a cash benefit to survivors when a policyholder dies.

Total return: An investment's income as well as any capital appreciation.

Treasuries: Any government security offered by the U.S. Treasury.

Treasury bill (T-bill): A short-term obligation of the federal government, maturing in 13 or 26 weeks.

Treasury bond: A federal-government obligation that matures in ten years or more after issuance.

Treasury Inflation-Protected Securities (TIPS): Government bonds that increase in value during inflationary times. The value of the TIPS principal is adjusted twice a year to reflect changes in the federal Consumer Price Index.

Treasury note: A federal government obligation that matures from two to ten years after issuance.

Turnover: The percentage of the stocks in a mutual fund's portfolio that are sold each year.

U

Universal life insurance: A cash-value life-insurance policy that provides a death benefit as well as an investment component.

V

Value averaging: Rebalancing your buckets by selling securities when you exceed your targets, and adding more to the buckets whose returns have dropped below your target figures.

Variable annuity: An investment product that is part insurance policy and part mutual fund and whose return is *variable,* depending on how the mutual-fund portion performs.

Variable universal life insurance (VUL): A policy providing a death benefit but also serving as a tax-deferred investment vehicle. The rate of return on the investment portion is determined by the performance of the underlying securities.

Volatility: The tendency for a security's price to fluctuate over time.

W

Whole life insurance: A policy providing a death benefit but also serving as a tax-deferred investment vehicle. Part of the premium pays for the death benefit, and the rest is invested for the policyholder.

Wrap account: An account in which a brokerage manages an investor's portfolio for a flat quarterly or annual fee covering all administrative, commission, and management expenses.

Y

Yield: Income received from an investment expressed as a percentage of the market price.

Z

Zero-coupon bond: A bond sold at a discount to its face value.

$ $ $ $ $

About the Authors

Raymond J. Lucia, Sr., Certified Financial Planner, is a nationally recognized expert in financial and business management. He's president and founder of the Raymond J. Lucia Companies, Inc., which oversees more than $1 billion in invested assets. Host of the nationally syndicated radio program *The Ray Lucia Show,* and author of the acclaimed book *Buckets of Money®: How to Retire in Comfort and Safety,* he's been called a "rising star in talk radio." Out of more than 250,000 registered representatives, he was named "One of the Ten Best Brokers in America in 2004" by *Registered Rep.* magazine.

Ray appears frequently on shows such as *Your World with Neil Cavuto, Forbes on Fox, Cashin' In, Cavuto on Business,* and *The Wall Street Journal Report with Maria Bartiromo.* He is currently presenting retirement seminars nationwide with noted economist, actor, and author Ben Stein. For more information about Ray Lucia, please visit: **www.RayLucia.com**.

$ $ $

Dale Fetherling has written or co-authored more than a dozen nonfiction books and taught writing and editing at five colleges and universities. He's based in San Diego, California.

$ $ $ $ $

NOTES

NOTES